Astral Magic in Babylonia

TRANSACTIONS

of the

American Philosophical Society

Held at Philadelphia for Promoting Useful Knowledge

VOLUME 85, Part 4, 1995

Astral Magic in Babylonia

ERICA REINER

THE AMERICAN PHILOSOPHICAL SOCIETY

Independence Square, Philadelphia

1995

Cover: Neo-Babylonian tablet with relief of a sundisk suspended before the sun god. Courtesy of the British Museum, no. 91000; published by L.W. King, *Babylonian Boundary-Stones* (London, 1912) pl. xcviii.

Reiner, Erica
Astral Magic in Babylonia
Includes references and index.
1. Babylonia 2. Magic
3. Religion 4. History, Ancient

ISBN: 0-87169-854-4 95-76539

TABLE OF CONTENTS

List of Illustrations vi
Foreword vii
Abbreviations x
Introduction 1
Chapter I: The Role of Stars 15
Chapter II: The Art of the Herbalist 25
Chapter III: Medicine 43
Chapter IV: Divination 61
Chapter V: Apotropaia 81
Chapter VI: Sorcerers and Sorceresses 97
Chapter VII: The Nature of Stones 119
Chapter VIII: Nocturnal Rituals 133
Index 145

ILLUSTRATIONS

1. Relief from Assurnasirpal's palace with the king wearing a necklace hung with emblems of the planets 4

2. Cylinder seal showing bearded Ištar 5

3, 4, 5. Representations of constellations incised on a Late Babylonian tablet 10, 11

6. Middle register of a bronze plaque, showing a patient being cured 45

7. Seal representing Gula with her dog 54

8. Gula and her dog represented on a boundary stone 54

9. Clay models of sheep livers inscribed with liver omens ... 60

10. Bronze bell decorated with scenes of exorcisms of demons .. 80

Foreword

> I, Muḥammad ibn Isḥāq, have lastly only to add that the books on this subject are too numerous and extensive to be recorded in full, and besides the authors keep on repeating the statements of their predecessors.
>
> al-Nadīm, *Fihrist*, vol. 1, p. 360

Magic, astrology, and witchcraft have become fashionable of late. The appeal of the mysterious and the occult to the contemporary public has spawned a considerable literature on magic, ancient and exotic alike. Classicists have mined Greek and Latin sources for elements of magic and sorcery, and have made forays into the neighboring territories of the ancient Near East for parallels, real or assumed.

Knowledgeable as he may be in his own field, the Classical scholar cannot be expected to be equally well versed in the literature of peoples whose records have survived in the cuneiform script only and are couched in dead languages that have been deciphered only in the last century. One, Sumerian, is not related to any known language; the other, Akkadian, even though it belongs to the Semitic family of languages, diverges from its relatives sufficiently to be difficult to master. Not surprisingly, the most apposite and interesting comparisons often suffer from a misunderstanding of the Near Eastern material. Connections between the oriental cultures and their echoes in the west become tenuous if one term of the equation is incorrectly expressed. To provide a foundation for comparisons the Near Eastern material needs to be presented in a reliable form. This is the purpose of my study. My sources are culled from such scientific texts as medicine, divination, and rituals, which are not usually included in anthologies of Mesopotamian texts and are rarely available in translation.

While I do not claim familiarity with the Classical data, it has seemed necessary that I refer to Greek and Latin sources as I attempt to point up parallels. Many suggestions for the paths to pursue and references to the literature came from David Pingree, whose wisdom and interest have sustained this work. My quotes from and my translations of Classical sources are neither independent nor original; I adduce them simply because they provide a context that the cuneiform sources lack, and therefore they situate in a broader background the Near Eastern texts' terse allusions. The point becomes evident from the examples of "drawing down the moon," and "seizing the mouth," discussed in Chapters V and VI.

In spite of some striking similarities which may simply attest to the universal and ubiquitous nature of magic practices, one must note that well-attested procedures in Hellenistic and later magic are not matched in their more specific details by the Mesopotamian material, as the comparison of rituals for the confection of amulets and prescriptions for molding figurines and their paraphernalia shows. Of course, the few Mesopotamian rituals with detailed descriptions of the materia and the dromena have been many times invoked by comparatists and historians of religion, from Mircea Eliade's *Cosmologie et alchimie babyloniennes* (Bucarest: Vremea, 1937 [in Rumanian]; French translation Paris: Gallimard, 1991) to Walter Burkert's *Die orientalisierende Epoche* of 1982 (Sitzungsberichte der Heidelberger Akademie der Wissenschaften, Philosophisch-historische Klasse, 1984/1 = *The Orientalizing Revolution*, Cambridge, Mass. and London: Harvard University Press, 1992), not to mention more romantic and popular books of the past.

There are other important differences between the Near East and Greece. In Mesopotamia, preserved are those rituals that exorcists set down in handbooks and handed on to their disciples and successors through generations; these can be regarded as the official scientific manuals of the experts. Magic was not a marginal and clandestine manipulation; it was an activity prescribed and overtly practiced for the benefit of king and court, or of important individuals—only noxious witchcraft was forbidden and prosecuted. The magic of the common folk probably was never written down, and we have not much to go on when seeking to compare it with the material from the West. Neither can we document from Mesopotamia, as we can from the Hellenistic world and Rome, the changes in the social and legal status of magic and its practitioners. Moreover, in the Classical world we are privileged to have a vivid documentation of the use of magic in the literary sources, whether they deal with mythological events or events deemed historical. Classical literature provides the background against which the spells on lamellae, amulets, or gems can be delimited. The accounts of the preparation of a magic ritual, its aims, and its effects found in Homer, Greek drama and novels, in epics such as Lucan's *Pharsalia*, or the stories of Lucian, are the envy of the Assyriologist who has to be content with the allusions, or tantalizing glimpses into the practice of magic, which Mesopotamian sources allow.

The Near Eastern material for this book was collected over many years of association with the *Chicago Assyrian Dictionary*; for the stimulation provided by discussions at the Institute for Advanced Study in Princeton (in the second term of 1990–91 and the summer of 1992), and for the opportunity to explore a variety of avenues there I am indebted especially to the faculty of the Institute's School of Historical Studies. The original impetus to study astral influences in Babylonia, as well as many suggestions, came from Otto Neugebauer; I could no longer seek his advice for the final manuscript in Princeton, but to his memory I would like to dedicate this work.

ABBREVIATIONS

ABL R. F. Harper, *Assyrian and Babylonian Letters.* 14 vols. Chicago: University of Chicago Press, 1892–1914

ABRT J. A. Craig, *Assyrian and Babylonian Religious Texts* (Assyriologische Bibliothek XIII/1–2). Leipzig: Hinrichs, 1895–97

ACh C. Virolleaud, *L'Astrologie chaldéenne.* Paris: Geuthner, 1905–12

AfK *Archiv für Keilschriftforschung.* Berlin, 1923–25

AfO *Archiv für Orientforschung.* Berlin, 1926–

AGM *Archiv für Geschichte der Medizin.* Leipzig, 1908–

AHw. W. von Soden, *Akkadisches Handwörterbuch.* Wiesbaden: Harrassowitz, 1959–81

AMT R. C. Thompson, *Assyrian Medical Texts from the originals in the British Museum.* London-New York: H. Milford, Oxford University Press, 1923

Analecta Biblica Rome, 1952–

Anatolian Studies London, 1951–

AOS American Oriental Series

ARM Archives Royales de Mari. Paris: Geuthner, 1941–

ARMT Archives Royales de Mari (texts in transliteration and translation). Paris: Imprimerie Nationale, 1950–

ArOr *Archív Orientální.* (Journal of the Czechoslovak Oriental Institute). Prague, 1929–

ARRIM *Royal Inscriptions of Mesopotamia, Annual Review.* Toronto, 1983–

AS Assyriological Studies. Chicago, 1931–

Aula Orientalis Sabadell (Barcelona), 1983–

BAM F. Köcher, *Die babylonisch-assyrische Medizin in Texten und Untersuchungen.* Berlin: de Gruyter, 1963–

BBR H. Zimmern, *Beiträge zur Kenntnis der babylonischen Religion* (Assyriologische Bibliothek XII). Leipzig: Hinrichs, 1896–1901

BE University of Pennsylvania, Babylonian Section, Series A, cuneiform texts. Philadelphia, 1893–1914

Bibliotheca Orientalis Leiden, 1943–

BMS L. W. King, *Babylonian Magic and Sorcery.* London: Luzac & Co., 1896

Boll, *Sphaera* F. J. Boll, *Sphaera.* Leipzig: Teubner, 1903

Boll-Bezold-Gundel Boll, Franz, and Carl Bezold, *Sternglaube und Sterndeutung.* 4th ed. revised by W. Gundel. Leipzig-Berlin: Teubner, 1931.

Borger, *Esarh.* R. Borger, *Die Inschriften Asarhaddons, Königs von Assyrien (AfO* Beiheft 9). Osnabrück: Biblio, 1967

BPO E. Reiner and D. Pingree, *Babylonian Planetary Omens* (Bibliotheca Mesopotamica, vol. 2). Malibu: Undena, 1975–

ABBREVIATIONS

BRM Babylonian Records in the Library of J. Pierpont Morgan, ed. Albert T. Clay. 4 vols. New York: Private print, 1912–23

CAD *The Assyrian Dictionary of the Oriental Institute of the University of Chicago.* Chicago and Glückstadt: J. J. Augustin, 1956–

CCAG *Catalogus Codicum Astrologorum Graecorum*, eds. F. Cumont, F. Boll, et al. Brussels, 1898–

CRAI *Académie des Inscriptions et Belles Lettres. Comptes rendus des Séances.* Paris, 1857–

CT Cuneiform Texts from Babylonian Tablets in the British Museum. London, 1896–

DACG R. C. Thompson, *A Dictionary of Assyrian Chemistry and Geology.* Oxford: Clarendon, 1936

Dover Fs *'Owls to Athens'. Essays on Classical Subjects Presented to Sir Kenneth Dover*, ed. E. M. Craik. Oxford: Clarendon, 1990

Dream-book A. L. Oppenheim, *The Interpretation of Dreams in the Ancient Near East* (Transactions of the American Philosophical Society, Vol. 46/3), 1956

DSB *Dictionary of Scientific Biography*, C. C. Gillispie, ed. New York: Scribner, 1970–

EPHE *Ecole Pratique des Hautes Etudes, IVe Section, Annuaire*

HAMA O. Neugebauer, *A History of Ancient Mathematical Astronomy.* 3 vols. Berlin-Heidelberg-New York: Springer, 1975

Hg. Lexical series *HAR-gud* = *imrû* = *ballu*, published MSL 5–11

Hh. Lexical series *HAR-ra* = *hubullu*, published MSL 5–11

History of Religions Chicago, 1961–

HKL R. Borger, *Handbuch der Keilschriftliteratur.* 3 vols. Berlin: de Gruyter, 1967–75.

Hopfner, *Offenbarungszauber* Th. Hopfner, *Griechisch-Ägyptischer Offenbarungszauber.* vol. I–II Leipzig, 1921 and 1924; new edition of vol. I and vol. II Part 1 Amsterdam: Hakkert, 1974 and 1983

Iraq London, 1934–

JAOS *Journal of the American Oriental Society.* New Haven, 1843–

JCS *Journal of Cuneiform Studies.* New Haven, 1947–

JEOL *Jaarbericht van heet Vooraziatisch-Egyptisch Genootschap "Ex Oriente Lux."* Leiden, 1933–

JNES *Journal of Near Eastern Studies.* Chicago, 1942–

JWCI *Journal of the Warburg and Courtauld Institutes.* London, 1937–

KAO E. F. Weidner, *Alter und Bedeutung der babylonischen Astronomie und Astrallehre, nebst Studien über Fixsternhimmel und Kalender* (KAO [Im Kampfe um den alten Orient] 4). Leipzig, 1914

KAR E. Ebeling, *Keilschrifttexte aus Assur religiösen Inhalts* (WVDOG XXVIII/1–4, XXXIV/1–5). Leipzig: Hinrichs, 1915–23

KB Keilinschriftliche Bibliothek. Berlin: Reuther's, 1889–

KBo Keilschrifttexte aus Boghazköi, eds. H. Figulla, E. F. Weidner, et al. Leipzig: Hinrichs, 1916–23

KMI E. Ebeling, *Keilschrifttexte medizinischen Inhalts* (Berliner Beiträge zur Keilschriftforschung, Beiheft 1–2). Berlin, 1922–23

Köcher, *Pflanzenkunde* F. Köcher, *Keilschrifttexte zur assyrisch-babylonischen Drogen- und Pflanzenkunde.* Deutsche Akademie der Wissenschaften zu Berlin, Institut für Orientforschung, Veröffentlichung Nr. 29. Berlin: Akademie-Verlag, 1955.

KUB Keilschrifturkunden aus Boghazköi

LAS S. Parpola, *Letters from Assyrian Scholars to the Kings Esarhaddon and Assurbanipal* (Alter Orient und Altes Testament, 5/1 and 5/2). Kevelaer: Butzon & Bercker, 1970 and 1983

LBAT *Late Babylonian Astronomical and Related Texts,* copied by T. G. Pinches and J. N. Strassmaier, prepared for publication by A. J. Sachs, with the cooperation of J. Schaumberger. Providence: Brown University Press, 1955

LKA E. Ebeling, *Literarische Keilschrifttexte aus Assur.* Berlin: Akademie-Verlag, 1953

Malku Synonym list *malku* = *šarru*

MAOG *Mitteilungen der Altorientalischen Gesellschaft, Berlin.* Leipzig: E. Pfeiffer, 1925-

MIO *Mitteilungen des Instituts für Orientforschung,* Akademie der Wissenschaften. Berlin, 1953-

MRS Mission de Ras Shamra. Paris, 1936-

MSL Materialien zum sumerischen Lexikon (from volume X on: Materials for the Sumerian Lexicon). Rome: Pontificium Institutum Biblicum, 1937-

MUL.APIN Hermann Hunger and David Pingree, *MUL.APIN. An Astronomical Compendium in Cuneiform. AfO* Beiheft 24. Horn, Austria: F. Berger, 1989.

NABU *Nouvelles Assyriologiques Brèves et Utilitaires.* Paris, 1987-

NH Pliny, *Natural History*

OIP Oriental Institute Publications. Chicago, 1924-

Or. NS *Orientalia,* Nova Series. Rome, 1932-

PBS University of Pennsylvania, University Museum, Publications of the Babylonian Section. Philadelphia, 1911-

PGM *Papyri Graecae Magicae. Die griechischen Zauberpapyri,* ed. K. Preisendanz. 2nd revised edition, 2 vols. Stuttgart: Teubner, 1973, 1974. English version: The Greek Magical Papyri in Translation, ed. H. D. Betz. Chicago: University of Chicago Press, 1986

R H. C. Rawlinson, *The Cuneiform Inscriptions of Western Asia.* 5 vols. London, 1861-84

RA *Revue d'assyriologie et d'archéologie orientale.* Paris, 1884-

RAC *Reallexikon für Antike und Christentum.* Stuttgart, 1941-

RBPH *Revue Belge de Philologie et d'Histoire.* Brussels, 1922-

RE *Pauly's Realencyklopädie der classischen Altertumswissenschaft,* pub. G. Wissowa. Stuttgart: Metzler, 1894-

RLA *Reallexikon der Assyriologie.* Berlin & Leipzig: de Gruyter, 1928-

RSO *Rivista degli studi orientali.* Rome, 1907-

SAA State Archives of Assyria. Helsinki: Helsinki University Press, 1987-

SAAB *State Archives of Assyria, Bulletin.* Helsinki, 1987-

SAHG A. Falkenstein and W. von Soden, *Sumerische und akkadische Hymnen und Gebete.* Zürich-Stuttgart: Artemis, 1953

SANE Sources from the Ancient Near East. Malibu: Undena, 1974–

SLB Studia ad Tabulas Cuneiformes a F. M. Th. de Liagre Böhl Collectas Pertinentia. Leiden, 1952–

SMEA *Studi Micenei ed Egeo-anatolici.* Rome, 1966–

SpTU *Spätbabylonische Texte aus Uruk* (I–III: Ausgrabungen der Deutschen Forschungsgemeinschaft in Uruk-Warka, vols. 9, 10, 12. Berlin: Gebr. Mann, 1976–; IV: Ausgrabungen in Uruk-Warka, Endberichte, vol. 12. Mainz am Rhein: von Zabern, 1993)

Strack-Billerbeck H. L. Strack, and P. Billerbeck, *Kommentar zum Neuen Testament aus Talmud und Midrasch.* Munich, 1922–28

Streck, *Asb.* Maximilian Streck, *Assurbanipal* (Vorderasiatische Bibliothek, 7). Leipzig: Hinrichs, 1916

STT O. R. Gurney, J. J. Finkelstein, and P. Hulin, *The Sultantepe Tablets* (Occasional Publications of the British Institute for Archaeology at Ankara, No. 3 and No. 7). London, 1957 and 1964

ŠÀ.ZI.GA R. D. Biggs, *ŠÀ.ZI.GA: Ancient Mesopotamian Potency Incantations* (Texts from Cuneiform Sources, 2). Locust Valley, NY: J. J. Augustin, 1967

Šu-ila O. Loretz and W. R. Mayer, *Šu-ila-Gebete* (Alter Orient und Altes Testament, 34). Kevelaer: Butzon & Bercker, 1978

TAPA *Transactions of the American Philological Association.* Hartford, 1871–

TCL Musée du Louvre – Département des Antiquités Orientales. Textes cunéiformes. Paris: Geuthner, 1910–

TDP René Labat, *Traité akkadien de diagnostics et pronostic médicaux* (Leiden: Brill, 1951)

Thompson Rep. R. C. Thompson, *The Reports of Magicians and Astrologers of Nineveh and Babylon in the British Museum.* London: Luzac & Co., 1900

TLB Tabulae Cuneiformes a F. M. Th. de Liagre Böhl Collectae. Leiden, 1954–

TSBA *Transactions of the Society of Biblical Archaeology.* London, 1872–93.

UET Ur Excavations. Texts. London and Philadelphia: Oxford University Press – University of Pennsylvania Press, 1928–

Weidner, *Handbuch* E. Weidner, *Handbuch der babylonischen Astronomie* (Assyriologische Bibliothek XXIII). Leipzig: Hinrichs, 1915

WO *Die Welt des Orients.* Göttingen, 1947–

WVDOG Deutsche Orientgesellschaft, Wissenschaftliche Veröffentlichungen. Leipzig, 1900–

WZKM *Wiener Zeitschrift für die Kunde des Morgenlandes.* Vienna, 1887–

YOS Yale Oriental Series, Babylonian Texts. New Haven, 1915–

ZA *Zeitschrift für Assyriologie und verwandte Gebiete,* Leipzig, 1886–

Introduction

> The nobles are deep in sleep,[1]
> the bars (of the doors) are lowered, the bolts(?) are in place—
> (also) the (ordinary) people do not utter a sound,
> the(ir always) open doors are locked.
> The gods and goddesses of the country—
> Šamaš, Sin, Adad and Ištar—
> have gone home to heaven to sleep,
> they will not give decisions or verdicts (tonight).

And the diviner ends:

> May the great gods of the night:
> shining Fire-star,
> heroic Irra,
> Bow-star, Yoke-star,
> Orion, Dragon-star,
> Wagon, Goat-star,
> Bison-star, Serpent-star
> stand by and
> put a propitious sign
> in the lamb I am blessing now
> for the haruspicy I will perform (at dawn).[2]

One of the rare prayers from Mesopotamia that strike a responsive chord in a modern reader, this prayer, or rather lyric poem, is known among Assyriologists as 'Prayer to the Gods of the Night.' The Gods of the Night of the title is but the translation of the Akkadian phrase *ilī mušīti* that appears in line 14 of this poem and in the incipit of various other versions of the prayer.

The Gods of the Night, as their enumeration in this poem

---

[1] The first word of the poem (here translated 'deep in sleep' from *bullulu* 'to become numb?' with *CAD* B p. 44a s.v. *balālu*) has been read *pullusu* by Wolfram von Soden, *ZA* 43 (1936) 306 and *AHw*. 814a; a reading *pullulu*, with the translation 'secured' was proposed by A. Livingstone, *NABU* 1990/86.

[2] The translation is that of Oppenheim, *Analecta Biblica* 12 (1959) 295f., with minor modifications.

shows, are the stars and constellations of the night sky. How prevalent is the appeal to stellar deities, and to what extent and in what circumstances are the gods and goddesses worshipped in Mesopotamia considered under their stellar manifestations, is the subject I wish to treat here.

The situational context for reciting this prayer is divination, and more specifically the preparation by the haruspex—Akkadian *bārû*—of the lamb that will be slaughtered so that the inspection of its entrails—exta—yield an omen, usually as answer to the diviner's query. This role of the *bārû* in Mesopotamian divination has not received particular attention in the many studies that deal with it and with its relationship to the Etruscan *disciplina.*[3]

Other areas of Mesopotamian life that rely on, appeal to, or use the power of the stars are magic machinations, meant to cause harm as well as to protect from harm; the confection of amulets and charms; the establishing of favorable or unfavorable moments in time; and the complex domain of medicine, from procuring the herb or other medicinal substance, through the preparation and administration of the medication.

There is a vast corpus of Babylonian literature, hardly exploited by Assyriologists even, and of which a small part only is available to the non-specialist in translation or in excerpt, that can be mined for references or allusions to astral magic, that is, efforts to use the influence of the heavenly bodies upon the sublunar world, for purposes beneficent to man as well as for evil machinations. Such astral magic, as the art of harnessing the power of the stars may be called, was practiced on the one hand by scholars, such as the professional diviners and exorcists, to foretell the future and to avert evil portents, and on the other by sorcerers and sorceresses who harnessed the same

[3] See especially Jean Nougayrol, "Trente ans de recherches sur la divination babylonienne (1935–1965)," in *La Divination en Mésopotamie ancienne et dans les régions voisines*, XIVe Rencontre Assyriologique Internationale (Paris: Presses Universitaires de France, 1966) 5–19; idem, "La divination babylonienne," in *La Divination*, A. Caquot and M. Leibovici, eds. (Paris: Presses Universitaires de France, 1968), vol. 1, pp. 25–81; see also Jean Bottéro, "Symptômes, Signes, Ecritures," in *Divination et Rationalité*, J.-P. Vernant, ed. (Paris: Editions du Seuil, 1974), 70–197.

powers to inflict harm upon an adversary. The former were knowledgeable in apotropaic rituals, the latter in black magic.

Of the stars that appear in these magic contexts it is not only the planets that are invoked for their influence, as they are in Hellenistic astrology, but also various fixed stars and constellations. Babylonian constellations take their names from the shapes that their configurations suggest: human figures, animals, or common objects, similar, and sometimes identical to the names they had in Classical antiquity, as we learn from the descriptions of celestial configurations known as the Greek and the Barbaric, i.e., non-Greek, spheres,[4] the latter usually taken to refer to the Egyptian or the Babylonian sphere.

Illustrations are rare and late in Mesopotamia; still, we are able to identify many constellations, even those whose names are uniquely Babylonian. The identifications are based mainly on astronomical data; these are complemented and confirmed by the single cuneiform text that gives a description of part of the heavens.[5] Thus, among the animal figures, the Goat is the constellation Lyra, and the Snake more or less corresponds to Hydra; among the demons and divine beings the Demon with the Gaping Mouth is roughly equivalent to Cygnus (with parts of Cepheus), and the True Shepherd of the god of the sky, Anu, is Orion; of the celestial counterparts of terrestrial objects the Arrow is Sirius, the Furrow, Spica, and the Wagon is Ursa Maior, our Big Dipper.

Mathematical astronomy in Mesopotamia appears in the fifth century B.C. The observation of the heavens and the recognition of the periodicities of heavenly phenomena go back, nevertheless, much farther in time. The identity of the appearances of Venus as Evening star and Morning star was known early, and so was, though possibly at a later date, that of the two appearances of Mercury. The telling names given to the fastest planet, Mercury: the Leaping One,[6] and to the slowest, Saturn: the Steady One[7] also testify to the astronomical knowl-

---

[4] Also called *Sphaera graecanica* and *Sphaera barbarica*, see Boll, *Sphaera* pp. 411f.

[5] E. F. Weidner, "Eine Beschreibung des Sternenhimmels aus Assur," *AfO* 4 (1927) 73–85.

[6] GUD.UD = Šihṭu, see A. J. Sachs, *LBAT* p. xxxvii.

[7] SAG.UŠ = kayamānu.

FIGURE 1. Relief from Assurnasirpal's palace with the king wearing a necklace hung with emblems of the planets. Courtesy of the British Museum, no. 124525.

edge of the Babylonians. Of the other planets Mars was, obviously, the Red planet, also known as the Enemy;[8] Jupiter was Heroic.[9] Sun and Moon were included in the number of the seven planets. The Sun, surveying the entire earth, omnipresent and omniscient, was as in other cultures the god of justice, as expressed in the great hymn to Šamaš, discussed below, and the Scales (the constellation Libra, Akkadian *Zibanītu*) have as epithet "Šamaš's star of justice," an association comparable to that of personified Justice holding the scales in her hand on medieval representations.[10]

The stars and planets may be addressed under their astral

[8] *Makrû* 'red,' and *Nakru* 'enemy.'

[9] Sumerian UD.AL.TAR, Akkadian *Dāpinu*; the meaning of Jupiter's most common name, SAG.ME.GAR, has so far remained opaque, not even the correct reading of the signs ME.GAR (that is, whether they are to be pronounced *megar* or not) is known.

[10] It was the constellation Virgo, which is adjacent to Libra, that was associated with Dikē, the goddess of Justice, see *RE* 9 (1903) 577ff., as in the Commentaries to Aratos' *Phaenomena* 602 (Maass): virgo iusta quae et libra vocatur. For the scales as attribute of the goddess Justitia see, e.g., *Lexicon der christlichen Ikonographie*, Engelbert Kirschbaum S. J., ed., vol. 2 (Rome: Herder, 1970) 467f.; see especially Karl Ludwig Skutsch, "Libramen Aequum," *Die Antike* 12 (1936) 49–64.

FIGURE 2. Cylinder seal showing bearded Ištar, published as no. 371 in Edith Porada, *Corpus of Ancient Near Eastern Seals in North American Collections*, I (The Bollingen Series XIV), Washington: Pantheon Press, 1948.

names or as the deities they represent: Ninurta, Ištar, Gula, etc.; the difference between the two designations may be expressed in the cuneiform writing by the sign that precedes their names: either the sign for "god" or the sign for "star." The prefixed cuneiform sign indicates, as do other so-called "determinatives," the class to which an entity belongs. The determinative for divine names, customarily transcribed as a raised letter *d* (^{d}), is abbreviated from the Sumerian word *dingir* 'god,' itself evolved from the pictogram representing an eight-pointed star; the determinative for stars is the word-sign for the Sumerian word *mul* 'star,' whose pictographic predecessor was a configuration of three stars. Thus, the spellings MUL.PA.BIL.SAG and ^{d}PA.BIL.SAG 'Sagittarius,' MUL.SIPA.ZI.AN.NA and ^{d}SIPA.ZI.AN.NA 'Orion,' MUL.GU$_4$.UD and ^{d}GU$_4$.UD 'Mercury,' MUL Delebat and ^{d}Delebat 'Venus' are interchangeable, sometimes even in one and the same text.[11]

The highest divine triad, Anu, Enlil, and Ea, are not identified with individual stars, constellations, or planets; rather, among them they represent the entire sky, not only in the person of Anu, the sky god par excellence, whose name in

---

[11] Late astrological and astronomical texts occasionally use other determinatives, such as the signs TE, ÁB, and GÁN, for which the readings múl, mul$_x$ and mul$_4$ were devised by Assyriologists; the reasons for the choice of these determinatives elude us; they may represent a learned pun or a cryptogram. For ÁB see the literature quoted by A. J. Sachs, *JCS* 21 (1967, published 1969) 200.

Sumerian, *an*, means 'sky,'[12] but especially as lords of the three "paths" in the sky, the "Path of Anu," the "Path of Enlil," and the "Path of Ea," which represent three segments of the horizon over which the stars rise.[13]

The two appearances of Venus, even though identified as the same planet, were attributed to two distinct manifestations of the same deity: As morning star, Venus was female; as evening star, male,[14] and the two aspects corresponded to the double character of Ištar as goddess of love and war. As the male deity Ištar is described as bearded,[15] and she is so represented on an Islamic bronze candelabra, now in the Musée des Arts Décoratifs.[16] As for Mercury who, just as in Hellenistic astrology, is both male and female,[17] the identity of the planet in his evening and morning visibilities was recognized long before astronomical tables calculating Mercury's period were composed: Mercury is addressed as "star of sunrise and sunset."[18]

Mars, the hostile planet, presides over destruction, and is

---

[12] The pictogram which evolved into the cuneiform sign AN, which also stands for *dingir* 'god,' is the image of an eight-pointed star.

[13] For this identification, see David Pingree, *BPO* 2 p. 17f. The three "paths" frequently occur in celestial omens.

[14] Usually the opposite is held, in conformity with Ptolemy's assignment of genders to planets in *Tetrabiblos* 1.6 and 7. The Babylonian evidence is based on an explanatory text dealing with Venus, published in *3R* 53 (K.5990, republished in *ACh* Ištar 8) from which the lines "Venus is female at sunset" and "Venus is male at sunrise" were communicated by Sayce, in *TSBA* 3 (1874) 196; the text is also cited by Parpola, *LAS* 2 p. 77 and n. 157. In fact, K.5990 is the only source holding that Venus is female at sunset, while others (BM 134543, K.10566, 81-2-4,239, etc., see Reiner and Pingree, *BPO* 3) hold that Venus *ina* ᵈUTU.È (KUR-*ma*) *sinnišat* 'is female (rising) in the east.' For Venus being female in the west see also Wolfgang Heimpel, "The Sun at Night and the Doors of Heaven in Babylonian Texts," *JCS* 38 (1986) 127–51.

[15] *ziqna zaqnat* in Tablet 61 of the celestial omen series *Enūma Anu Enlil*, and in its parallel sections in the series *iqqur īpuš* for which see Chapter V. She is also often represented with a beard on Mesopotamian cylinder seals, see fig. 2.

[16] Listed as No. 3057 in the *Amtlicher Katalog* of the 1910 München exhibit, cited by F. Saxl, *Der Islam* 3 (1912) 174 n. 4: "Venus (wohl mißverständlich) bärtig."

[17] Akkadian *zikar sinniš* (NITA SAL) 'male (and) female,' K.2346 r. 29, compare Ptolemy *Tetrabiblos* 1.6 and 7.

[18] *AfO* 18 (1957–58) 385ff. CBS 733 + 1757:11 (prayer to Marduk as Mercury, edited by W. G. Lambert).

equated with Nergal, god of pestilence. His rising – first visibility – is a bad omen, portending death of the herds: "Mars will rise and destroy the herd,"[19] the only prediction of an astronomical event, apart from omens predicting an eclipse, appearing in other than celestial omens. His Akkadian name, *Ṣalbatānu*, has no known meaning or etymology.[20] Learned Babylonian commentaries have explained this name as 'He who keeps plague constant' by breaking up the name into its syllabic components and interpreting these syllables in Sumerian, thus arriving at the assumed Akkadian reading *Muštabarrû mūtānu*.[21]

The names of most planets have no identifiable meaning in either Sumerian or Akkadian, neither the just mentioned name of Mars, Ṣalbatānu, nor Jupiter's most common name SAG.ME.GAR (see note 9); nor the name of Venus, written *Dil-bat* (preferably to be read *Dele-bat* following the Greek transcription *Delephat*). No clear etymology or explanation exists for the Akkadian or Sumerian word for 'planet' itself. In Greek, *planetes* are the 'errant ones' because they roam the sky amidst the fixed stars; the Akkadian word for planet, *bibbu*, 'wild sheep,' may also refer to their irregular movement.[22]

---

19 References to this prediction from lunar omens have been collected by Francesca Rochberg-Halton, in *A Scientific Humanist. Studies in Memory of Abraham Sachs*, Erle Leichty, M. deJ. Ellis, P. Gerardi, eds. (Philadelphia: The University Museum, 1988) 323–28. The omen also appears as apodosis of a liver omen, *RA* 65 (1971) 73:62, cited *CAD* N p. 266, as also noted by M. Stol, *Bibliotheca Orientalis* 47 (1990) 375, and in a celestial omen on solar eclipses, with the name of Mars replaced by MUL.UDU.BAD 'planet,' *ACh* Šamaš 8:62.

20 Even the correct reading of the polyvalent signs NI = ṣal and BE = bat with which the name is customarily written has only recently been confirmed with the help of a spelling ṣa-al-ba-ta-nu, in the liver omen cited in the preceding note, see Jean Nougayrol, *RA* 65 (1971) 82 ad line 62.

21 In the list *5R* 46 no. 1:42, based on the equations ZAL = *šutabrû* (infinitive) 'to last long,' participle *muštabarrû*; BAD = *mūtu*, with phonetic complement *-a-nu* = *mūtānu* 'plague' or 'great death.'

22 The Sumerian word which is equated with *bibbu*, UDU.BAD, also contains the word 'sheep' (UDU), but the second element, the polyvalent sign BAD, once thought to have the reading *idim* 'wild,' has recently been found glossed *til*, in the gloss to line 34 of Tablet XI of HAR-ra = *hubullu*, which lists hides, among them [KUŠ.U]DU.BAD (gloss: [u]-du-ti-il) = *mašak bi-ib-bi*; see MSL 7 124:34, and for the gloss, MSL 9 197. Since in Sumerian *til* means 'finished' or 'complete,' the once assumed meaning 'wild sheep' for the Sumerian word is no longer tenable.

But of all the planets it was the Moon that was of the greatest importance to the Babylonians. It was the Moon, from its first sighting to its last, that regulated the calendar, which was based on lunar months. The Moon is a "Fruit, lord of the month,"[23] constantly renewing himself, as his epithet *eddešû* 'ever-renewing' stresses. The Moon's waxing and waning does not determine a stronger or weaker influence on, say, the growing of crops as it does in Hellenistic astrology, but its phases signal the timing of various ritual acts. The Moon god, Sin, the father of both Šamaš (the Sun) and Ištar, is a male deity, not the Selene or Luna of the Greeks and Romans, but he still has an affinity with women magicians, sorceresses who are able to "draw down the Moon" (see Chapter VI). The eclipse of the Moon, in particular, remained a terrifying event, whose dire predictions had to be averted by penitential rites,[24] including, under the Sargonid kings in the eighth and seventh centuries B.C., the installation of a substitute king. This substitute king reigned for one hundred days and was then put to death, thus taking upon himself the misfortune and death portended for the king.[25]

Sun, Moon, and Venus, represented by their emblems the sundisk, the lunar crescent, and the eight-pointed star, are commonly depicted on monuments—steles, boundary stones—as guardians of the provisions sworn to in the treaty or deed recorded therein.

The influence of these stellar deities on man is twofold: they are both the origin of ills that beset him and the beneficent powers that can be made favorably disposed toward a supplicant. They may cause affliction, exerting nefarious influence on their own or through sorcerers' manipulations, and they may herald ill fortune by their motions and configurations that are recorded in the extensive collection of celestial omens.

However, through proper prayers and rituals the stars' influence can avert the portended misfortune and assist the exorcist and the physician in healing illness.

---

[23] *Inbu bēl arhi*; this metaphor is also the name of a Babylonian royal hemerology, for which see pp. 113f.

[24] The text (BRM 4 6) is treated by Erich Ebeling, *Tod und Leben nach den Vorstellungen der Babylonier* (Berlin and Leipzig: de Gruyter & Co., 1931) no. 24, pp. 91–96.

[25] For this ritual see Parpola, *LAS* 2 pp. xxii–xxxii.

Astral magic and the role of astral deities have been amply studied in connection with Hellenistic Egypt and the corpus of Hermetic texts and magical papyri originating in Egypt.[26] The cuneiform evidence from Mesopotamia has been largely neglected by Assyriologists, and has been at the most utilized at second hand by other scholars who had to rely on often inexactly edited Babylonian sources. But even if comparison with neighboring civilizations had not so suggested, the power attributed to the heavenly bodies and their significance and impact according to the Babylonians' conception in their cosmology should have been evident from such Mesopotamian images as the poetic phrase "writing of heaven" (*šiṭir šamê* or *šiṭir burūme*) applied to the starry sky,[27] and from King Esarhaddon's remark that he depicted on steles "*lumāšu*-stars which represent the writing of my name."[28] Uncertain is the reference, unfortunately still opaque, to the "reading" or "meaning" of Assurbanipal's name that was revealed in a dream to Gyges, king of Lydia.[29]

Poetic texts are also the first to adumbrate how the moon and the stars give signs and warnings to men, even before the art of celestial divination had assumed the status of a scholarly discipline. The so-called "King of Battle" (*šar tamhāri*), an Old Babylonian poem dealing with the exploits of King Sargon of Akkad

---

[26] Garth Fowden, *The Egyptian Hermes: a historical approach to the late pagan mind* (Cambridge: Cambridge University Press, 1986) can be consulted for earlier references.

[27] See *CAD* Š/3 p. 146 s.v.; cited (after Zimmern) already by Franz Dornseiff, *Das Alphabet in Mystik und Magie*, Stoicheia Heft 7 (Leipzig and Berlin: Teubner, 1922) 89f.

[28] *lumāšē šiṭir šumiya*, Borger, *Esarh.* p. 28:11, *lumāšē tamšīl šiṭir šumiya*, Borger, *Esarh.* p. 27 Ep. 40:9. An attempt at correlating this phrase with the symbols depicted on the stone monument was made by D. D. Luckenbill, "The Black Stone of Esarhaddon," *American Journal of Semitic Languages* 41 (1924–25) 165–73; see also, with reference to Sargon's use of the phrase, C. J. Gadd, *Ideas of Divine Rule in the Ancient East*, The Schweich Lectures of the British Academy 1945 (London, 1948) 93–95.

[29] See for this episode Mordechai Cogan and Hayim Tadmor, "Gyges and Ashurbanipal," *Or.* NS 46 (1977) 75, though they, by preferring the manuscript tradition which writes *nibīt šarrūtiya* 'the mention of my kingship' over *nibīt šumiya* 'the "reading" of my name,' divorce this occurrence from the other occurrences of this well-attested phrase.

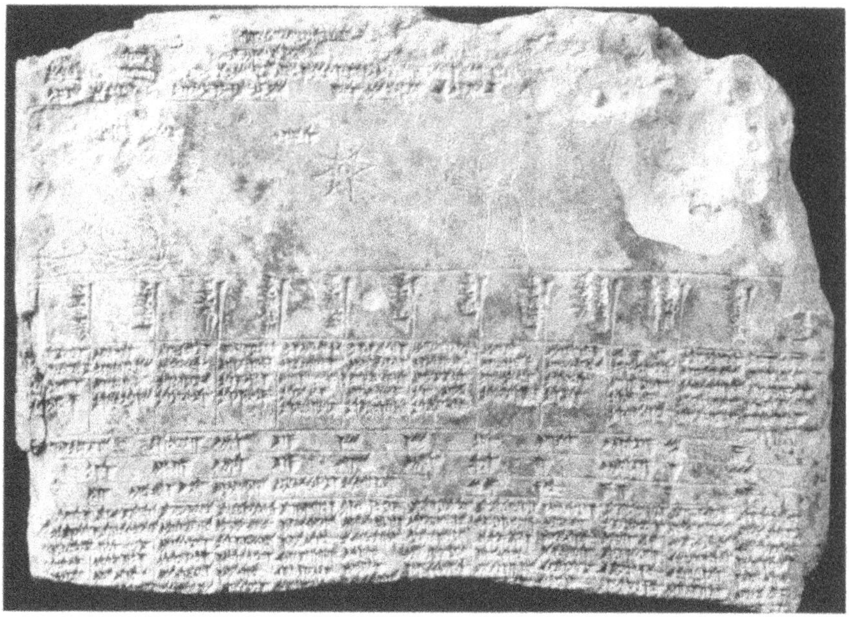

FIGURE 3

FIGURE 4

FIGURE 5

FIGURES 3, 4, 5. Representations of constellations incised on a Late Babylonian tablet. Fig. 3, courtesy of the Louvre, no. AO 6448; fig. 4 courtesy of Staatliche Museen zu Berlin, no. VAT 7847; fig. 5 courtesy of Staatliche Museen zu Berlin, no. VAT 7851.

(c. 2400 B.C.),[30] relates how 'the sun became obscured, the stars came forth for the enemy,'[31] a celestial portent that must refer to a solar eclipse during which the stars became visible, an event that was evidently to be interpreted as the stars portending victory for Sargon against his enemy.

Allusions to celestial portents given to Sargon appear in liver omens, the earliest recorded mode of divination, which is attested long before celestial omens were collected and codified. A particular configuration of the sheep's liver is said to refer to King Sargon of Akkad as one who "traversed darkness and light came out for him."[32] This description must record an eclipse occurring under Sargon, in spite of its peculiar phraseology; indeed, omens from lunar eclipses were the first to be committed to writing, possibly as early as 1800 B.C.[33] More

[30] Joan G. Westenholz, *Legends of the Kings of Akkad . . .* (forthcoming).

[31] id'im šamšum kakkabū ú-ṣú-ú ana nakrim, *RA* 45 (1951) 174:63–64; for a different interpretation see J.-J. Glassner, *RA* 79 (1985) 123.

[32] For omens referring to Sargon of Akkad see H. Hirsch, *AfO* 20 (1963) 7ff.

[33] F. Rochberg-Halton, *Aspects of Babylonian Celestial Divination: The Lunar*

important, Sargon's later namesake, Sargon II of Assyria, also records, no doubt intentionally referring to his illustrious predecessor's example, that a lunar eclipse portended victory for him on his campaign against Urartu in 714 B.C.[34]

Portents from lunar and solar eclipses, as well as from other lunar, solar, stellar, and meteorological phenomena eventually were collected and more or less standardized in the omen collection called from its incipit *Enūma Anu Enlil* 'When Anu (and) Enlil' comprising seventy books (Akkadian: "tablets"[35]) along with various excerpts from these and commentaries to them.[36] But while these prognostications provided warnings for king and country—though rarely for an individual—the stars and planets were not thought to affect man's destiny by their direct influence, as they were in Greek horoscopic astrology. In Otto Neugebauer's words:

> Before the fifth century B.C. celestial omina probably did not include predictions for individuals, based on planetary positions

Eclipse Tablets of Enūma Anu Enlil, Archiv für Orientforschung, Beiheft 22 (Horn, Austria: Ferdinand Berger, 1989). See also P. Huber, "Dating by Lunar Eclipse Omens with Speculations on the Birth of Omen Astrology," in *From Ancient Omens to Statistical Mechanics. Essays on the Exact Sciences Presented to Asger Aaboe,* J. L. Berggren and B. R. Goldstein, eds., Acta Historica Scientiarum Naturalium et Medicinalium, 39 (Copenhagen: University Library, 1987) 3-13. For attempts at using omens that connect lunar eclipses with historical events (the so-called "historical omens") for the purposes of dating these events, see Johann Schaumberger, "Die Mondfinsternisse der Dritten Dynastie von Ur," *ZA* 49 (1949) 50-58, and idem, "Astronomische Untersuchung der 'historischen' Mondfinsternisse in Enūma Anu Enlil," *AfO* 17 (1954-56) 89-92.

[34] A. L. Oppenheim, "The City of Assur in 714 B.C.," *JNES* 19 (1960) 133-47.

[35] The term "tablet" is used in Assyriology to designate a chapter, book, or other unit of a series of clay tablets, so named because it is written on one clay tablet, and normally bears in its colophon a subscript naming it the nth tablet of the series.

[36] The collection is in the process of being edited by Reiner and Pingree, Rochberg-Halton, and van Soldt; so far published are *BPO* fascicles 1 and 2 (by Reiner and Pingree) covering E(nūma) A(nu) E(nlil) Tablets 50-51 and 63, *AfO* Beiheft 22 by F. Rochberg-Halton (see note 33) covering Tablets 15-22, and *Solar Omens of* Enuma Anu Enlil: *Tablets 23(24)-29(30)* by Wilfred H. van Soldt (Leiden: Nederlands Instituut voor het Nabije Oosten, 1995). An edition of Tablet 14 was published by F. Al-Rawi and A. R. George, *AfO* 39 (1991-92) 52-73.

in the signs of the zodiac and on their mutual configurations. In this latest and most significant modification astrology became known to the Greeks in the Hellenistic period. But with the exception of some typical Mesopotamian relics the doctrine was changed in Greek hands to a universal system in which form alone it could spread all over the world. Hence astrology in the modern sense of the term, with its vastly expanded set of "methods" is a truly Greek creation, in many respects parallel to the development of Christian theology a few centuries later.[37]

Yet besides Greek deterministic astrology, that is, genethlialogy, or horoscopic astrology, to which the quoted strictures of Neugebauer apply, and Mesopotamian omen literature with which he contrasted it, there exist areas in which the Babylonians acknowledged the influence of the stars. These are, firstly, catarchic astrology, which endeavors to find the most auspicious moment for commencing an undertaking; secondly, belief in the stars' power to imbue ordinary substances with supernatural, magic effectiveness, which I discuss in Chapters II and III; and thirdly, the apotropaic and prophylactic application of astral influence, both benefic and malefic, especially in the machinations of black magic, insofar as stars can protect from and avert the evil wrought by sorcerers or portended by an ominous sign. Cuneiform sources reveal how the Babylonians conceived the celestial bodies, what power they attributed to them, what they expected to obtain through these powers, and what were the means they used to gain their influence. Documentation for these concerns is found not so much in the literature that concerns itself with celestial omens but in the scientific writings of the Mesopotamian intellectuals. These writings include, in addition to fields that are generally acknowledged as science today, such as medicine, others that are not, such as divination and various activities around it. Much new material can be found in the recently reexamined correspondence of Assyrian and Babylonian scholars in the letters they addressed to the kings of Assyria in the eighth and seventh centuries,[38] and in their reports on astronomical observations which include pre-

[37] O. Neugebauer, *HAMA* 613.

[38] Published by Simo Parpola, *LAS,* revised and expanded in his *Letters from Assyrian and Babylonian Scholars,* SAA 10 (1993).

dictions based on the phenomena observed as well as the means to avert portended evil.[39] We may follow them in making no distinction between scientific astronomy and magic operations.

Parallels with beliefs and practices of the Hellenistic world, as I try to show in these pages, strengthen my claim of the uses made of the astral powers; Mesopotamian sources not customarily adduced for the history of culture may thereby add their evidence to the history of magic, especially astral magic.

[39] Published by Hermann Hunger, *Astrological Reports to Assyrian Kings*, SAA 8 (1992).

CHAPTER I

The Role of Stars

Stars function in a dual role in relation to man: they exert a direct influence and serve as mediators between man and god. Directly, through astral irradiation, they transform ordinary substances into potent ones that will be effective in magic, medicine, or ritual, as *materia medica,* amulets, or cultic appurtenances. Stars also provide reliable answers to the query of the diviner. More important, in their second role stars are man's medium of communication with the divine.

The role of the stars as mediators emerges from the descriptions given in Mesopotamian poetry. For poetry can be found not only in the much-anthologized pieces from Gilgameš and other myths or epic tales, or in the hymns and prayers of the official cult that have from early on attracted attention and comparison with the psalms of the Old Testament. It is often hidden in the scientific texts, those that constitute the corpus of the professional exorcist and diviner, disdained by the scientist and dismissed as boring by the literary historian.

The mediating role of the stars – not unlike the role of saints – is most clearly stated in the prayer of the supplicant to the Yoke star, approximately our Boötes, in an apotropaic ritual against mistakes occurring while executing temple offices:

> Yoke star standing at the right, Yoke star standing at the left,
> the god sends you to man, and man to the god,
> (and now) I send you to (my personal) god who eats my food-offering,
> drinks my water (libation),
> accepts my incense offering.[40]

---

[40] MUL.ŠUDUN Á.ZI.DA GUB.BA MUL.ŠUDUN Á.GÙB.BA GUB.BA
išapparkunūši ilu ana amēli amēlu ana ili
anāku ašpurkunūši ana DINGIR ākil NINDA.MU NAG! A.MU
māhiru sirqīya
KAR 38 r. 24ff. and duplicates, see Caplice, *Or.* NS 39 (1970) 124ff.

Stars are messengers who are to take the supplicant's prayer to the deity, as in:

may the star itself take to you (goddess) my misery;
let the ecstatic[41] tell you, the dream-interpreter repeat to you,
let the (three) watches of the night speak to you . . .[42]

Other stars of the night sky appear in a like role. Besides the prayer to the Yoke star, the cited apotropaic ritual contains appeals, first, to the "gods of the night," then to Venus, and finally to the Pleiades, adjured to be at the supplicant's right, and to the Kidney star, adjured to be at his left.[43]

Stand by me, O Gods of the Night!
Heed my words, O gods of destinies,
Anu, Enlil, Ea, and all the great gods!
I call to you, Delebat (i.e., Venus), Lady of battles (variant has: Lady of the silence [of the night]),
I call to you, O Night, bride (veiled by?) Anu.
Pleiades, stand on my right, Kidney-star, stand on my left!

Of the several copies some preserve only the partial invocation "[. . .] Pleiades, stand at my left, [I? send] you to the god and goddess [who ate my food offering,] drank my water [libation], [. . .] intercede for me!"[44] Rare as such explicit state-

---

[41] The translation of the word "ecstatic" presupposes the reading *zabbu* selected here, on account of its parallelism with *šabrû*, 'interpreter of dreams.' However, in the reading *zappu*, equally possible, the word means 'Pleiades' and possibly this is what was originally meant. As for the parallel, *šabrû* (or *šaprû*), it does not refer, to my knowledge, to a star or constellation.

[42] muruṣ libbiya MUL-ma lūbilakki
zabbu liqbâkimma šabrû lišannâki
EN.NUN.MEŠ ša mūši lidbubanikki

LKA 29d ii 1ff. The lines speaking of "the watches of the night" also occur in *LKA* 29e right col. 1 and its parallel *STT* 52:2ff., see W. G. Lambert, *RA* 53 (1959) 127. The "three watches of the night" are also addressed in *KAR* 58 rev. 7, along with Nusku. Of course there remains the problem of the meaning of "send" and "take" in the cited prayers.

[43] *KAR* 38:12f., see E. Ebeling, *Aus dem Tagewerk eines assyrischen Zauberpriesters*, MAOG 5/3 (Leipzig: Harrassowitz, 1931) 45ff.; also edited by Ebeling, *RA* 49 (1955) 184, and, with duplicates, by R. I. Caplice, *Or.* NS 39 (1970) 124ff. A poetic German translation appears in *SAHG* no. 69.

[44] [. . .] MUL.MUL ina GÙB.MU i-zi-za [. . . -ku]-nu-ši ana DINGIR u dIštar [. . .] iš-tu-ú me-e-a [. . .] abūtī ṣabta, *RA* 18 (1921) 28:5ff. The ritual seeks to

ments are, they shed light on other appeals that leave the mode of the stars' intercession unspecified.

Just as the Sun sees all of the earth by day, so do the stars by night. They are also often addressed with the same words: "You who see the entire world."[45] Rarely do we find, however, prayers of such elaborateness as those whose title designates them as "lifting-of-the-hand,"[46] a name referring to the appropriate prayer gesture accompanying them. Such prayers are prescribed in the elaborate rituals,[47] often extending over several days, intended to purify the temple or the king. Our knowledge of the existence of some of the prayers to stars comes solely from the listing of their incipits in these ritual texts.

Lifting-of-the-hand prayers to the constellations Wagon (Ursa Maior), True Shepherd of Anu[48] (Orion), the Pleiades,[49] the Scorpion[50] (Scorpius), and to the Arrow Star[51] (Sirius) are known.[52] That the planets Venus and Jupiter were invoked is known from incipits of lifting-of-the-hand prayers, but it is not

---

avert the evil portended by a mistake committed while serving in a temple office (HUL GARZA), see Caplice, *Or.* NS 39 (1970) 124f.; a further duplicate (with the star names not preserved) is published in Hermann Hunger, *SpTU*, vol. 1 no. 11 r. 4–8.

45 *hā'iṭ kibrāti*, see CT 23 36 = *BAM* 480 iii 52, cited Chapter III.

46 German: *Handerhebung*, translating the Sumerian term *šu-ila*, 'hand-lifting,' written *šu.íl.la*, from which the loanword *šuillakku* has been derived in Akkadian. The most recent study, with a catalogue of these prayers, including the category "Gebete an Gestirne," and an edition of a number of them, is that of Werner Mayer, *Untersuchungen zur Formensprache der babylonischen "Gebetsbeschwörungen,"* Studia Pohl: Series Maior, 5 (Rome: Biblical Institute Press, 1976). An earlier edition, with transliteration and translation of the then known texts is by Erich Ebeling, *Die akkadische Gebetsserie "Handerhebung"* (Berlin, 1953).

47 For these rituals (*bīt rimki* 'House of Bathing'; *bīt salā' mê* 'House of Sprinkling Water') see Parpola, *LAS* 2 p. 198f. ad no. 203. For *bīt mēsiri* 'House of (ritual) enclosure' see R. Borger, *JNES* 33 (1974) 183ff. and *HKL* 2 (1975) p. 195f. ad G. Meier, *AfO* 14. For *mīs pî* 'mouth-washing' see Chapter VIII.

48 A literal translation of the Sumerian compound SIPA.ZI.AN.NA.

49 Sumerian MUL.MUL 'Stars,' Akkadian *zappu* = 'Bristle.'

50 Sumerian GÍR.TAB = Akkadian *Zuqaqīpu*.

51 Sumerian KAK.SI.SÁ = Akkadian *Šukūdu*.

52 The existence of others can be seen from *ABL* 23 (= *LAS* no. 185), in which such prayers are prescribed to the god Nusku, the Moon, the Pleiades, Sirius, Mars, and Bē[let-balāṭi?], see Parpola, *LAS* 2 pp. 177f. and p. 349 n. 643, and from *ABL* 1401 = *LAS* no. 233.

known whether they were addressed as deities or planets, while surviving prayers to Mars[53] show that he was addressed both under his planetary name *Ṣalbatānu* and as the deity, Nergal, whose astral manifestation Mars is. Ambiguity obtains of course in prayers addressed to the Moon, whose name *Sin* applies equally to the Moon god and to the Moon as one of the seven planets. Lifting-of-the-hand prayers are also addressed, collectively, simply to "stars," or "all stars"[54] often called "gods of the night."[55]

Unequivocally astral names are used in the treaties that Esarhaddon concluded with the vassals of Assyria to secure the rights of succession of his son Assurbanipal; they were put under the protection of not only the major gods Šamaš, Sin, and Ištar, who are elsewhere too identified with Sun, Moon, and the planet Venus, but also of other astral deities. Thus Jupiter introduces the list of six astral deities in Esarhaddon's Succession Treaty, the other five being Venus, Saturn, Mercury, Mars, and Sirius, in this order.[56] Similarly, Jupiter precedes Sirius[57] in another treaty[58] which is known only from its mention in a letter of Esarhaddon's son Šamaš-šumu-ukīn.[59] The treaties concluded in Anatolia between the kings of the Hittites and their neighbors some six hundred years earlier were also put

---

[53] Among them the prayer to *Ṣalbatānu* (Mars), listed as Nergal 1 in Werner Mayer, *Untersuchungen* (note 46 above) 402. For prayers to Sirius, Venus, the Pleiades, and Išum see Parpola, *LAS* 2 p. 349 n. 643.

[54] ŠU.ÍL.LÁ MUL.MEŠ DÙ.A.BI [. . .] *LKA* 58 rev., edited Ebeling, *Die akkadische Gebetsserie "Handerhebung,"* (Berlin, 1953) 152f., cited Werner Mayer, *Untersuchungen* (note 46 above) 429. For lines 1–3 see R. D. Biggs, *ŠÀ.ZI.GA. Ancient Mesopotamian Potency Incantations*, Texts from Cuneiform Sources, 2 (Locust Valley, NY: J. J. Augustin, 1967) 75.

[55] See Werner Mayer, *Untersuchungen* (note 46 above) 427f.; the prayer is also cited *ABL* 370 = *LAS* no. 203.

[56] SAG.ME.GAR, Delebat, dUDU.BAD.SAG.UŠ, dUDU.BAD.GUD.UD, Ṣalbatānu, KAK.SI.SÁ in Esarhaddon's Succession Treaty, newly published in Simo Parpola and Kazuko Watanabe, *Neo-Assyrian Treaties and Loyalty Oaths*, SAA 2 (1988) no. 6 lines 13ff., also *LAS* no. 1 rev. 18f., see Parpola, *Iraq* 34 (1972) 32 n. 57 and *LAS* 2 p. 5.

[57] MUL.SAG.ME.GAR and MUL.KAK.SI.SÁ.

[58] See Parpola, *Iraq* 34 (1972) 32 n. 57.

[59] Edited by S. Parpola, "A Letter from Šamaš-šumu-ukīn to Esarhaddon," *Iraq* 34 (1972) 21–34.

under the protection of the planets and stars, particularly of Venus, called "resplendent Ištar (variant: Venus)"[60] as well as of the storm god and such cosmic powers as mountains and rivers, and of the "gods of the nether world" for which a variant substitutes Ereškigal, the queen of the nether world.[61] The appeal to Babylonian deities in their astral manifestation can still be found in Syriac magic texts.[62]

Invocations to stars are not necessarily long and elaborate. A few lines, often a few words suffice to state the petitioner's appeal. In extreme cases, divine favor is requested by a simple enumeration of star names beside names of gods, natural forces, and other entities such as the days of the month, in a litany-like sequence, as in the type of text composed to gain absolution that I have called *lipšur* litanies from their kenning *lipšur* 'may absolve.'[63] For example, in one such litany[64] an enumeration of various gods is followed by "Gods of the night, Pleiades, Virgo, Orion, Jupiter?," and the names of the rivers Tigris, Euphrates, and other rivers.[65]

Of all the stars, it is Sirius that is especially often addressed, both under its stellar name 'Arrow,'[66] and as the star's divine manifestation, the god Ninurta. The hymnic invocation "Arrow-star by name, making battle resound?, . . . paths, making

60 ^{d}*Ištar* (variant: MUL *Dil-bat*) *mul-tar-ri-hu*, also ^{d}*A-šur kakkabu*, variant: ^{d}*Ištar* MUL *Dil-bat* (Treaty between Šuppiluliuma and Šattiwaza, KBo 1 1, variants from KBo 1 2, see E. F. Weidner, *Politische Dokumente aus Kleinasien*, Boghazköi-Studien 8 [Leipzig, 1923] 30ff. r. 45 and 57), and ^{d}*Ištar*-MUL (Treaty between Šattiwaza and Šuppiluliuma, see Weidner, ibid. 54 r. 42).

61 E.g., MRS 9 85ff. RS 17.338+ lines 105–10, a text edited by Guy Kestemont, *Ugarit-Forschungen* 6 (1974) 85–127, for lines 105–110 see ibid. 116–17. For Ereškigal's occurrence in Greek magic texts see Hans Dieter Betz, "Fragment from a Catabasis Ritual," *History of Religions* 19 (1979–80) 287–95. A Babylonian ritual against snakes (*Or.* NS 36 [1967] 32 rev. 5) also prescribes a prayer to be recited before Ereškigal; the connection of the chthonic goddess with snakes is obvious.

62 See Philippe Gignoux, *Incantations magiques syriaques* (Louvain: E. Peeters, 1987).

63 Reiner, "'Lipšur' Litanies," *JNES* 15 (1956) 129–49.

64 *ABRT* 1 56–58 K.2096 and duplicates, see *JNES* 15 144ff.

65 DINGIR.MEŠ MI MUL.MUL MUL E-ru MUL SIPA.ZI.AN.NA MUL Š[ul?-pa-è] *ABRT* 1 57:23, dupl. K.6308:1–2. These and the following lines are not treated in *JNES* 15.

66 (MUL.)KAK.SI.SÁ = Šukūdu.

everything perfect"[67] is part of a collection of incantations, some in Sumerian and others in Akkadian,[68] known under the title HUL.BA.ZI.ZI 'Begone, Evil!,' literally "Evil (HUL) Be gone (BA.ZI.ZI)."[69] The last incantation of the collection conjures the evil in the name of Jupiter, the Pleiades, and the god Irragal: "Be conjured by the powerful, fearsome, brilliant Jupiter, by the Pleiades and Irragal, let 'any evil' not come close."[70]

A magic effect is sought by praying to a deity called First-born of Emah:

> O First-born of Emah, First-born of Emah, you are the eldest son of Enlil
> You descended from Ekur, and you stand in the middle of the sky with the Wagon.[71]

The stellar nature of the divine being addressed is evident from the second line, where he is described as standing in the middle of the sky, with the Wagon star. As for the astronomical identity of the "First-born of Emah," such a star, described as "first-born son of Anu," is listed in an astronomical compendium from about 1000 B.C.[72] as the star that stands in the "rope" of the Wagon,[73] and has been identified with the Pole

---

[67] MUL.KAK.SI.SÁ MU.NE mu-šá-lil qab-li muš-te-'-u ur-he-ti mu-šak-lil mim-ma šum-šú *STT* 215 i 65–66, duplicates *KAR* 76:14f., *KAR* 88 i[!] 10f., or a short exclamation "By the Arrow-star" (nīš MUL.KAK.SI.SÁ nīš MUL. KAK.SI.SÁ *KAR* 76 r. 25f., and duplicates).

[68] Part of this collection was first edited by Ebeling under the title "Sammlungen von Beschwörungsformeln," as "Gattung IV," *ArOr* 21 (1953) 403–23.

[69] It is being prepared for publication by I. L. Finkel under this title. The title is taken from a rubric in the last line but it seems that the subscript HUL.BA.ZI.ZI refers to one or more of the preceding incantations, not necessarily to the entire collection.

[70] nīš gašru rašbu šūpî [d]Šul-pa-è-a nīš MUL.MUL u [d]Ìr-ra-gal lu tamât mimma lemnu aj iṭhâ, *STT* 215 vi 15–17.

[71] ÉN DUMU.UŠ É.MAH DUMU.UŠ É.MAH aplu rabû ša Enlil attama
ištu Ekur [t]ūridamma ina qabal šamê itti MUL.MAR.GÍD.DA tazzaz
[. . . . . .] KAL-an-ni li-iz-ku-ta at-ta-ma
[. . . . . .] UZU.HAR.BAD NU (variant: ul) NAG TU_6 ÉN
(text from *BAM* 542 iii 13–16 and dupl. ND 5497/21+ ii 4′–9′).

[72] MUL.APIN I i 21f., edited by Hermann Hunger and David Pingree, *MUL.APIN.*

[73] MUL ša ina ṭurrišu izzazzu MUL.DUMU.UŠ.É.MAH māru rēštû ša Anim 'the star that stands in its rope' (i.e., of MAR.GÍD.DA.AN.NA 'Wagon of Heaven,' Ursa Minor). C. Bezold, *Zenit- und Äquatorialgestirne am baby-*

Star. A prayer to it is prescribed in the hemerology for the month of Ulūlu (month VI).[74]

But the First-born of Emah is also a deity, since he is addressed as the son of Enlil, one of the three supreme gods, whose temple Ekur in the ancient city of Nippur is the earthly counterpart of, we assume, a celestial Ekur in one of the heavens where the gods dwell. Some descriptions of the heavens speak of seven heavens, and some of three only, each made of a different precious stone.[75]

It is noteworthy that the address to the "First-born of Emah" appears in a medical text in which remedy for toothache is sought from the "first-born of the Mountain, Marduk"; it is to be recited in connection with a ritual that includes fashioning a clay model of a jaw with the aching tooth. The "Mountain" is an epithet of the god Enlil, and so far the two appeals to the "first-born of the Mountain" and to the "First-born of Emah, . . . the eldest son of Enlil" seem to be identical, except that, of course, Marduk is not the son of Enlil, but of Ea, the third god of the supreme triad, the god of the subterranean waters and also the god of cunning.

The reason for addressing the deity of a particular celestial body is not normally stated, and can be inferred in obvious and

---

lonischen Fixsternhimmel (Heidelberg, 1913) 43, identified it with Polaris (presently α, in c. 1000 B.C., β Ursae Minoris, see F. X. Kugler, *Sternkunde und Sterndienst in Babel. Ergänzungen zum ersten und zweiten Buch* [Münster, 1913] 57). The identification is partly based on the occurrence in Astrolabe B iii 11. The star is mentioned in the so-called "Stevenson Omen Text" (*Babyloniaca* 7 231 = pl. XVII) ii 4 and 5: šumma UL.DUMU.UŠ.É.MAH ša UL.MAR.GÍD.DA GAL-ti ana UL.ME.GAR is-niq BE.ME GÁL-ši, šumma KI.MIN issi SU.KÚ GÁL-ši 'if the First-born of É.MAH, (part) of the Great Wagon, approaches Jupiter, there will be pestilence; if ditto recedes, there will be famine.' A variant of the star's name, DUMU.UŠ AN.MAH, would mean 'First-born of Lofty Anu,' see Hunger ad loc. (note 72 above) p. 125.

[74] *4R* 32 i 48 and 33* i 49, see KB 6/2 p. 12, also Benno Landsberger, *Der kultische Kalender der Babylonier und Assyrer*, Leipziger Semitistische Studien 6/1–2 (Leipzig: Hinrichs, 1915) 128.

[75] The pertinent lines of the text, *KAR* 307, have been variously treated by Benno Landsberger, "Über Farben im Sumerisch-Akkadischen," *JCS* 21 (1967, published 1969) 139–73, on pp. 154f.; by A. L. Oppenheim, "Man and Nature in Mesopotamian Civilization," *DSB* 15 pp. 640f.; and by A. Livingstone, *Mystical and Mythological Explanatory Works of Assyrian and Babylonian Scholars* (Oxford: Clarendon, 1986) 82–87.

trivial cases only. Thus, for example, the prayer to Mars in his manifestation as the god Nergal (the god of the plague) was to be recited by the Babylonian king Šamaš-šumu-ukīn, the son of Esarhaddon, mentioned above, during a plague epidemic.[76] Rarely is reference made to phenomena most characteristic of the celestial body, such as the eclipse of the moon.[77] Only in the Hymn to the Sun[78] is there an allusion, clad in poetic terms, to the sun's daily course and yearly cycle, reflecting the Babylonians' characteristic preoccupation with calendric matters, a preoccupation that also surfaces in the description of the creation of the cosmos in Tablet VI of the Poem of the Creation, also known, from its incipit, as *Enūma eliš*.

Some prayers are written, it appears, in the Sumerian language, but in fact are simple transpositions of Akkadian phraseology into Sumerian words and phrases. They may have been recited—as in various rituals—by the priest or exorcist *utraque lingua eruditus*[79] while the client's prayer was couched in the vernacular, Akkadian. Such a prayer, to be recited three times to avert "any evil"[80] from a baby, appeals to 'Ninmah, standing in the sky, mistress of all lands'[81] and to the stars standing at the right and the left.[82] The "mistress" is probably Venus the morning star, and the prayer is to be recited before sunrise,[83] and is followed by a fragmentary prayer to the Sun, Šamaš; with this the tablet breaks off. We thus envisage a dawn ceremony in

---

[76] See Ebeling, *Die akkadische Gebetsserie "Handerhebung,"* (Berlin, 1953), 8ff. and von Soden, *SAHG* 300f.; it is listed as Nergal 1 by Werner Mayer, *Untersuchungen* (note 46 above) 402.

[77] The well-known rituals to avert the evil portent of the eclipse, such as BRM 4 6, and the notorious "substitute king ritual" that such a portent necessitated under the Sargonids are treated by S. Parpola in *LAS* 2 pp. xxii–xxxii.

[78] Known to Assyriologists as the Šamaš hymn, a 200-line learned composition, for which see my book *Your Thwarts in Pieces, Your Mooring Rope Cut. Poetry from Babylonia and Assyria*, Michigan Studies in the Humanities, 5 (Ann Arbor, 1985), Chapter IV.

[79] 'Learned in both languages,' see Tadeusz Kotula, *"Utraque lingua eruditi.* Une page relative à l'histoire de l'éducation dans l'Afrique romaine," *Hommages à Marcel Renard*, vol. 2, Coll. Latomus 102 (Brussels, 1969) 386–92.

[80] Akkadian *mimma lemnu*, possibly with a specialized meaning.

[81] [. . .] ^{d}Nin.mah an.na gub.ba nin.kur.kur.ra.[ke$_4$] *LKA* 142:6ff.

[82] For the "right" and "left" Yoke star (*KAR* 38 r. 24) see above p. 15.

[83] *lām Šamaš ittapha*, line 3.

which the morning star Venus was addressed, followed by a sunrise ceremony. Prayers to Venus as morning star, addressed as a female deity, are attested through the Middle Babylonian personal name Ina-niphiša-alsīš 'I called to her at her rising.'[84]

The unnamed star addressed as "You have risen, star, you are the first one"[85] no doubt also is Venus, this time, as the masculine gender of the pronoun and the adjective indicate, as evening star.

Lovers too turn to Venus, the planet of the goddess of love, Ištar. Their prayer is addressed to the goddess, but her astral character is evident from her epithet "luminary of heaven"[86] and from the sacrifices to Ištar-of-the-Stars.[87] The ritual directs: "you set up a reed altar before Ištar-of-the-Stars, you make offerings"[88] and, having prepared six times two figurines, "you burn (them) before Ištar-of-the-Stars."[89]

A "woman whose husband is angry with her"[90] recites a prayer to Ištar,[91] calling to her "in the midst of the sky."[92] The

---

[84] PBS 2/2 53:20 and 32.

[85] MUL tappuha panû atta, *KAR* 374:1. The pronoun *atta* 'you' and the adjective *panû* 'first' are masculines. See also the "unnamed star" quoted Chapter III.

[86] nannarat šamê, see Biggs, *ŠÀ.ZI.GA* p. 28:25, and see *CAD* N/1 p. 261a.

[87] Ištar-kakkabī, see next note.

[88] ana IGI 15.MUL.MEŠ (variant: [I]š-tar MUL.MEŠ) paṭīra tukân niqê tanaqqi (variant: teppuš) Biggs, *ŠÀ.ZI.GA* p. 27ff. (*KAR* 236:18ff. and duplicates) lines 19f.; another ritual is probably also performed before Ištar-kakkabī: ana IGI d15.[MUL.MEŠ?] ibid. p. 65 K.9036:6′, also [ana IGI d15?]. MUL GAR-an ibid. 12′. The readings given in *ŠÀ.ZI.GA* p. 65 have been slightly emended in lines 10′ (after *AHw.* s. v. *urbatu*) and 12′.

[89] ina IZI ana IGI 15.MUL.MEŠ tašarrap, see Biggs, *ŠÀ.ZI.GA* p. 28:24.

[90] SAL šá DAM-sà UGU-šá šab-su *STT* 257 r. 10 (subscript). I am indebted to my colleague Christopher A. Faraone for drawing my attention to the use of the κεστός to diminish anger between a woman and her husband, see his "Aphrodite's ΚΕΣΤΟΣ and Apples for Atalanta: Aphrodisiacs in Early Greek Myth and Ritual," *Phoenix* 44 (1990) 222.

[91] *STT* 257 rev. 2–9, listed as Ištar 28 in Werner Mayer, *Untersuchungen zur Formensprache der babylonischen "Gebetsbeschwörungen,"* Studia Pohl: Series Maior, 5 (Rome: Biblical Institute Press, 1976) 392.

[92] ašassīki Ištar . . . ina qereb šamāmi *STT* 257 rev. 5f. Since astronomically such a position for Venus is excluded "midst" must be taken figuratively. The topos is also known from Sumerian, expressed as *an.šà.ta*, in e.g., the Iddin-Dagan hymn line 161 edited by Daniel David Reisman, "Two Neo-Sumerian Royal Hymns" (Ph.D. diss., University of Pennsylvania, 1969).

charm is one of the few love charms spoken by women to reconquer their lovers, best known from Theocritus' Second Idyll and Virgil's Eighth Eclogue, while in the Greek magical papyri it is men who desire to secure the love of women. The reference to Venus is indubitable, even though the first few words in the pertinent ritual are broken,[93] since the prayer addresses the star? (the word is broken) of the morning.[94]

To Venus also, as Ištar-of-the-Stars, turns the exorcist before administering the potion to the love-stricken patient.[95] Most often, however, it is the multitude of stars, the entire starry sky, and not a particular planet or constellation that is invoked. A ritual designed to have the king triumph over his enemies[96] is performed "before all? stars,"[97] it is accompanied by the recitation of a prayer addressed to the stars of the night.[98] The next ritual[99] prescribes the fashioning of two figurines holding the lance and the scepter (the royal insignia) but clothed in everyday garments, the making of offerings to Ursa Maior, and the burying of the figurines in enemy territory. A possibly related ritual for diverting the enemy from the homeland is a fragmentary text in which the names of the gods to whom the prayer is addressed are not preserved, only the epithets 'Brightly shining gods, (you who are?) judges.'[100] How the stars responded to such appeals, and how they exerted their influence upon earthly matters, will be the subject of the following chapters dealing with such areas affecting man as medicine, herbalistry, and both apotropaic and noxious magic.

---

93 Possibly ⌈MUL?⌉ [Dil-bat?].

94 É[N x] ⌈x⌉ še-re-e-ti ⌈x⌉ [x] ⌈x⌉-tú (or: [d]i?-par) šá mu-še-r[i? . . .] r. 17.

95 Thus in the *Šaziga* texts, as in *AMT* 88,3:6, see Biggs, *ŠÀ.ZI.GA* p. 52.

96 [eli nākirī]šu [uzuzzima?] līta [šakāni] *STT* 72:23.

97 IGI MUL.MEŠ gim-r[i . . .] line 24.

98 MUL mu-ši-⌈i?⌉-[ti?] *STT* 72:1–22, with the ritual beginning in line 24, see *JNES* 26 (1967) 190f.

99 Lines 41–51, to which *STT* 251:7′–16′ is a duplicate.

100 DINGIR.ME šūpûtu mārū dajānī, Hermann Hunger, *SpTU*, vol. 1 no. 12 line 17.

CHAPTER II

The Art of the Herbalist

> For, who can forget the powerful and noxious herbs of Medea, the enchanting herbs of Lucan, the fatal herbs of Claudian, the flourishing plants of Maro, and lastly those venomous plants, of which abundance was to be found in Colchis and Thessally?
>
> *De Vegetalibus Magicis,* written by M. J. H. Heucher (1700) edited by Edmund Goldsmid, F.R.H.S.F.S.A (Scot.) Privately printed, Edinburgh. 1886, pp. 11–12.

Among the many "firsts" that can be attributed to the Mesopotamians[101] we may certainly count the first herbals and the first lapidaries, and a case may be made for the first bestiary too. The cuneiform handbooks can be compared to their later counterparts because they already exhibit their characteristic structure, and go beyond simple enumerations of stones and herbs we see in the Egyptian Onomastica.[102] Such simple lists were among the very first documents written in Mesopotamia or indeed anywhere. The organizing principle they exhibit is due to the character of the cuneiform writing system.

In the Sumerian writing system names of members belonging to a class are preceded by a class mark, called "determinative," that indicates their nature; only in a few classes does the determinative follow. Names of professions and other human classes, as well as bodily characteristics or deformities, are preceded by the word for 'man' written with the sign *lú;*

---

[101] For the role of the Sumerians, see Samuel Noah Kramer, *History Begins at Sumer* (Garden City, NY: Doubleday and Co., 1959); 3rd, revised ed., with additions, with the subtitle *Thirty-Nine Firsts in Man's Recorded History* (Philadelphia: University of Pennsylvania Press, 1981).

[102] Alan H. Gardiner, *Ancient Egyptian Onomastica* (Oxford: Oxford University Press, 1947), for which see Oppenheim, "Man and Nature in Mesopotamian Civilization," *DSB* 15 p. 634.

of textiles and clothing by the word for 'wool' (*síg*), 'linen' (*gada*), or 'cloth' (*túg*); of cities, rivers, and other geographical units by the appropriate determinative; similarly, objects made of wood, stone, clay, reed, etc., are preceded by a class mark indicating the nature of the item: the word for 'wood,' 'stone,' 'clay,' 'reed,' etc. Names of garden plants, birds, and fish are, however, followed by their respective class marks *sar*, *mušen*, and ku_6.

The earliest lists written in cuneiform, as early as the third millennium, simply catalogue objects or living beings; the principle of classification is obviously semantic, based on the presence of the determinative and therefore seemingly acrographic, that is, the items are grouped according to the first sign used to write them. Consequently, in any list, objects belonging to a particular class are listed together, and the classification according to the determinative doubles as a topical arrangement. This principle is useful for mnemotechnical and didactic purposes and at the same time displays a classification of the world, a feature that may be taken, with von Soden, as a sign of the intellectual curiosity of the Mesopotamian man.[103] Similarly complex is the structure of the much later, late antique and medieval, collections of lists and glossaries.[104]

These Sumerian unilingual lists were eventually provided with an additional column of Akkadian translations, but their sequence remained the "acrographic" principle displayed by the Sumerian.

The best known such bilingual lists, consisting of a Sumerian column and a corresponding Akkadian column, form part of the series known, from its incipit, as *HAR-ra* = *hubullu*, a compendium of twenty-odd chapters enumerating objects of the physical world. To these lists a later commentary (called *HAR-gud*) adds a third column, also in Akkadian, which gives alternative translations, usually by substituting more common

[103] Wolfram von Soden, "Leistung und Grenze sumerischer und babylonischer Wissenschaft," in *Die Welt als Geschichte*, vol. 2 (Stuttgart, 1936); reprinted, with additions and corrections, in Benno Landsberger, *Die Eigenbegrifflichkeit der babylonischen Welt* (Darmstadt, 1965). See also Oppenheim, "Man and Nature in Mesopotamian Civilization," *DSB* 15 pp. 634ff.

[104] See James A. H. Murray, *The Evolution of English Lexicography*, The Romanes lecture 1900.

words for terms of the second column that had become obsolete, without thereby changing the sequence or purpose of these lists. In certain cases the third column contains not just another equivalent or synonym, but an attempt at *scholia*; for example "Egyptian squash" to a variety of squash listed in Tablet XXIII[105] or "mourning garment" to explain the poetic word *karru* in Tablet XIX.[106]

Among the chapters[107] of *HAR-ra = hubullu*, the XVIIth, incompletely preserved, deals with plants. In it, the acrographic principle applies in the first section, where each plant name begins with the Sumerian word *ú*, 'herb.' In the second section, the names are not preceded by *ú*, but followed by *sar*, 'plant,' the postposed class mark for such garden plants as vegetables, and other cultivated plants. Note that Greek too makes a distinction between βοτάνη 'simple' (medicinal plant) and λαχανόν 'vegetable.'[108]

Within a section no classificatory principle is discernible, except that varieties of the same species, whether botanically accurately classified or not, are by orthographic necessity enumerated together, as for example the alliaceae, whose names in Sumerian are composed with the element *sum* 'garlic' and a descriptive element, such as *sum.sag.dili* 'one-headed garlic'[109] while the Akkadian name is *turû* or the cucurbitaceae, whose names are composed with *ukúš* 'squash' and a descriptive element, e.g., *ukúš.šir.gud* with Akkadian equivalent *iški alpi* 'ox-testicle (squash).'[110] These lists continued to serve as pedagogical tools for learning Sumerian.

---

105 Hg. D 249.

106 Hg. E 76 and duplicates; this explanation is also given in a late synonym list (Malku VI 61), which gives synonyms for rare or obsolete words.

107 Usually called "tablets" in Assyriological parlance, see note 35.

108 Cited Margaret H. Thomson, *Textes Grecs inédits relatifs aux plantes* (Paris: Les Belles Lettres, 1955) 91, ad "Second traité alphabétique sur les plantes, tiré d'Aétius."

109 Literally (Sumerian:) "garlic–head–single" see Marten Stol, *Bulletin on Sumerian Agriculture* 3 (1987) 57–compare μονόκλωνος *PGM* IV 808.

110 Literally (Sumerian:) "squash–testicle–ox" Hh. XVII 377a and Hh. XXIV 310. Compare, e.g., *testiculus vulpis* (= *Orchis*), *testiculus canis* (= *Orchis militaris L.*), cited Hermann Fischer, *Mittelalterliche Pflanzenkunde* (Hildesheim: Olms, 1967) 276, and *Orchis alopekos*, cited from the lexicon by Nicolas Hieropais, in A. Delatte, *Anecdota atheniensia*, Bibliothèque de la Faculté

A more practical purpose was served by a work composed of four or possibly more chapters (again called "tablets") known from its incipit as *Uruanna = maštakal* or, for short, *Uruanna*. The two columns of this list place side by side two plant names. Sometimes the left-side entry is a Sumerian name and the right-side one its Akkadian equivalent as in the cited incipit; in other instances several left-side entries, either Sumerian or Akkadian, are equated with one (usually Akkadian) name. The explanation sometimes is a name that simply gives the indication: herb for snake bite[111] (compare our "cough drop" or the trade name "After-Bite") or the plant is compared to another, better known plant or even, though more rarely, warrants a brief description quite similar to the entries in the Herbal (see p. 30). Sometimes to the term in the right-hand side is added the remark "in Subarian," "in Elamite," or "in Kassite," to specify that the name in the left column comes from one or another of the foreign languages of the areas surrounding Mesopotamia.

Uruanna could thus serve as a pharmaceutical handbook, used to look up Sumerian and other foreign names, and may also have served to indicate what herb could be substituted for another. The pharmaceutical as opposed to purely lexical character can also be inferred by the inclusion in the list of other pharmacological substances, such as minerals (including salts), insects, and oils.

Eventually, however, presumably around 1000 B.C., a different type of list was composed, a treatise that might more properly be called a precursor of herbals; in the Assyriological literature it usually goes under such a name as a "pharmaceutical handbook," or "vade mecum of the physician." The ancient Babylonians simply called it DUB.Ú.HI.A 'tablet about/on herbs.'[112] In outward appearance this list too is divided in three columns but not on linguistic grounds: the first column gives the name,

---

de philosophie et lettres de l'Université de Liège, fasc. 88, vol. 2 p. 408 line 14. Note also the names *Phallus impudicus* (*Fungus Melitensis*) 'devil's horn'; Arabic *zubb-eḍ-ḍîb* 'penis lupi,' and *zubb-el-ḥamād* 'desert penis' quoted Immanuel Löw, *Die Flora der Juden* (Vienna and Leipzig: R. Löwit, 1926), vol. 1 p. 44, cited M. L. Wagner, *Romanica Helvetica* 4 (= Festschrift Jaberg, 1937) 106 n. 1.

111 šammu nišik ṣēri, Uruanna I 391.

112 Compare Ebeling, *KAR* 44 rev. 3, see Köcher, *BAM* V p. xi and n. 9.

Sumerian or Akkadian, of the plant; the second, the indication, that is, the symptoms or name of the disease it is supposed to counteract; and the third, the mode of application: how it is to be prepared (e.g., ground, diluted in beer) and how it is to be administered (e.g., as a potion, a salve, a lotion). The arrangement follows the middle column so that the herbs are grouped according to the disease they are good for; this layout is convenient for finding the remedies for a particular ailment by simply going down the middle column of the list.

For example: Yellow saffron : for constricted bladder : to chop, to administer as a potion in fine beer; Kaniš-acorn : for the same : to chop, to administer as a potion in fine beer; Garlic : for the same : to chop, to administer as a potion in oil or fine beer;[113] Pistachio-herb : herb for the lungs : to chop, to administer as a potion without eating;[114] Dog's tongue : herb for cough : to press out its juice and administer as a potion.[115]

This "vade mecum" has a counterpart that deals with stones, also simply called DUB.NA$_4$.MEŠ 'tablet about/on stones';[116] nevertheless, these compilations are only partially comparable to those of the late herbals and lapidaries.

The type of text that seems truly the precursor of the medieval handbooks is the one that I will call the *šikinšu* type, from the opening words. Three such handbooks are known, one (*abnu šikinšu*) dealing with stones and minerals, another one (*šammu šikinšu*) with herbs, and a third (*ṣēru šikinšu*), of which only a small fragment survives, with snakes. These three books thus represent the three categories lapidaries, herbals, and bestiaries, of which latter the snake book is possibly the sole surviving chapter.

All three handbooks evince a common structure. Each entry begins the description with the word *šikinšu*, a word not easy to translate if we consider its literal meaning alone: the word *šiknu* may mean "appearance, looks, character," and the like;

---

113 *BAM* 1 i 26–28.

114 *BAM* 1 ii 24; see note 197.

115 Ibid. ii 35. A text published by René Labat, "La pharmacopée au service de la piété," *Semitica* 3 (1950) 5–18, prescribes the use of herbs and other ingredients in order to secure divine favor as well as to avert evil and illness.

116 Cf. Ebeling, *KAR* 44 rev. 3, see Leichty apud Köcher, *BAM* IV p. vii.

the possessive suffix *-šu,* 'its,' points back to the antecedent (*abnu* 'stone,' *šammu* 'herb,' or *ṣēru* 'snake'). If we take our cue from handbooks of a later period, we may choose the English term "nature," simply because medieval texts begin the description with this word (either with *natura,* if in Latin, or with the form equivalent to *natura* in the Romance language used).[117] And so we may translate the opening words as "the nature of the herb (stone, snake) is."

What these handbooks lack are the illustrations of the later herbals.[118] The absence of illustrations is only partly due to the nature of the writing and the writing material; illustrations, even though only rarely and mostly in schematic drawing, do appear on liver models and in some divinatory texts and on some clay tablets inscribed with liver omens to illustrate marks on the liver or lungs,[119] or with physiognomic omens to illustrate drawings on the forehead or the hand, omens that may be taken as remote precursors of metoposcopy[120] and chiromancy. There exist sketches to indicate the emplacement of paraphernalia in rituals and, even more rarely, in magic texts, as models of figures to be drawn.[121] In lieu of illustrations, descriptions, often very precise, have to serve: they are couched, as in later herbals, in terms of the plant's resemblance to and difference from other plants with which it is compared.[122]

For example, "The herb whose nature is like the *amhara* plant's, (but) its leaves are small, and it has no milky sap, its

---

[117] For example, "La natura del pavon es aital . . . ," "La natura de la furmicz es aital . . ." Der waldensische Physiologus, ed. Alfons Mayer, *Romanische Forschungen* 5 (1890) 390–418, nos. 4 (Pavon) and 42 (De la furmicz).

[118] Illustrations appear late also in Byzantine, Arabic, and other later herbals.

[119] See Nougayrol, *RA* 68 (1974) 61f.

[120] Angus G. Clarke, "Metoposcopy: An Art to Find the Mind's Construction in the Forehead," in *Astrology, Science and Society: Historical Essays,* Patrick Curry, ed. (Woodbridge, Suffolk: The Boydell Press, 1987) 171–95.

[121] See Reiner, "Magic Figurines, Amulets and Talismans," in *Monsters and Demons in the Ancient and Medieval Worlds. Papers Presented in Honor of Edith Porada,* Ann E. Farkas et al., eds. (Mainz on Rhine: Philipp von Zabern, 1988) 27–36.

[122] Texts: Köcher, *Pflanzenkunde* 33, 34b, and 35, see Reiner, *Bibliotheca Orientalis* 15 (1958) 102f.; *BAM* 327, 379 and dupl. Egbert von Weiher, *SpTU,* vol. 3 no. 106; *STT* 93.

seed resembles linseed, that plant is called *labubītu*. The herb whose nature is like that of the *amhara*-plant's, but its seed is red like that of the *abulilu*-plant, that herb is called [. . .], it is good for removing paralysis; to dry, to crush, and to apply as a salve (mixed) in oil."[123]

Or: "The herb's nature is: its thorn is like the thorn of cress, its leaves are as large as cress leaves, that herb is called *namhara*, whoever drinks it will die."[124]

An even more detailed description runs: "The herb's nature is like that of the 'dog's tongue,' or, according to a second source, like the *haltappānu*-herb; its leaves are long, its fruit is like the Adad-squash,[125] it grows tall, its seed, like the *tubāqu* plant's, is divided(?)[126] in three: that herb is called *šunazi*, and in the language of Hatti they call it *tubāqānu* [that is, the *tubāqu*-like herb]; it is good for scorpion sting; its mode of preparation: to dry, to crush, to administer as a potion in beer."[127]

Obviously, these descriptions are very much like those found not only in herbals such as Dioscorides,[128] but also in the spells collected in Hellenistic magical papyri, written in Greek[129] or in Demotic, as in "The ivy—it grows in gardens; its leaf is like the leaf of a *shekam* plant, being divided into three

[123] Köcher, *Pflanzenkunde* 33:4–7.

[124] Köcher, *Pflanzenkunde* 33:12–13.

[125] Written with the Sumerogram Ú.UKÚŠ.dIM.

[126] The verb form used is *ummud*.

[127] Köcher, *Pflanzenkunde* 33:15–16.

[128] E.g., "hic autem folia habet similia porro, sed oblonga et tenueiora," Dioscorides Longobardus Book I 5c, De quiperu indicu, ed. Konrad Hofmann–T. M. Auracher, *Romanische Forschungen* 1 (1883) 58. Or also "Poligonon masculus aut carcinetron aut . . . vocant. Erba est virgas habens teneras molles et multas, nodosas, spansa super terra, sicut agrostis. Folia habet ruta similia, sed oblonga et mollia. Semen habet foliis singulis, unde et masculus dictus est, flore albu aut fenicinu habens. Virtus est illi stiptica et frigida, unde sucus eius bibitus emptoicis medicatur . . . De poligono femina. Poligonon femina frutex est .i. Virga habens, molle et cannosa, . . . omnia suprascripta facere potest, sed minus virtute habet," Dioscorides Longobardus Book IV 11c d,' De poligonon, ed. Hermann Stadler, *Romanische Forschungen* 11 (1901) 11f. (= Dioscorides IV 4). For Dioscorides see now John M. Riddle, *Dioscorides on Pharmacy and Medicine* (Austin: University of Texas Press, 1985).

[129] For example, *PGM* IV 798–810.

lobes like a grape leaf. It is one palm in measurement; its blossom is like silver (another [manuscript] says gold)."[130]

Some of the more exotic names raise the question whether names designating parts of the body of animals that are listed among the *pharmaka* actually refer to animal substances or are to be taken as descriptive names of plants, as the "dog's tongue" in the previous quote, a literal translation from Akkadian,[131] equivalent–in name at least–to cynoglossum. R. Campbell Thompson thought that "The Assyrian was as ready to call what was almost certainly opium by name of 'lion fat' (*lipî nēši*) or 'human fat' (*lipî amēlūti*) or castor oil as 'the blood of a black snake' (*dami ṣīri ṣalmi*) as later alchemists were to give ridiculous synonyms for mercury, cinnabar, cadmia, and such."[132]

That some of the strange names were indeed used to refer to plants is shown by an often quoted passage from the Greek magical papyri:[133]

> Because of the masses' eagerness to practice magic, the temple scribes inscribed the names of the herbs and other things which they employed, on the statues of the gods, so that the masses, as a consequence of their misunderstanding, might not practice magic. . . . But we have collected the explanations [of these names] from many copies [of the sacred writings], all of them secret.
>
> Here they are:
>
> A snake's head: a leech.
>
> . . .
>
> Blood of a snake: haematite.
>
> Lion semen: human semen.

[130] Demotic Magical Papyrus XIV 735, translated by Janet H. Johnson, in *The Greek Magical Papyri in Translation*, H.-D. Betz, ed. (Chicago and London: University of Chicago Press, 1986) 234.

[131] Akkadian *lišān kalbi* 'tongue of dog'; the corresponding Sumerian compound is *eme.ur.gi₇*.

[132] *DACG* p. xiii, cited–disapprovingly–by Dietlinde Goltz, *Studien zur Geschichte der Mineralnamen in Pharmazie, Chemie und Medizin von den Anfängen bis Paracelsus*, Sudhoffs Archiv, Beiheft 14 (Wiesbaden: Franz Steiner, 1972). Note also the article "Mageia" by Hopfner in *RE* 27 (1928) 301-93, and especially the fancy names of remedies ridiculed by Artemidorus, *Onirocriticon* 4, 22 (Pack, Teubner 1963; French translation: *Artémidore. La Clef des Songes*, transl. A. J. Festugière [Paris, Vrin 1975]).

[133] Papyrus Leiden xii 17ff. (=*PGM* XII 400ff.), cf. Hopfner, *Offenbarungszauber*, vol. 1 §493, also Dioscorides, cited Hopfner, ibid. §494.

Semen of Hermes: dill.
Blood from a head: lupine.
Blood of Hephaistos: artemisia.
Human bile: turnip sap.
Fat from a head: spurge.
but "blood of porcupine: really from the porcupine."[134]

Yet, we might question whether these terms were indeed used as "secret" names, as the papyrus indicates. The use of "secret" or "cover" names (German: "Decknamen") is not necessarily intended to keep the craft or learning from the uninitiated or, in case of a lucrative profession, from the competition. Complicated and rare words and spellings may simply attest to the sophistication of the writer, and enhance his reputation. The practice may be comparable to the use of outlandish sign values in a Middle Babylonian glass text, once thought to have been used to safeguard professional secrets.[135]

Still, late herbals speak of these substances as if they indeed were animal (see note 110). Other plant names are less fanciful, even though they may betray wishful thinking: *imhur ešrā* 'it cures twenty'—that is, twenty ailments, and even *imhur-līmu* 'it cures a thousand,' just as in Hungarian there is an herb called *ezerjófű*, 'thousand-good-herb.' The German *Tausendgüldenkraut*, literally 'thousand-gold-pieces-herb,' on the other hand, seems to be a calque on Latin *centaurium* (compare English centaury), etymologized as 'hundred' (*centum*) 'gold pieces' (*aurum*).[136] The name of the herb centaury (Greek κενταύρειον) is said to derive from the word Centaur, so named after the centaur Chiron, who healed his wound with it.[137]

---

134 ἀληθῶς χοιρογρύλλου, *PGM* XII 414.

135 For the use of outlandish sign values in the Middle Babylonian glass text and the implications of this scribal practice see A. Leo Oppenheim, *Glass and Glassmaking in Ancient Mesopotamia* (Corning, NY: The Corning Museum of Glass, 1970) 59ff.

136 See *Handbuch des deutschen Aberglaubens* s.v.

137 Suggested by Reinhold Strömberg, *Griechische Pflanzennamen*, Göteborgs Högskolas Årsskrift 46, 1940:1 (Göteborg, 1940) 100: "Man hat geglaubt dass Cheiron diese Heilpflanzen zuerst verwendet hätte"; he is followed by the Greek etymological dictionaries of Frisk and Chantraine. The connection of the plant with Chiron comes from Theophrastus, *Historia Plantarum* 3.3.6 and Pliny, *NH* 25.66.

In ancient natural histories it is often added to the description of the plant that the species comes in two sexes: male and female, as the above cited *poligonon* (see note 128). These designations have nothing to do with the plant's sex essential for propagation, but refer to its potency. This is evident from the fact that stones too—that is, beads of semi-precious stones—come in both masculine and feminine varieties; this was known in Greek literature since Theophrastus (end of the 4th c. B.C.) but, like many small and perhaps insignificant details of the transmission of beliefs and knowledge, harks back to Babylonian sources. Not only Classical authors[138] noted this division but modern jewelers as well.[139] The division of *materia medica* into masculine and feminine is well known from Greek and Latin authors; according to commentators, among them Pliny the Elder, masculine herbs are stronger and more effective than the feminine ones. Note *mascula tura* "male incense" in Virgil,[140] explained by the commentator as *mascula tura, id est fortia* "male incense, hence stronger."[141] In Babylonian

---

[138] Joan Evans, *Magical Jewels of the Middle Ages and the Renaissance* (Oxford: Clarendon Press, 1922, republished New York: Dover, 1976) 15. See also, for Pliny, *NH* 36.39 (aetites), 37.119 (cyaneus), 37.25 (magnet) and for *Orph. lithica kerygmata* (topaz) Hopfner, *Offenbarungszauber*, vol. 1 §564 and §565. The Orphic lapidaries are now edited by Robert Halleux and Jacques Schamp, *Les Lapidaires grecs* (Paris: Les Belles Lettres, 1985); see ibid. 151, *Orphei lithica kerygmata* 8.6: Οὗτός (scil. τοπάζιος) ἐστιν ὁ ἄρσην, ὁ δὲ θηλυκὸς ἐλαφρότερος 'C'est la variété mâle. La variété femelle est plus légère . . .' See also J. C. Plumpe, "Vivum saxum, vivi lapides. The concept of 'living stones' in Classical and Christian Antiquity," *Traditio* 1 (1943), 1–14; R. Halleux, "Fécondité des mines et sexualité des pierres dans l'antiquité gréco-romaine," *RBPH* 48 (1970) 16–25, both cited in Robert Halleux and Jacques Schamp, *Les Lapidaires grecs* (Paris: Les Belles Lettres, 1985) 326.

[139] "Les pierres précieuses masculines sont celles qui possèdent une couleur plus vive, les féminines celles qui ont une couleur plus pâle." G. Boson, *Les métaux et les pierres dans les inscriptions assyro-babyloniennes.* Inaugural-Dissertation . . . (Munich: Akademische Buchdruckerei von F. Straub, 1914) 73 n. 4 (possibly quoting "Dies ist ein terminus technicus der Edelsteinhändler . . . Männliche Steine sind die sattgefärbten, weibliche die blassen Steine," Oefele, "Gynäkologische Steine," *ZA* 14 [1899] 356ff.) In Akkadian too the *šubû* stone comes in a male and a female variety (*BAM* 112:10), and so do the *šû* stone (see the dictionaries), the *arzallu* stone, black frit, and others. See also Chapter VII, notes 591–92.

[140] *Ecl.* 8, 65.

[141] Philargyrius 2.3, cf. Pliny, *NH* 12.61; note also *tritu cum ture masculo*

medical texts the substance UB.PAD (to be read probably *uppattu* or *upputtu*) comes in male and female varieties.[142]

Sometimes the etymology of the name is transparent. While 'sunflower' (*ú.*ᵈUTU *šammi šamaš*) probably describes any heliotrope, that is, a flower that always looks at the sun: "the flower of Šamaš that faces the setting of the sun,"[143] other names composed with a name of a god or goddess are more suggestive. We do not know to what botanical species for example the herb called "Ninurta's aromatic" (Sumerian *šim.* ᵈ*Ninurta*, equated in Akkadian with *nikiptu*)[144] refers, both varieties of which, masculine and feminine, are mentioned in recipes; however, the name of the herb called *šim.*ᵈ*Išhara*, 'aromatic of the goddess Išhara,' which is equated with Akkadian *qunnabu*, 'cannabis,'[145] may indeed conjure up an aphrodisiac through the association with Išhara, goddess of love, and also calls to mind the plant named *ki.ná Ištar*, in Akkadian *suhsi Ištar* or *majāl Ištar*, both meaning 'bed of Ištar.'

The pharmaceutical lists, whether of the *Uruanna* or the *šikinšu* type, provide the physician or the pharmacist with the knowledge about the appropriate herb to be used for a particular ailment. However, it is important to know not only your roots and herbs, and what they are good for but also the proper time and manner for picking the herb, or digging up the root, so as to maximize its healing power and, not least, to guard against the evil consequences of your acts. Then, and perhaps most important, one has to know the proper time to administer the medicine, by selecting an astrologically propitious moment. A sixteenth-century doctor urged: "Above all things next to grammar a physician must have surely his Astronomye, to know how, when and at what time every medicine ought to be administered."[146]

'crushed with male incense,' Dioscorides (Lombardus) II 48a (*Romanische Forschungen* 10 [1899] 204f.).

142 *AMT* 104:15.

143 šammi Šamaš ša ana ereb šamši panūsu šaknu, *AMT* 74 ii 25, cf. KBo 9 44 r. ii 6.

144 The Akkadian word is probably derived from the Sumerian word *ligidba* which is the gloss given to the compound *šim.*ᵈ*Ninurta*.

145 *ZA* 73 (1983) 243 no. 12. Compare the *scholion* or variant ŠIM.GIG : *qu-un-nab* in the medical text CT 55 377:4.

146 Katherine Oldmeadow, *The Folklore of Herbs* (Birmingham, n.d.) 6. For

The rules and precautions to be followed at the gathering of a plant are not set out in the pharmaceutical handbooks; they have to be culled from prescriptions in medical texts and some rituals. The directions given to the herbalist are very similar to those observed by the 'root-cutter' (the literal translation of Greek *rhizotomos*) in antiquity, in the Middle Ages, and in folk medicine, as collected in Armand Delatte's *Herbarius*,[147] to which these examples from Mesopotamia may serve as supplement:

> (Look for) a gourd which grows alone in the plain;
> when the Sun has gone down,
> cover your head with a kerchief,
> cover the gourd too, draw a magic circle with flour around it,
> and in the morning, before the Sun comes out,
> pull it up from its location,
> take its root . . .[148]

These instructions specify the time for picking the plant, and the precautions to be observed in regard to both the plant and the herbalist. The scene is night (between sunset and sunrise); the plant is isolated by a magic circle and covered; and the herbalist protects himself by covering his head.

Nighttime may be specified in other ways: sometimes it is sufficient to say that the sun must not "see" the herb: for example, a root "which the sun did not see when you pulled

---

preparing and administering the medicine at a propitious moment see Chapter III.

[147] Armand Delatte, *Herbarius. Recherches sur le cérémonial usité chez les anciens pour la cueillette des simples et des plantes magiques*, Bulletins de l'Académie Royale de Belgique, Classe des Lettres, t. 22 (1936); re-edited Paris: Droz 1938.

[148] ú.ukúš.ti.gil.la an.edin.na AŠ.a mú.a ^{d}Utu.è.a.na ku$_4$.ra.na túg sag.zu u.me.ni.dul ú.ukúš.ti.gil.la u.me.ni.dul zíd u.me.ni.hur á.gú.zi.ga.ta ^{d}Utu nam.ta.è ki.gub.ba.a.ni.ta u.me.ni.sír erina.bi šu u.me.ti : tigillâ ša ina ṣēri edißšišu aṣû kīma Šamaš ana bītišu erēbi ṣubāta qaqqadka kuttimma tigillâ kuttimma qēma eṣirma ina šēri lām Šamaš aṣê ina manzazi(šu) usuhšuma šurussu leqēma, CT 17 19 i 17–24 and dupls. Egbert von Weiher, *SpTU*, vol. 2 no. 2 i 29–40, etc., see Borger, *HKL* 2 (1975) 289. The translation 'gourd' here used is intended to serve as allusion to the gourd (Hebrew *qiyqayon*; see Jack M. Sasson, *Jonah*, The Anchor Bible, vol. 24B [New York: Doubleday, 1990] 291), that provided shade for the prophet Jonah; other terms such as squash, cucumber, melon, are equally possible translations of the Akkadian word, for which see M. Stol, *Bulletin on Sumerian Agriculture* 3 (1987) 81ff.

it up."[149] A medical text enjoins "you crush the root of the namtar-plant which was not exposed to the sun when it was dug up."[150] Recall the

> Root of hemlock digg'd i'the dark,

as well as

> . . . slips of yew
> Sliver'd in the moon's eclipse

that the witches, in *Macbeth,* throw into their caldron.[151]

Covering the plant and surrounding it with a magic circle are necessary because the plant may not willingly give up the root, leaf, or shoot needed for preparing the medicine; one must buy it from the plant, or at least give some compensation for it. Theophrastus notes, "That one should be bidden to pray while cutting is not perhaps unreasonable, but the additions made to this injunction are absurd: for instance, as to cutting the kind of all-heal (*panakes*) one should put in the ground in its place an offering made of all kind of fruits and a cake; and that, when one is cutting gladwyn [Gk. ξίρις = iris?], one should put in its place to pay for it cakes of meal from spring-sown wheat, and that one should cut it with a two-edged sword, first making a circle round it three times. . . ."[152]

In Babylonia the acacia shrub (Ú.GÍR) is such a plant. When collecting acacia shoots, you spread them under an acacia shrub that grows on a mud wall[153] and say: "You have received the

---

[149] Akkadian: *ša ina nasāhika Šamaš la īmuru,* e.g., [Ú . . .] GIŠ.Ú.GÍR ša ina ZI-ka ᵈUTU NU IGI.DU₈.A (*BAM* 1 i 7); Ú šurši GIŠ.NIM ša ina ZI-ka ᵈUTU NU IGI.DU₈.A (*BAM* 1 i 10); (išid) lišān kalbi ša ina nasāhika Šamaš NU IGI.[DU₈] (*BAM* 396 iii 7, also *BAM* 575 iii 25); ᵈUTU NU IGI.LÁ (*BAM* 55:12); see *CAD* N/2 s.v. *nasāhu* meaning 2d-1′.

[150] SUHUŠxŠE nam-tar-ru šá ina na-pa-li ᵈUTU NU IGI.BAR tasâk—unpublished medical text from Emar, line 46, courtesy A. Tsukimoto, and the similar šuruš GIŠ.NAM.TAR NITÁ u sin-niš MAN NU IGI-rum KÚ NAG ina GÚ GAR.GAR 'root of the *namtar* (or read: *pillû*) plant, male and female, (that) the sun did not see, to give to eat (or) drink (or) put around the neck' and šurši GIŠ.NIM.BABBAR ša ina nasāhika ᵈUTU NU IGI.DU₈, CT 14 23 K.229:10, and, with šurši GIŠ.Ú.GÍR ibid. 7. For *napālu* 'to dig up' see Marten Stol, *Bulletin on Sumerian Agriculture* 3 (1987) 65.

[151] Act IV, Scene 1.

[152] Theophrastus, *Historia Plantarum* 9.8.7. Cf. also L. B. Lawler, "Three cakes for the dogs," *Classical Bulletin* 30 (1954) 25–28.

[153] Typical of the shrub acacia (*Prosopis farcta,* Arabic *šok*).

present intended for you, now give me the plant of life."[154] At the very least, the herbalist must propitiate the plant by speaking a greeting or a prayer, for which I may again quote Pliny (*NH* 25.145): "Some instruct the diggers [of the pimpernel] to say nothing until they have saluted it before sunrise, and *then* to gather it and extract the juice, for so they say its efficacy is at its greatest." Even Christian monks recommended that while gathering herbs it would be holy to speak the salutation:

All hail, thou holy herb, vervin,
Growing on the ground.[155]

The two-edged sword, or any other tool used, must not be made of iron, a precaution that is well known from Classical Greek and Latin texts, as can be seen from a passage in Pliny's *Natural History* (24.103): "The plant called *selago* is gathered without iron with the right hand, thrust under the tunic through the left arm-hole, as though the gatherer were thieving."[156] The earliest attestation for this practice too comes from Babylonia, as was recognized as early as 1941. The Babylonian herbalist, too, draws a circle around the herb, in the cited text[157] with flour; in other recipes with an instrument but not with one made of iron. The precaution of approaching the herb the head covered with a cloth and covering the plant itself seems aimed at "blinding" the plant so that it does not recog-

---

[154] ŠE.KAK tašabbuš ina šapal Ú.GÍR ša eli pitiqti aṣû tatabbak kīam taqabbi umma attama qīštaka mahrāta šamma ša balāṭi idnamma, *BAM* 248 iv 34, dupl. *AMT* 67,1 iv 27. Incidentally, not only plants receive a bakshish for yielding up their bounty (for offerings to plants, described in Pliny, see the references collected by Delatte, *Herbarius* [note 147 above]) but also other participants in the magic actions: the claypit (*kullatu*) from which the clay for fashioning figurines is taken (*Bibliotheca Orientalis* 30 178:5) and the river that carries away the contaminated material (*KAR* 227:18, see Erich Ebeling, *Tod und Leben nach den Vorstellungen der Babylonier* [Berlin and Leipzig: de Gruyter & Co., 1931] 125).

[155] T. F. Thiselton Dyer, *The Folk-lore of Plants* (New York: Appleton, 1889) 285. Or: "Hail thou holy herb Growing in the ground," as quoted in Katherine Oldmeadow, *The Folklore of Herbs* (Birmingham, n.d.) 6.

[156] "sine ferro dextra manu per tunicam qua sinistra exuitur, velut a furante," quoted Delatte, *Herbarius* (note 147 above) 175f. [= pp. 139ff.], with variant interpretations, e.g. " L'étoffe qui recouvre la main sert d'isolateur . . ."

[157] See note 148.

nize the herbalist.[158] The reference to "as though . . . thieving" also indicates that the gatherer of the herbs pretends to be someone else, so as not to bring down upon himself the herb's revenge, an evil from which the Babylonian herbalist would have protected himself by an apotropaic ritual, but I know of no such ritual.

The plant "growing alone in the plain" or the "lone tamarisk" is singled out already by its habitat;[159] other habitats are also singled out as significant. Especially effective, apparently, are plants growing on a grave (Akkadian *kimahhu*), as the texts often specify: "root of camel thorn from a grave, root of an acacia-shrub from a grave";[160] or "acacia-shrub which grew on a grave."[161] Compare:

> Iubet sepulcris caprificos erutas,
> iubet cupressos funebris . . . aduri
>
> "(Canidia) orders wild fig trees uprooted from the tombs, funereal cypresses."[162]

Most efficacious are plants growing in the mountains; there on the mountains' heights they are better exposed to the influence of the stars, not only because they are closer to them but also because the atmosphere is thinner.[163] Among addresses

---

[158] ". . . nous reconnaissons quelques précautions parmi les plus courantes: l'heure du premier contact et celle de la cueillette, qui sont surtout de nuit ou de l'aurore plutôt que diurnes, et surtout le cercle magique délimité autour de la plante. Le plus souvent, il est tracé sur le sol avec un instrument (rarement en fer), qui l'entame assez profondément; dans notre texte, il sera dessiné avec de la farine répandue. Pourquoi un cercle? On y voit symboliquement une prise de possession isolant la plante de tout secours, mais aussi une véritable purification, le cercle la soustrayant aux mauvaises influences extérieures. Une particularité de ce rituel est l'approche . . . 'la tête couverte d'un vêtement'; . . . cette précaution se double de celle de couvrir la plante elle-même; le but visé paraît être d'"aveugler" la plante et d'empêcher que l'herboriste soit connu d'elle . . ." G. Contenau, "Herbarius," *RA* 38 (1941) 53–55, ad *4R* 3a:32–41, now CT 17 19, cited above.

[159] For the "lone (or single) palm tree" see Babylonian Talmud P^e^sachim 111^a^, also 111^b^, cited Strack-Billerbeck, vol. 4/1 p. 518.

[160] šuruš balti ša eli [kimahhi] šuruš ašāgi ša eli kimahhi, *AMT* 102:38.

[161] ašāgu ša ina muhhi kimahhi aṣû, *AMT* 99,3 r. 15, and passim.

[162] Horace, *Epod.* 5.17 sq. Note also Et strigis inventae per busca iacentia plumae "a screech-owl's feathers found among sunken tombs," Propertius III 6,29.

[163] See the texts quoted by Hopfner, *Offenbarungszauber,* vol. 1 §466.

to herbs whose healing properties are sought, several begin by describing the plant as mountain-grown: "The heartsease grows in the mountains . . ."[164]

Herbs can serve not only to heal but also to diagnose a condition. The patient's reaction to a medicine may very well indicate what his illness is and what the prognosis may be. Rare as they are, the attestations of this diagnostic method indicate that they may have been used more often than the extant texts reveal. One of the few is a Babylonian medical text that testifies to the use of a so-to-speak patch test. The sick man is bandaged with a poultice made of ingredients that act as an irritant and produce a blister. After having applied the poultice for three days, on the fourth day you remove it and inspect the blister that was produced by the poultice. The color of the blister, whether it is white, red, yellow, or black, will predict the course of the man's illness: "if the blister is white, his intestines will quiet down; if it is red, his intestines 'hold too much heat'; if it is green, (the affliction is due to) overexposure to sun; if it is black, the affliction will cause him suffering and he will not live."[165] Only after the diagnosis is made does the physician apply a medication to alleviate the condition provoked.

A similar test is described in a recently found medical text from Emar on the Euphrates:[166] "he chops? herbs for 'leprosy' with a fig-tree branch, he grinds? figs and raisins and ties them on in a bandage; on the next day at night he removes them, if they are white, he replaces the bandage, on the third day he

---

[164] *šammu ša libbi ina šadî aṣîma,* see my *Your Thwarts in Pieces, Your Mooring Rope Cut. Poetry from Babylonia and Assyria,* Michigan Studies in the Humanities, 5 (Ann Arbor, 1985), Chapter V.

[165] Edith K. Ritter, "Magical-Expert (= *Āšipu*) and Physician (= *Asû*). Notes on two Complementary Professions in Babylonian Medicine," *Studies in Honor of Benno Landsberger on His Seventy-Fifth Birthday, April 21, 1965,* AS 16 (Chicago: University of Chicago Press, 1965) 304, see also *CAD* B s.v. *bubu'tu.*

[166] Ú.MEŠ ša epqanni ina PA (= haṭṭi?) ša GIŠ.PÈŠ imahhaṣma GURUN GIŠ.PÈŠ u GIŠ.GEŠTIN.UD.DU i-haš-šal-ma irakkas-šunūti ina UD.2 GI_6 ipaṭṭaršunūti šumma peṣû appūna irakkas-šunūti ina UD.3.KAM ipaṭṭaršunūti šumma peṣû appūna irakkas-šunūti šumma peṣû ihalliqu u šumma peṣûšunu la iggamar TA NA_4.ZÚ uhappašunūtima . . . šumma pani simmišu mithuruma sāmu $ŠE.MUŠ_5$ . . . izarrūma iballuṭ šumma la iballuṭ . . . tartanakkasšu iballuṭ (Emar med. text 72–94, courtesy A. Tsukimoto).

removes them, if they are white, he replaces the bandage, (but) if the white (color?) disappears or if their white (color) is not absorbed? he crushes them with an obsidian stone . . . if the surface of his wound is uniformly red, he strews 'bitter barley' (etc., over it) and he will get well, if he does not get well, you keep placing a bandage (made with various ingredients) on him and he will get well."

A rare pregnancy testing text from Babylonia has also come to light. It was used to test whether a woman is able to conceive. The test consists of inserting a pessary made from medications wrapped in a wad of wool, or of giving the woman a potion to drink. If the potion causes her to vomit, she is pregnant; if the wad of wool has turned green, she is pregnant. While similar tests had been known from Egyptian medicine, and they have been compared with Classical parallels,[167] the newly identified Babylonian pregnancy test is the first Mesopotamian example of this practice.[168]

The fame of Babylonian herbalists is attested in a ninth-century A.D. Arabic book, known as *Nabatean Agriculture,* which reports that certain medicinal plants were introduced by Babylonian kings, whose names it lists.[169] In fact, we know from Babylonian medical texts that certain salves[170] and strings of amulet stones were attributed to a famous king of the past, for example, to Hammurapi, Narām-Sin, and Rīm-Sin.[171] Another, perhaps not quite trustworthy, witness to the fame of

---

[167] Erik Iversen, *Papyrus Carlsberg No. VIII with Some Remarks on the Egyptian Origin of Some Popular Birth Prognoses,* Kgl. Danske Videnskabernes Selskab, Historisk-filologiske Meddelelser 26,5 (1939), and J. B. deC. M. Saunders, *The Transitions from Ancient Egyptian to Greek Medicine* (Lawrence: University of Kansas Press, 1963) 15–18. See also the article "Empfängnis" by Erna Lesky, in *RAC* 4 (1959) 1248–52.

[168] The text is edited and commented on in Erica Reiner, "Babylonian Birth Prognoses," *ZA* 72 (1982) 124–38.

[169] D. Chwolson, *Über die Überreste der altbabylonischen Literatur in arabischen Übersetzungen* (St. Petersburg, 1859) 42. Unfortunately, the new translation of the *Nabatean Agriculture* announced by T. Fahd has not yet been published.

[170] tēqīt īnī ša Hammurapi latku 'proven eye-salve from Hammurapi' *BAM* 159 iv 22; tēqītu ša Hammurapi latiktu, Egbert von Weiher, *SpTU,* vol. 2 no. 50:12.

[171] See Chapter VII.

Babylonian drugs is the woman scorned in Theocritus' *Second Idyll*, who swears:

> If he continues to grieve me, I call on the Fates as my witness
> Soon he shall knock at the portals of Hades, such sinister drugs I
> Keep in my medicine chest, which I learned about from a
> Chaldean.[172]

[172] Theocritus 2.160–162, translated by Daryl Hine, *Theocritus Idylls and Epigrams* (New York: Atheneum, 1982). (Greek: φάρμακα . . . 'Ασσυρίω . . . παρὰ ξείνοιο μαθοῖσα).

CHAPTER III
Medicine

> For when those who first wrote on the subject gave their attention almost solely to meditation about the stars, and believed natural philosophy and the healing art to be intimately connected with these heavenly bodies, they disseminated seeds of magic, from which that science grew to such a degree that it over-spread the whole world with its pollution.
>
> *Bibliotheca Curiosa.* Magic Plants; being a translation of a curious tract entitled *De Vegetalibus Magicis,* written by M. J. H. Heucher (1700) edited by Edmund Goldsmid, F.R.H.S.F.S.A (Scot.) Privately printed, Edinburgh. 1886, pp. 13–14.

The Tale of the Poor Man of Nippur, the earliest example[173] of the folktale motif "The First Larrikin" best known from the *Thousand and One Nights* has often served to show that ancient Mesopotamian literature too knew the physician as a comic figure. This tale narrates how a poor man, wronged by the corrupt mayor of the city of Nippur, takes his revenge by giving the mayor three good thrashings for the one he received. He administers the second thrashing in the garb of a doctor from the city of Isin, under the pretense of tending the wounds that he himself had inflicted when he thrashed the mayor in a different disguise. Another humorous story, only recently published, The Tale of the Illiterate Doctor from Isin,[174] also pokes fun at the medical profession represented here again by a physician from Isin.

He is depicted as an illiterate who, when invited to Nippur to a banquet, cannot find his way to the house of his host be-

[173] O. R. Gurney, "The Tale of the Poor Man of Nippur and its folktale parallels," *Anatolian Studies* 22 (1972) 149–58.

[174] Erica Reiner, "'Why Do You Cuss me?'," *Proceedings of the American Philosophical Society* 130 (1986) 1–6.

cause he does not understand Sumerian, the elite language still spoken by the inhabitants. Even the old woman on the street corner who gives him directions is bilingual. She addresses him in Sumerian but has to repeat everything she said in the only language he knows, in Akkadian. The doctor's ignorance of Sumerian, the language of learning, is as ridiculous as a physician's ignorance of Latin would have been in the not-so-distant past. Through the person of the physician the story also makes fun of the city of Isin itself, as famous in Mesopotamia for its physicians and as synonymous with medicine as medieval Salerno was to become. The most famous in the ancient world were of course the Egyptian physicians; so great was their fame that their neighbors in Anatolia begged them to come and provide treatment and medication, a topic that has been amply treated by Egyptologists.[175]

The two humorous tales that show that the physician was a comic figure in Babylonian literature just as he was in Molière—and still is—have contributed to rekindle the interest in Mesopotamian medicine. The study of Mesopotamian medicine has also benefited from the upsurge of interest in the history of ancient medicine,[176] and has attracted a number of Assyriologists competent to deal with the original material. They contribute to collective works on the history of medicine[177] but in the main their studies have focused on the identification of the diseases and of the materia medica used in the prescriptions. This, however, is the area that is fraught with the greatest difficulties, since we are rarely able to identify the substances—plants, minerals, and other matter—that enter as ingredients in recipes, or even to give a precise translation of the symptoms

---

[175] E.g., Elmar Edel, *Ägyptische Ärzte und ägyptische Medizin am hethitischen Königshof* (Opladen: Westdeutscher Verlag, 1976).

[176] To mention, e.g., the studies on Hippocratic medicine resulting from the *Colloque* of Strasbourg in 1972, and the books of G. E. R. Lloyd, the most recent being *The Revolutions of Wisdom*. Sather Classical Lectures, vol. 52 (Berkeley–Los Angeles–London: University of California Press, 1987).

[177] For example, *Krankheit, Heilkunst, Heilung*, H. Schipperges, E. Seidler, P. U. Unschuld, eds., Veröffentlichungen des Instituts für Historische Anthropologie e. V., vol. 1 (Freiburg: Alber, 1978), or *Diseases in Antiquity; a survey of the diseases, injury, and surgery of early populations*, Don R. Brothwell and A. T. Sandison, eds. (Springfield, Ill.: C. C. Thomas, 1967).

FIGURE 6. Middle register of a bronze plaque, showing a patient being cured. Courtesy of the Louvre, no. 22205.

described. The conceptual advance represented by the structural approach of Dietlinde Goltz[178] has remained largely without following, as have the more philosophically oriented studies of Lloyd; even though we no longer give credence to Herodotus' report on the lack of physicians[179] or make fun of the Babylonians' "*Dreckapotheke.*" Herodotus' report that the Babylonians bring their sick to the market in order to inquire of passers-by what remedies they would suggest has served as argument in the market-economy dispute more importantly than in the history of medicine, and we realize that the *Dreckapotheke* was a well-known pharmaceutical handbook of the seventeenth century.[180]

Understanding Babylonian medicine is especially seriously hampered by the character of the prescriptions, as they nowhere explain the reasons for the treatment indicated nor the property of the ingredient that recommends its use.

In this respect the medicine of the Babylonians is not different from the rest of their scientific literature which knows only two forms: the list—from sign lists and Sumerian and Akkadian bilingual word lists and grammatical paradigms to mathematical and astronomical tables—and the procedural

---

178 Dietlinde Goltz, *Studien zur altorientalischen und griechischen Heilkunde*, Sudhoffs Archiv, Beiheft 16 (Wiesbaden: Franz Steiner, 1974).

179 Hdt. 3.1, see A. Leo Oppenheim, *Ancient Mesopotamia* (Chicago: University of Chicago Press, 1964) 294f. The anecdote is repeated in Strabo XVI 1.20.

180 The 1696 work *Neu-vermehrte, heylsame Dreckapotheke . . .* by Christian Frz. Paullini.

text. In medicine, the list form is used in the pharmaceutical compendia and the procedural in prescriptions. Even procedure texts do not constitute a proper handbook, however. Scientific texts in Babylonia deal with the particular, not the general; they describe procedures but not the justification, the underlying reasons, for the procedures; they are casuistic and not universalistic; they deal not with theory but with application. This holds, as has been many times stated, for Babylonian collections of laws, which hence it is no longer customary to call "law codes"; for Babylonian mathematics, which deal with problems and not with proofs; for the few "procedure" texts which describe step by step how to make glass, how to dye wool purple, how to train horses and, we can now add from a recently published manual, how to prepare meat dishes.[181]

In addition to the comparison of Babylonian and Greek medicine on the epistemological and structural level as Goltz has done, the examination of the astral components of Babylonian medicine, what in antiquity was called iatromathematics, is of interest for identifying the direct threads that connect the two. A guide for discovering the rationale—if one may call it that—behind the instructions to the physician found in these sources is handily provided by Greek and Latin, Classical and late, and even medieval texts. The non-Mesopotamian texts may serve as guides, inasmuch as they can provide the general background for the beliefs and practices we find in Mesopotamia; comparisons, illuminating as they may be, should not be taken as attempts to ascertain the priority of the Babylonian over the Greek or the direction of influences, if any.[182]

Treatment and cure of diseases in Babylonia were the purview of two different kinds of practitioners: the *āšipu* and the *asû*.[183] The *āšipu* was the expert who performed apotropaic rit-

[181] Jean Bottéro, *Textes culinaires Mésopotamiens* (Winona Lake: Eisenbrauns, 1995).

[182] For these questions a summary with previous bibliography is found in Christopher A. Faraone, "Hephaestus the Magician and Near Eastern Parallels for Alcinous' Watchdogs," *Greek, Roman, and Byzantine Studies* 28 (1987) 257–80, especially 277ff. A revised version is found in Christopher A. Faraone, *Talismans and Trojan Horses* (Oxford University Press, 1992) 18–35, Chapter 2, "Beastly Guardians at the Gate."

[183] For literature see Edith K. Ritter, "Magical-Expert (= *Āšipu*) and Physician (= *Asû*). Notes on two Complementary Professions in Babylonian

uals, recited incantations, and executed magic manipulations; hence the term is often translated as 'conjurer,' 'exorcist,' or the like. It fell to him to examine the patient and to make a diagnosis of the illness, to prognosticate its outcome, and also often to determine its aitiology: whether the illness had a somatic cause or whether it was brought about by a god or demon, or by the infringement of a taboo. His role is evident from the handbook known, from its incipit, as *enūma ana bīt marṣi āšipu illiku*, "when the exorcist goes to the house of the sick person," a handbook comprising forty chapters, to many of which ancient commentaries have also been preserved.[184]

The treatment of the patient was the domain of the other practitioner, the *asû*, whose title may be appropriately translated as 'physician.' He was in charge of the preparation and administration of the medicine and of other treatments among which those we might call magical must also be counted. Several chapters of the corpus of the physician are extant, but they seem not to have been organized into a single treatise such as the exorcist's were. These chapters have such titles[185] as "if a man's eyes are 'sick,'"[186] "if a man's head is feverish,"[187] and commentaries to several of these chapters, as well as to others that are not extant, are also known.

Although elsewhere it is the exorcist who performs exorcistic and apotropaic rituals, the rituals and procedures designed to make the medical treatment more effective belong in the

---

Medicine," *Studies in Honor of Benno Landsberger on His Seventy-Fifth Birthday, April 21, 1965*, AS 16 (Chicago: University of Chicago Press, 1965) 299–321; R. D. Biggs, "Babylonien," in *Krankheit, Heilkunst, Heilung*, H. Schipperges, E. Seidler, P. U. Unschuld, eds., Veröffentlichungen des Instituts für Historische Anthropologie e. V., vol. 1 (Freiburg: Alber, 1978) 91–114.

184 Edited by René Labat, *Traité akkadien de diagnostics et pronostics médicaux* (Leiden: Brill, 1951); additional pieces of the treatise and commentaries have been published by Hermann Hunger, *SpTU*, vol. 1 nos. 27–42, and Egbert von Weiher, *SpTU*, vol. 3 nos. 87–89. A catalogue of the series is published by I. L. Finkel, "Adad-apla-iddina, Esagil-kīn-apli, and the Series SA.GIG," in *A Scientific Humanist. Studies in Memory of Abraham Sachs*, Erle Leichty, M. deJ. Ellis, P. Gerardi, eds. (Philadelphia: The University Museum, 1988) 143–59.

185 Titles appear as subscripts on the cuneiform tablets.

186 E.g., *BAM* nos. 510–16.

187 E.g., Hermann Hunger, *SpTU*, vol. 1 nos. 44, 46, and 48.

physician's domain. Foremost among them are those designed to ascertain that the celestial powers make the medication efficacious; to attain this goal the medicine has to be prepared under the stars' benefic influence, and administered at a propitious time.

The most commonly occurring phrase among the instructions to this effect is "you let (the preparation) spend the night under the stars."[188] Since the instruction refers to a medication prepared ahead of time, on the eve before it is administered to the patient, it could be taken as the normal way of expressing "to let stand overnight," as in fact it has been translated in the *Chicago Assyrian Dictionary.*[189] There are indeed practical reasons for letting the preparation stand overnight: the ingredients must be steeped in the carrier–oil for salves, liquids for potions and baths–in order to be properly blended.[190] The mixture is sometimes put in the oven to steep or simmer overnight, and removed in the morning and cooled before use. Nevertheless, the practical reason alone does not explain or justify the procedure: exposition of the medication "to the stars" is necessary to obtain astral irradiation.

The phrase is first encountered in medical texts written in Akkadian at the Hittite capital Hattuša (present-day Boghazköy) in Anatolia where they were excavated in the early years of this century; they can be dated to c. the thirteenth century B.C. As these texts themselves are no doubt copies of, or modeled on originals written in Babylonia, they take us back to the middle of the second millennium and possibly even earlier, to the Old Babylonian period from which few medical texts are extant. The Boghazköy material, in structure, content, and terminology, resembles the large corpus of medical texts from the first millennium more than it does the few known Old Babylonian and Middle Babylonian exemplars; since much of the intellectual as well as political history of Babylonia is hidden in

---

188 *ina kakkabi tušbât*, literally, 'you have (it) spend the night *in* the star,' the singular form (M)UL being more frequent than the plural (M)UL.MEŠ.

189 Sub vv. *bâtu* and *kakkabu*.

190 Dietlinde Goltz, *Studien zur altorientalischen und griechischen Heilkunde*, Sudhoffs Archiv, Beiheft 16 (Wiesbaden: Franz Steiner, 1974) 51 with n. 300: "Das Ziel des Stehenlassens ist eine Mazeration."

the so-called "dark ages," roughly from c. 1600 to c. 1400, the break in the tradition, also evidenced by the Boghazköy texts, remains difficult to date and to explain. Nevertheless, one of the Old Babylonian prescriptions already mentions that the medication "should spend the night under the stars."[191] The only difference between the Old Babylonian and the more recent version is that the latter speaks to the physician, and the early prescription speaks of the medicine.

A typical prescription found in a Boghazköy text reads:

> you mix (the ingredients) in first-quality beer, you let it spend the night under the stars, in the morning you *strain* the first-quality beer and you give it to him to drink.[192]

Another prescription:

> you [steep] (the *materia medica*) together in water, you let it spend the night under the stars, in the morning you [. . .] that water.[193]

Several other texts, many of them fragmentary, contain similar instructions, for example: "you let that water (mixed with the blood of a bat?) spend the night under the stars";[194] note especially "you let it spend the night [. . .], in the morning [. . .]."[195]

The same instructions, occasionally in an amplified version, occur frequently in the large corpus of medical texts written in

---

191 [*i-n*]*a* MUL *li-bi-it-ma*, YOS 11 29:6–7 (collated by Walter Farber), i.e., *ina* MUL = *ina kakkabim* "in the star," and *libīt* from the same verb, *bâtu* (Old Babylonian *biātum*), 'to spend the night,' conjugated in the intransitive rather than in the factitive stem.

192 ina KAŠ.SAG tamahhaṣ ina MUL.MEŠ tušbât ina šērti KAŠ.SAG tuzâk . . . tašaqqīšuma, KUB 37 55 iv 15.

193 iltēniš ina mê ta[rassanšunūti] ina MUL.MEŠ tušbât ina šērtim mê šunūti [. . .], KUB 37 50:4ff. and parallel 55 iv 8ff.

194 *mê šunūti ina* MUL *tuš-bat*, KUB 4 48 i 15 (edited Biggs, *ŠÀ.ZI.GA* p. 54f.), *ana* MUL *tušbât*, ibid. iii 15 (ibid. p. 55), *ina* MUL *tušbât*, KUB 37 43 ii 4 and, with added injunction for not exposing it to sunlight (see p. 37) in the parallel 44:17, also KUB 37 49:6′, and, with only the verb *tušbât* preserved, [*ina* MUL *tu*]-*uš-bat*, KUB 4 27:10 and [*ina* MUL *t*]*u-uš-bá-a-at*, ibid. rev. 5.

195 [. . .] *tuš-ba-at a-ku-zi-en-ga* [. . .], KUB 37 56:4. The spelling *a-ku-zi-en-ga* represents, in "phonetic" spelling, the Sumerogram Á.GÚ.ZI.GA = Akkadian *šērtu* 'morning.' From another western source, the ancient city of Emar in Syria (modern day Meskene), come the similar phrases *ina* MUL *tuš-bat* and *ina* MUL *tuš-bat ina še-*[*er-ti* . . .] Arnaud, *SMEA* 30 (1992) 226 no. 27 i 5′ and 20′.

Mesopotamia. We know these texts both from the library of Tiglath-Pileser I in Assur from the eleventh or tenth centuries B.C. and from the seventh-century library of Assurbanipal at Nineveh, but their date of composition is uncertain. For example:

> If a man's left temple hurts him and his left eye is swollen and tears, you crush dates, Telmun-dates, *ašû*-plant, and cedar resin in myrrh oil, you expose it overnight to the stars,[196] in the morning, without eating,[197] you daub (his eyes with it)[198]
>
> You dry and crush 'dog's tongue'[199] which, when you pulled it up, the sun [did not see],[200] [you mix it] into beer from the tavern-keeper, you expose it overnight to the star(s), [he drinks it] without eating [and gets well].[201]
>
> You expose (the emetic) overnight to the star(s), he drinks it and will vomit.[202]

Powdered minerals are added to beer and then mixed with juniper oil,[203] exposed to the stars, and in the morning, before the sun rises, "you anoint the patient's entire body";[204] a sim-

---

196 A less literal translation of the phrase "you let it spend the night under the stars." The phrase is comparable to Greek *astronomeîn*, that is, to expose to stellar irradiation, for which see Delatte, *Herbarius* (note 147 above) 192, with reference to *CCAG* 12 pp. 127,16; (τρεῖς νύκτας νὰ ἀστρονομίσῃς) 128,8; cf. 129,15; (τρεῖς νύκτας ἔξω ἐν τοῖς ἄστροις) 131,12 De septem herbis planetarum, ex codice 3 (= Cod. Mus. Paleogr. Acad. Scient. Petropolitanae). The German verb 'besternen' was used by H. Ritter in his translation of the Arabic Picatrix as a single-word equivalent to "dem astralischen Einfluss aussetzen."

197 The injunction could refer not only to the patient's fasting, as it has usually been taken and as it also seems to mean here, either because it was recognized that ingesting medicine on an empty stomach makes it more effective or because fasting is essential for cultic purity, but it could refer, as in other cultures, to swallowing medicine and the like without chewing or, as Pliny puts it, without the teeth touching it (quoniam dentibus tactis nihil prosint 'because if the teeth are touched [the medication] is useless' Pliny, *NH* 30.35). Probably for similar reasons is the use of a reed tube (Akkadian *takkussu*, cf. Pliny's *per harundinem*) for administering medicine recommended.

198 ina UL tušbât ina šērim balu patān teqqi, *BAM* 482 iii 2.

199 A plant whose Akkadian name corresponds to cynoglossum, but whose botanical identity is not known, see p. 32 and note 131.

200 For this precaution see Chapter II.

201 ina UL tuš-bat balum patān [išattīma ina'eš], *BAM* 396 iii 7–9.

202 ina UL tuš-bat išattīma i'arru, *BAM* 578 iii 1 and 2.

203 šaman šurmēni.

204 kala zumrišu tapaššaš, *AMT* 90,1 iii 6.

ilar recipe directs: "you set out a holy water vessel, put tamarisk, *maštakal*-plant, sweet reed, and cedar oil into it, expose it to the stars overnight, draw [a magic circle around it],[205] and in the morning, facing the sun, you massage [. . .]."[206]

The texts are sometimes explicit about prescribing the administration of the drug "in the morning,"[207] sometimes adding "facing the sun,"[208] but more often mention only the exposure to the stars,[209] occasionally adding "at night,"[210] or amplifying the phrase as "to the stars of the night."[211]

To the stars are exposed other substances as well. To protect from ghosts, a clay pot covering a figurine is exposed for three days, to the sun during the day and to the stars at night: "you make a figurine of 'any evil,' clothe it in a lion skin, you string carnelian and put it around its neck, you provide it with a sack and give it travel provisions, for three days you place in front of it nine food portions, . . . -soup, you place it on the roof of the patient's house, and libate for it . . . -flour mixed in water and beer, you erect around it three cuts of cedar, you surround it with a circle of flour, you upend over it an unfired . . . -pot, by day let the sun see the . . . -pot, at night let the stars see it, on the third day at midday? 22? . . . you place a censer with

---

205 For restoration see *BAM* 578 i 37–41, cited p. 59 n. 245.

206 agubbâ tukân ana libbi bīni maštakal [GI?].DÙG.GA šaman erēni ana libbi tanaddi [ina] UL tušbât [x (x)]-eṣ-ṣir ina šēri ana IGI dŠamaš [. . . tu]mašša', *AMT* 70,7:10–12.

207 *ina šēri*, written syllabically, for example, *ina mūši ana* IGI MUL *tuš-bat ina še-rim tušabšal . . . lām Šamaš napāhi tašaqqīšu* "at night you expose it to the stars, in the morning, before sunrise, you give it to him to drink," *BAM* 57:10–13, or written with the Sumerogram Á.GÚ.ZI.GA 'morning,' e.g., *AMT* 90,1 iii 6, *BAM* 514 ii 29, and (in an apotropaic ritual for digging a well) CT 38 29:48.

208 ina Á.GÚ.ZI.GA ina IGI MAN (variant: dUTU), *BAM* 449 iii 6 and 15 (= *AMT* 90,1), ina še-rim ana IGI dUTU, *AMT* 70,7:12, both "in the morning before the sun." For the meaning of the phrase "before the sun," scil. the Sun as supreme judge, in magical rituals see Parpola, *LAS* 2 p. 182 ad no. 187.

209 *ina* MUL *tušbât*, *AMT* 62,3 r. 4 = Biggs, *ŠÀ.ZI.GA* p. 51; *ina* MUL *tuš-bat*, *AfK* 1 (1923) 36:4 and 9 (copy p. 38); *KAR* 65 r. 7 = *RA* 48 (1954) 132 no. 7; *ina* UL *tušbât*, *AMT* 37,2 r. 8, *AMT* 1,3:9, *BAM* 396 ii 24, 480 ii 7, 482 ii 3, 499 iii 13, 516 i 63, 575 i 17, *STT* 102:11, *AMT* 91,2 and dupl., see Caplice, *Or.* NS 36 (1967) 25:12; 79-7-8-115:7ff., see Caplice, *Or.* NS 36 (1967) 32.

210 ina mūši ina UL tušbât 'at night you expose it to the stars,' *BAM* 152:7.

211 *ana* MUL *mušīti Or.* NS 36 (1967) 287:9, 295:25, both belonging to the class of apotropaic rituals. Another apotropaic ritual preserves only [. . . *tu*]š-*bat ina* Á.GÚ.ZI.GA . . ., *Or.* NS 40 (1971) 164 no. 63:5'.

juniper before Šamaš, at night you pour out millet-flour before the stars, for three days he should recite over it" (the incantation follows).[212]

Nowhere is it stated in what way the stars are expected to act on the medication or what specific effect their irradiation is to achieve. Again, were it not for the knowledge we gain from the Greeks, we might have been satisfied with the rationalist explanation mentioned earlier. Still, there exist clues that should have made us Assyriologists realize that more than a practical result was desired by the nocturnal exposition. For the instructions do not confine themselves to prescribe overnight exposition to "stars" in general, but sometimes specify to which star or constellation the preparation should be exposed. For example, a variant to one of the just cited prescriptions, instead of exposition to "the stars of the night," specifies exposition to the Goat star.[213] The instructions of another prescription are: "at night you place it in front of the Goat star, and in the morning, before sunrise, before he sets foot on the ground, he drinks it."[214] Or also, for a salve for the eyes: "at night on the roof [you expose it] to the Goat$^?$ star, in the morning, before sunrise [you . . .] these herbs."[215]

The Goat star, which corresponds to the constellation Lyra, is the celestial manifestation of the goddess Gula. Gula is the goddess of healing; a chthonic goddess with a dog as her companion, and in other respects too resembling Hecate. This

---

[212] ṣalam mimma lemnu teppuš mašak nēši tulabbassu sāmtu tašakkak ina kišādišu tašakkan naruqqa tušaṣbas[su] u ṣudê tanaddinšu UD.3.KAM 9 kurummassu UTÚL ṣirpēti ana panīšu tašakkan ina ūr bīt marṣi tušzassuma ZÍD.ŠE.SA.A ina mê u šikari tamahhaṣma tanaqqīšu 3 silti GIŠ.ERIN.NA itātišu tuzaqqap zisurrâ talammīšu DUG.NÍG.DÚR.BÚR NU AL.ŠEG$_6$.GÁ elišu tukattam ina ūmi DUG.NÍG.DÚR.BÚR ^{d}UTU līmuršu ina mūši MUL.MEŠ līmurušu UD.3.KAM BAR.BAR ūmi 22 NÍG x nignak burāši ana pan Šamaš tašakkan ina mūši ZÍD.ZÍZ.ÀM ana pan MUL.MEŠ mušīti tasarraq ana pan Šamaš u MUL.MEŠ UD.3.KAM ana muhhi ⌈li$^?$⌉ -im-tan-⟨an⟩-nu, *BAM* 323:4–13 (= *KAR* 184), edited by Jo Ann Scurlock, "Magical Means of Dealing with Ghosts in Ancient Mesopotamia" (Ph.D. diss., University of Chicago, 1988), Prescription 56.

[213] *BAM* 578 i 38–41, variant from *BAM* 159 i 34; parallel also *BAM* 60:7–11.

[214] ina MI ana IGI MUL.ÙZ tašakkan ina šērti lām Šamaš aṣê lām šēpšu ana qaqqari išakkanu išatti, *AMT* 59,1 i 29.

[215] ina MI ina ÙR ana IGI MUL.Ù[Z$^?$ . . .] ina šēri lām Šamaš aṣê Ú.HI.A annû[ti . . .], *BAM* 516 i 57f.

aspect of the goddess also explains the fact that votive dogs have been found in great numbers in the Gula temples, including the recently excavated temple in Nippur. We should also note that the goat is the animal of Hecate—and of her manifestation as Selene—too.[216]

As most specific instructions mention the constellation of Gula, the Goat, or rather She-goat,[217] it should be evident that the aim of the procedure is irradiation by the star of the goddess of healing. The star of Gula, especially the 0.1 magnitude Vega in the constellation Lyra, the fourth brightest of all the stars, is particularly prominent in the summer sky, but can be seen at varying times any night of the year.[218] Other prescriptions state: "These 24 herbs and aromatics you arrange before the Goat star, you moisten them with beer, in the morning you boil it";[219] "at night you let it stand overnight before the Goat star, in [the morning] you boil it,"[220] and so on.[221]

Any doubts about this identification should be dispelled by the explicit instruction: "at night you let it stand overnight before the Goat star, (you draw a magic circle around it with flour, you cense it) and you invoke the names of Gula and of Bēlet-ilī."[222] The Goat star of one prescription is further identified as the "cattle-pen" of Gula.[223] Instead of Goat star, some texts simply say "before the goddess Gula."[224]

---

216 Wilhelm Heinr. Roscher, *Über Selene und Verwandtes. Studien zur Griechischen Mythologie und Kulturgeschichte vom vergleichenden Standpunkte.* Viertes Heft (Leipzig: Teubner, 1890) 43 and 105. Greek magical papyri also occasionally interchange the moon goddesses Hecate and Selene, for example *PGM* IV 2525, 2711, and 2821.

217 Akkadian *enzu*.

218 To quote H. A. Rey, *The Stars. A New Way to See Them* (Boston: Houghton Mifflin, 1952, twelfth printing 1970) 38.

219 . . . ana IGI MUL.ÙZ tukân ina šikari tulabbak . . . ina šērti tušabšal, *BAM* 579 iv 19.

220 ina MI ana IGI MUL.ÙZ tu[š-b]at ina [šērti] tušabšal, *BAM* 579 iv 5f.

221 ina MI ana (variant: ina) IGI MUL.ÙZ tuš-bat, *BAM* 574 i 29, variant from 575 iv 49; and, with parallel MUL MI 'the star(s) of the night,' *BAM* 159 i 34, *BAM* 578 i 40.

222 ina mūši ana IGI MUL.ÙZ tušbât . . . šum Gula u DINGIR.MAH tazakkar, *BAM* 49:17ff., also ibid. r. 37ff., 50 ii 14ff., 54:10.

223 ana IGI MUL.ÙZ TÙR ^{d}Gu-la tušbât, *BAM* 579 iv 38ff.

224 *ana* IGI ^{d}*Gu-la* 'before Gula,' *BAM* 575 iii 54; cf., in a healing ritual, "you sweep the roof *ina* IGI ^{d}*Gu-la* 'before Gula,'" *KAR* 73:6.

FIGURE 7. Seal representing Gula with her dog. Courtesy of the British Museum, BM 89846, published by Dominique Collon, "Neo-assyrian Gula in the British Museum," in *Beschreiben und Deuten in der Archäologie des Alten Orients* (Altertumskunde des Vorderen Orients, 4), Münster: Ugarit-Verlag, 1994, pp. 43ff.

FIGURE 8. Gula and her dog represented on a boundary stone. Courtesy of the Louvre, no. SB 22, published by V. Scheil, Mémoires de la Délégation en Perse, vol. 2 (Paris: Leroux, 1900), pl. 24.

A further proof for the identity of the Goat star and the goddess of healing is the recipe: "You take equal amounts of various herbs, chop them, sprinkle them with pure juniper juice, and place the mixture before Gula" while a duplicate to this text says "place it before the Goat star."[225] Even the veterinarian exposed the tonic he prepared for horses to the Goat star: "take one-third liter each from the 23 plants enumerated above, . . . leave them overnight exposed to the Goat star, in the morning boil them, . . . this is a tonic for horses."[226]

The same sources from Anatolia that provided the earliest references to the practice of nocturnal exposition are also those that give the reasons for it. They are, however, written in the Hittite language, and thus were less accessible to Assyriologists. One text, from about the thirteenth century, directs the exorcist: "Take it (the substance to be used) up to the roof, and recite as follows: 'From on high in the sky may the thousand stars *incant* it, and may the Moon god *incant* it.' And it remains under the stars."[227]

The Hittite verb used for the celestial irradiation, *hukkišk-*, can be more easily translated into German, with the verb 'besprechen,' as the editor of the text, Kronasser, had done. For lack of a similarly appropriate term in English, I have applied the verb 'to incant,' reminiscent of "*incantation*," to express influence through irradiation. The Hittite text emphasizes the power the stars exercise and the way in which this power is manifested, while the Akkadian texts highlight the practitioner's act of the *exposition*. The result expected in both cultures, however, is not in doubt: the stars will make the potion or salve potent and efficacious.

It was not always Vega, the Goat, that was invoked to irradiate the medication, possibly because its position in the sky was not favorable or the day not propitious for praying to the

---

225 malmāliš tušamṣa UR.BI takassim mê burāši ellūti tasallah ina pan ᵈGula (variant: MUL.ÙZ) tukân, *BAM* 168:35f., dupl. *STT* 97 ii 6ff.

226 *BAM* 159 v 41–46. Herbs are exposed to the Goat star also in *BAM* 90:7′, 561:5′, 579 iv 5f., iv 19, and (in broken context) *BAM* 38 rev. 11.

227 KUB 7 no. 1 ii 20–24 (§6), see Kronasser, *Die Sprache* 7 (1961) 149 (transcription) and 151 (translation). Cf. §7 (ii 27ff.) "In der Nacht haben es die tausend Sterne und der Mondgott besprochen . . ." See also Ernst Tenner, *ZA* 38 (1929) 187f. ad lines 21ff.

goddess Gula. Corresponding in prominence to Vega in Lyra, the brightest summer star, the brightest winter constellation is Orion, known as the True Shepherd of Anu according to its Sumerian name, Sipazianna.[228] While Orion too was worshipped as a deity in Mesopotamia,[229] few medical texts invoke it. A fragmentary text[230] that preserves a ritual, including libations, before the constellation probably belongs in the medical corpus, judging by the few preserved ends of lines: "you salve him,"[231] the name of the herb 'it-cures-twenty,'[232] and the injunction "without eating" (line 8).[233] An equally fragmentary text invokes Orion against vertigo.[234]

More rarely, medical texts contain appeals to the Yoke star, a constellation roughly equivalent to Boötes (see Chapter I), the Scorpion, and Centaurus. But the constellation most frequently beseeched to irradiate the substance exposed to it is Ursa Maior, our Big Dipper, which occurs frequently in the Greek magical papyri too under its more common Greek name, Bear (ἄρκτος 'she-bear'). The Babylonians called it Wagon,[235] after the shape of the seven most conspicuous stars, a name that is also used by various Eurasian peoples: in English (Charles')

---

228 The constellation's Akkadian name, *Šitaddalu* or *Šidallu*, is a word of unknown meaning and etymology.

229 For Sipazianna's role in Babylonian ritual see Chapter VIII. He was invoked in the Hellenistic magical papyri as Saint Orion (*PGM* I 29–36).

230 *BAM* 502.

231 ŠÉŠ-*su* line 5.

232 Ú.IGI.20 = *imhur-ešrā* line 6.

233

1	[. . .] Sipa-zi-an-na ÙR SAR	[before] Orion you sweep the roof
2	[. . .] x GAR-an KAŠ SAG BAL-qí	you set out [. . .], you libate first quality beer
3	[. . .] TI? BÍ.ZA.ZA SIG$_7$.SIG$_7$	. . . a green frog
4	[. . .] x KU eṣ-ret (or: GIŠ.ŠID)	. . .
5	[. . .] ŠÉŠ-su	you salve him
6	[. . . Ú].IGI.20	"it-cures-twenty"-herb
7	[. . .]-x-haṭ (possibly: [mêšunu taṣ]ahhaṭ)	'you squeeze their juices'
8	[. . . balu] pa-tan	[without] eating
9	[. . .] ⌜e⌝	

234 ÉN MUL.SIPA.ZI.AN.NA [. . .] mukkišu GIG [. . .] E$_{11}$-la-ta ina šamê nap-[ha-ta . . .] ṣīdānu [. . .] mahraka AN [. . .], *LKA* 25 ii 20–24 (end of obverse?); the duplicates to this text (see p. 136) omit the prayer to Orion.

235 Sumerian MAR.GÍD.DA = Akkadian *Eriqqu*.

Wain, in Latin *plaustrum, carrus,* in French *chariot* (*le chariot du roi David*), in Italian *Carro,* in German *Wagen,* in South Slavic (*Velika* 'Big') *Kola,* in Hungarian *Szekér* (*Göncölszekér*), etc. Both Bear and Wagon are attested in Homer: "the Great Bear that mankind also calls the Wagon; she wheels on her axis always fixed, watching Orion, and she alone is denied a plunge in the Ocean's baths."[236] Only in Babylonia, however, do we have a more detailed description of this constellation as well as the enumeration of its parts: the yoke, the pole, and the side-pieces, which in these prayers are equated with divine beings.[237]

Since Ursa Maior is a circumpolar constellation, and thus never sets—"she alone is denied a plunge in the Ocean's baths"—or, as the Babylonians put it, "it stands there all year,"[238] it could be invoked at any season of the year, so that practical considerations could have played a role in its choice. We should also note that the Akkadian word for Wagon, *eriqqu,* is of feminine gender. Thereby the Wagon constellation may be identified with the goddess Ištar, and with her heavenly manifestation, the planet Venus. The identification is attested not only in the ancient star lists and commentaries according to which "The

---

236 Ἄρκτον θ', ἣν καὶ Ἅμαξαν ἐπίκλησιν καλέουσιν,
ἥ τ' αὐτοῦ στρέφεται καί τ' Ὠρίωνα δοκεύει,
οἴη δ' ἄμμορός ἐστι λοετρῶν Ὠκεανοῖο.

Il. XVIII 487–89 and Od. V 273–75, translation from *Homer, The Iliad.* Translated by Robert Fagles (New York: Viking Penguin, 1990). The passage is cited, among others, by Festugière, *La Révélation d'Hermès Trismégiste*² (1950) vol. 1 pp. 182f. and Eric P. Hamp, "The Principal Indo-European Constellations," *Proceedings of the Eleventh International Congress of Linguists,* Luigi Heilmann, ed. (Bologna: il Mulino, 1974) 1239. Most recently, the fact that the Greek name *amaxa,* 'chariot,' was borrowed from Babylonia has been pointed out by Duchesne-Guillemin, *CRAI* 1986 p. 237.

237 *STT* 73:61–64 and 71–75, see *JNES* 19 (1960) 33; a duplicate to this text, UET 7 118:8–10 and 17–20, writes the name of the constellation as MUL.MAR.GÍD.DA.AN.NA, which elsewhere designates Ursa Minor, see the references collected by Wayne Horowitz, "The Akkadian Name for Ursa Minor," *ZA* 79 (1989) 242. Another prayer to Ursa Maior, addressing her as MUL.MAR.GÍD.DA.AN.NA GIŠ.MAR.GÍD.DA *šamāmi,* is published in Egbert von Weiher, *SpTU,* vol. 4 no. 129 v 21ff., and an unpublished text, BM 33841 + 48068, signaled by W. G. Lambert to von Weiher, is mentioned on p. 39 ad loc.

238 *BPO* 2 Text III 28c: kal šatti izzaz.

Wagon is Venus in the East"[239] but is also evident from the inclusion of omens from the Wagon among celestial omens derived from phenomena of Venus observed.[240] In her manifestation as the year-round visible, circumpolar constellation Ursa Maior, the Big Dipper, Ištar can exert her influence even when her planet, Venus, is invisible.[241]

Other stars remain nameless. The chapter "if a man's head is feverish" of the medical compendium includes recipes to stop loss or thinning of hair, and the treatment is accompanied by the recitation of charms. The last of a series of six such charms (labeled "incantation") is addressed to an unnamed star, identified only as the "first" star, and is accompanied by offerings consisting not only of the usual foodstuffs (dates, flour, a sweet confection, ghee, herbs and spices, etc.) but also of a lamb. The address to the star is as follows:

> You, star, who illuminates [. . .] the midst of heaven, who surveys (all four) regions,
> I, so-and-so, son of so-and-so,[242] prostrate myself before you this night, decide my case, give me a verdict,
> let these herbs wipe away the evil that affects me.[243]

Just as a magic circle around the herb itself before it was dug up was indicated, a magic circle around the medicinal preparation was supposed to enhance the effect expected from the nocturnal exposition. Thus, a recipe directs: "you place (the three herbs steeped in beer) before the Goat star (variant: the stars of the night), you draw a circle around it,[244] in the morning [. . .] you strain it, he drinks it without eating."[245]

---

239 [MUL.MA]R.GÍD.DA MUL Dil-bat ina d[UTU.È].A, *LBAT* 1564:13, see Weidner, *Handbuch* 118, and the unpublished tablet BM 37391.

240 See *BPO* 3; note also that a *scholion* gives Venus as explanation to the Goat star: MUL.ÙZ d*Dil-bat* (Hermann Hunger, *Astrological Reports to Assyrian Kings*, SAA 8 [1992] no. 175 r. 7).

241 For rituals performed before Ursa Maior see Chapter V.

242 Here the name and patronymic of the patient are to be supplied.

243 atta kakkabu munammir x x x x qereb šamê hāʾiṭ kibrāti
anāku annanna mār annanna ina mūši annê maharka kamsāku dīnī dīn purussāʾa purus
šammū annûtu lipsisu lumnī,

BAM 480 iii 52–54.

244 Literally "surround it with a 'drawing.'"

245 ana pan MUL.ÙZ tašakkan uṣurta talammi ina šērti [x x] nu tašahhal

A medication prepared with herbs gathered in the proper fashion, and exposed to irradiation by the stars often is also administered at an astrologically propitious moment. Favorable days for commencing some activity or enterprise are listed in the hemerologies, but administering medicine is not singled out, apart from the injunction "the physician must not treat a patient"[246] which is mentioned among forbidden activities on certain unpropitious days. The choice of particular times of the month or year and the role of constellations and planets is significant not only in medicine but also in various domains of magic; it will be given an appropriate place in Chapter V.

Stars can be efficacious in healing illness since they may have been its cause. Poetic texts speak of illness "drizzling down from the udders of heaven"[247] or "raining down from the stars"; charms for protection against some illness may state that it "has come down from the stars in the sky";[248] dew coming from stars may be evil as well as beneficial, as the phrases "evil dew of the stars" and the "pure dew of the stars"[249] show. More specific is the attribution to the planets Jupiter and Mars of spleen and kidney ailments. We have here the first occurrence of melothesia[250] and the only known Babylonian ex-

---

balu patān išatti, *BAM* 578 i 38–41, variant from *BAM* 159 i 34; parallel also *BAM* 60:7–11. For 'without eating' see note 197.

[246] asû ana marṣi qāssu la ubbal, *KAR* 176 r. ii 26, and passim.

[247] *JCS* 9 (1955) 8ff. (the cuneiform text is now published as YOS 11 no. 8), see Oppenheim, "Man and Nature in Mesopotamian Civilization," *DSB* 15 p. 640, while other texts speak of illness sprung up from the bowels of the earth (Ludlul II 52), see E. Reiner, *Your Thwarts in Pieces, Your Mooring Rope Cut. Poetry from Babylonia and Assyria*, Michigan Studies in the Humanities, 5 (Ann Arbor, 1985) 115.

[248] The *maškadu*-disease *ištu* MUL.MEŠ *šamāmi urda, urdamma ištu* MUL.MEŠ *šamāmi* 'descended from the stars of the sky, it indeed descended from the stars of the sky,' *BAM* 390:5–7. For the disease *maškadu*—its "true" name, see E. Reiner, "Nocturnal Talk," in *Lingering over Words: Studies in Ancient Near Eastern Literature in Honor of William L. Moran*, Tzvi Abusch et al., eds., Harvard Semitic Studies, 37 (Atlanta: Scholars Press, 1990) 424 n. 18, while its "common" name is *šu'u*—see *CAD* s. vv.

[249] *nalšu lemnu ša kakkabī* and *nalšu ellu ša kakkabī*, Hermann Hunger, *SpTU*, vol. 1 no. 48 and dupl., cited Walter Farber, *Schlaf, Kindchen, Schlaf! Mesopotamische Baby-Beschwörungen und -Rituale* (Winona Lake: Eisenbrauns, 1989) 63.

[250] A. Bouché-Leclercq, *L'Astrologie grecque* (Paris, 1899, reprinted Aalen: Scientia, 1979) 320ff.

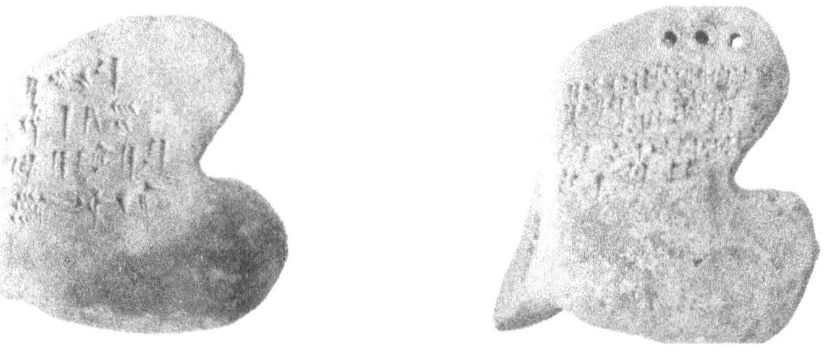

FIGURE 9. **Clay models of sheep livers inscribed with liver omens. Courtesy of the Louvre, nos. AO 19829 and AO 19834.**

ample. The commentary to a medical text in which it occurs does not make this connection clear. It cites the entry from a medical text and then comments upon it. The first entry is "If a man's spleen hurts him"; this is followed by the phrase that normally introduces *scholia*: "as they say" (or "as it–scil. the commentary–says"), and finally the *scholion* or explanation itself: "in the spleen = Jupiter"; a lexical equation, ŠÀ.GIG = *ṭu-li-mu* 'spleen,' ends the quote. The next entry is similarly structured: "If a man's kidney hurts him, (the disease comes from the god) Nergal, as they say: 'The Kidney-star is Mars.'"[251] In this last *scholion* the *tertium comparationis*, namely "Nergal is Mars," has been omitted. It is well known, from Ptolemy and others, that Mars "governs" the kidneys; Jupiter "governs" the liver and the stomach.[252]

---

251 šumma amīlu ṭulīmšu īkulšu . . . ša iqbû ina ŠÀ ŠÀ.GIG : ^{d}SAG.ME.GAR : ŠÀ.GIG = ṭu-li-mu, . . . šumma amīlu kalīssu īkulšu ^{d}Nergal ša iqbû MUL.BIR = ^{d}Ṣalbatānu (Civil, *JNES* 33 [1974] 336f., Text 3); see E. Reiner, *NABU* 1993/26. The unfortunately fragmentary commentary to a medical text comments on the ingredient "blood from a bull's kidney," with the equation MUL.BIR // ka-li-ti 'Kidney-star : kidney,' Hermann Hunger, *SpTU*, vol. 1 no. 54:11′.

252 *CCAG* 7 p. 216.5. *CCAG* 6 p. 83:9–13 (*De septem stellarum herbis*) attributes to Mars the shoulders (*metaphrena*) and kidneys, to Jupiter ὦμοι και θώραξ, cf. Demophilus ap. Porphyry, p. 198. Tycho-Brahe, in a lecture from 1574 (*De disciplinis mathematicis oper. omn.*, J. L. E. Dreyer, ed., vol. 1 [1913] 157) adduced by Boll-Bezold-Gundel p. 55, assigns the heart–the source of heat–to the Sun, the brain to the Moon, the spleen to Saturn, the liver to Jupiter, the gallbladder to Mars, the kidneys to Venus, the lungs to Mercury. For planetary melothesia see Alessandro Olivieri, *Melotesia planetaria Greca* (Napoli: Accademia di Archeologia Lettere e B. Arti, 1934).

CHAPTER IV

Divination[253]

They gaze at the stars (and) slaughter lambs
(*Neo-Assyrian letter*)

Mesopotamian man sought to learn what the future holds from every conceivable event and manifestation of the world around him. Gods gave signs through such happenings, and these signs, the gods' warnings, could be read, and the future that they predicted could be averted through penitence, prayer, and appropriate apotropaic rituals, just as even the stern God of the Old Testament could be swayed by the Ninivites' repentance, as the Book of Jonah teaches.

Some signs came unprovoked, through fortuitous happenings in house and fold and in the sky; others were specifically requested as answers to questions put to the gods through a variety of media.[254]

The fortuitous occurrence and a subsequent good fortune or misfortune were linked in the mind of Mesopotamian man, as they were in many early cultures and still are in primitive societies, not so much as cause and effect, but as signals or forewarnings and events. Such linked pairs, consisting of a protasis (if-clause) and an apodosis (forecast), a pair called by the technical term "omen," were collected in lists, and these lists even-

---

[253] For literature see A. L. Oppenheim, "The Arts of the Diviner," in *Ancient Mesopotamia* (note 179 above) 206–27; idem, "Man and Nature in Mesopotamian Civilization," *DSB* 15 pp. 634–66; Jean Bottéro, "Symptômes, Signes, Ecritures," in *Divination et Rationalité*, J.-P. Vernant, ed., 70–197. A concise summary of ancient divination is given in Georg Luck, *Arcana Mundi* (Baltimore and London: Johns Hopkins University Press, 1985) 229–31 and 251–57.

[254] In the Classical world these two types of omens are called *omina oblativa* '(freely) brought about omens' and *omina impetrativa* 'asked for omens,' see Bouché-Leclercq, *Histoire de la divination dans l'antiquité* (Paris: Leroux, 1879–82), vol. 4 p. 184.

tually developed into the large compendia that we call omen series. Usually, topically connected lists in the cuneiform writing system are acrographic as well, that is, each item—each line—begins with the same cuneiform sign or group of signs, a feature that articulates the ancient syllabaries and vocabularies, as we saw earlier. Lists can therefore often be expanded indefinitely through the addition of items that repeat the protasis with further specifications;[255] the forecasts connected with these additional omens are accordingly modified. For example, a phenomenon occurring on the right side of the liver was paired with the same one occurring on the left, with the opposite forecast. If one color occurred in the omen, similar omens with other colors—five in all: white, black, red, green, and variegated, always in this sequence—could be added. Numbers were increased from one or two to three and more, even if the increase resulted in an absurdity, as for example in the enumeration of multiple births up to eight or nine.[256] "[T]he original practical purpose of such collections of omens was soon expanded, and even superseded, by theoretical aspirations. Instead of expressing general principles of interpretation in abstract terms, the scribes strove to cover the range of possibilities by means of systematic permutations in pairs (left-right, above-below, and so on) or in long rows."[257] The Babylonian omen series kept growing in this way.

Omens could be provoked by observing the shapes taken by oil poured on water, a procedure called lecanomancy (from Greek *lekanē* 'basin'), and by observing the configurations of the smoke rising from an incense-burner, libanomancy (from Greek *libanos* 'frankincense'). These techniques were in vogue in the Old Babylonian period, in the first half of the second millennium B.C., but die out with it.[258] But the most ancient and the most tenacious in surviving of all the Babylonian divinatory

[255] Oppenheim, *DSB* 15 p. 642 with note 98.

[256] Erle Leichty, *The Babylonian Omen Series* šumma izbu, Texts from Cuneiform Sources, 3 (Glückstadt: Augustin, 1969) Tablet I 131.

[257] Oppenheim, *Ancient Mesopotamia* (note 179 above) 211.

[258] A few later excerpts of lecanomancy and libanomancy are extant but their existence as a written tradition need not indicate that the techniques were still in use, even though Nougayrol, *Or.* NS 32 (1963) 381 n. 1, argues in favor of their survival.

techniques is divination from the entrails (exta) of the lamb, extispicy, a term more general, since it includes divination from the gall bladder, the spleen, and the lungs, than the more commonly known term, hepatoscopy, 'inspection of the liver.' As is well known, hepatoscopy was practiced in Italy by the Etruscans, so that the Romans called this divination the "Etruscan discipline"; just as the hepatoscopy of the Etruscans ultimately goes back to Mesopotamian origins[259] so another technique practiced by the Etruscans, divination from thunder, brontoscopy, also had its antecedents, no doubt, in Babylonia where the meteorological omens formed part of the larger collection of celestial omens.[260] Hepatoscopy remained the main means of consulting the will of the gods, even as divination from celestial bodies was gaining in importance; as late as in the reign of King Nabonidus the portents of celestial omens had to be tested, as we shall see, by submitting queries about them to the haruspex.

The diviner par excellence was the haruspex, whose name, *bārû*, literally means 'observer, seer.' The term was also applied to those diviners who observed the configurations of the oil or smoke, while the scholars who made astronomical observations and recorded the forecasts derived from celestial phenomena were called *ṭupšar Enūma Anu Enlil*, a term meaning "scribe of (the celestial omen series entitled) 'When Anu, Enlil . . .,'" and best translated, albeit freely, "expert in celestial matters." An abundant correspondence from the Neo-Assyrian empire attests the importance at the royal court of the diviners and the astronomers who apprised the king of the portents, and the exorcists who were expert in averting ill-boding forecasts by their rituals.[261] The astronomers regularly conveyed to the king such routine reports as the monthly sighting of the new

---

[259] Jean Nougayrol, "Les rapports des haruspicines étrusque et assyro-babylonienne, et le foie d'argile de *Falerii Veteres* (Villa Giulia 3786)," *CRAI* 1955, pp. 509–19.

[260] Bouché-Leclercq, *Histoire de la divination dans l'antiquité* (Paris: Leroux 1879–82) vol. 4 pp. 32ff.

[261] This correspondence was recently reedited and commented by Simo Parpola, *LAS*, and revised in his *Letters from Assyrian and Babylonian Scholars*, SAA 10 (1993). See also Oppenheim, "Divination and Celestial Observation in the last Assyrian Empire," *Centaurus* 14 (1969) 97–135.

moon and the date of the opposition of sun and moon as well as special reports on various predictable and predicted celestial and meteorological phenomena, such as conjunctions, occultations, and rain and thunder.[262] More than a thousand years earlier, in Mari, the correspondents reported on such extraordinary events as torrential rains and thunder.[263]

Of the diviner we know from as early as the Old Babylonian period that he accompanied the king on his campaigns;[264] most diviners were attached to the court, though at least some villages had a resident *bārû*, as is shown by the complaint of an Old Babylonian correspondent that there are not enough lambs in the village even to provide the *bārû*.[265] Nevertheless, some diviners had to live by their wits. This is shown by the apotropaic ritual aiming at "achieving renown for the diviner."[266] Such renown, based on correct predictions, would attract the customers that the haruspex needed for his livelihood since he belonged to the professionals—the diviner and the physician—who made their living from private clients, as did also the innkeeper and baker with whom the diviner and the physician are joined in another ritual to ensure brisk business.[267]

---

[262] These are edited by Hermann Hunger, *Astrological Reports to Assyrian Kings*, SAA 8 (1992).

[263] ARMT 23 90 and 102, also ARMT 13 133, ARM 14 7, cited Joannès, ARMT 23 p. 100 sub a.

[264] For example, "The diviner, Ilušu-naṣir, servant of my lord, will lead the troops of my lord, and a Babylonian diviner will go with the Babylonian troops," ARM 2 22:24f., cited *CAD* B p. 124. For the role of the diviner in Mari, see J.-M. Durand, Archives épistolaires de Mari I/1 (= ARM 26, Paris: Editions Recherche sur les Civilisations, 1988) 3-80.

[265] "There are few ewes in the village, they are hardly sufficient to (provide) lambs for the diviner" TCL 18 125, cited *CAD* B p. 121.

[266] tanatti bārûti amāru u šuma ṭāba leqû 'to find praise for the diviner and to obtain fame (literally: a good name),' *BBR* no. 11 r. iii 15 and no. 19 r. 15.

[267] Ritual to be performed "in order that brisk trade not bypass the house of a tavern keeper, or of a diviner, or of a physician, or of an exorcist, or of a baker" *ZA* 32 (1918/19) 164-84. See Oppenheim, *Ancient Mesopotamia* (note 179 above) 303. For considering the primary reason for this ritual the purification of the tavern in order to return business to it see Stefan Maul, "Der Kneipenbesuch als Heilverfahren," in *La circulation des biens, des personnes et des idées dans le Proche-Orient ancien*, Actes de la XXXVIIIe Rencontre Assyriologique Internationale (Paris, 8-10 juillet 1991), D. Charpin & F. Joannès, eds. (Paris: Editions Recherche sur les Civilisations, 1992) 389-96, esp. p.

The standing of the haruspex at the Neo-Assyrian court and the respect accorded to his craft is evident from a "letter of recommendation" addressed to the king.[268] The writer of the letter recommends various scholars to the king as well-trained, and justifies his opinion by characterizing even the expert in the celestial omen series with the words *bārûti ile'i* 'he is expert in *bārûtu*', although it is possible that the word *bārûtu* is here used as a general term for 'divination' and not solely for 'hepatoscopy.'[269]

Before proceeding to the examination of the ominous parts of the lamb sacrificed for this purpose, the diviner appealed to his patron deities. These were, in the first millennium at least, the sun god, Šamaš, and the storm god, Adad; the haruspex invoked them at the beginning of his query as "O Šamaš, lord of judgment, O Adad, lord of divination."[270] In the earlier, Old Babylonian, period prayers of the diviner for a successful extispicy are similarly addressed to both deities[271] but also to Šamaš alone. The appeal to Šamaš is easily understood since the Sun, Šamaš, sees everything from above—the verb used is *barû* 'to see.'[272] More difficult to explain is the statement in these prayers that he also "inscribes the omens in the entrails of the

395. Note that the Latin Picatrix speaks of Ymago ad faciendum ut phisicus lucretur. . . . et videbis [laminam ymaginem habentem] mirabiliter trahere homines ad illum locum. Picatrix I v 30 (Pingree p. 21f.).

[268] CT 54 57, edited by Hermann Hunger, "Empfehlungen an den König," AOS 67 (1987) 157-66; new edition in Simo Parpola, *Letters from Assyrian and Babylonian Scholars*, SAA 10 no. 160.

[269] On the relationship of the various experts at the Assyrian court see Simo Parpola, "Mesopotamian Astrology and Astronomy as Domains of the Mesopotamian 'Wisdom,'" in *Die Rolle der Astronomie in den Kulturen Mesopotamiens*, Hannes D. Galter, ed., Grazer Morgenländische Studien, 3 (Graz, 1993).

[270] Šamaš bēl dīni Adad bēl bīri, see Werner Mayer, *Untersuchungen zur Formensprache der babylonischen "Gebetsbeschwörungen,"* Studia Pohl: Series Maior, 5 (Rome: Biblical Institute Press, 1976) 423 sub [2.]

[271] For example, YOS 11 22, edited by Goetze, *JCS* 22 (1968) 25–29, also AO 7032, see Nougayrol, *RA* 38 (1941) 87 (copy only); and see for these prayers Ivan Starr, *The Rituals of the Diviner* (Malibu: Undena, 1983) 44ff.

[272] The epithet 'Divine Seer of the land,' Akkadian ^{d}*bārû ša māti* (written ^{d}HAL *šá* KUR), cited Werner Mayer, *Untersuchungen* (n. 270 above) 411 sub 10 after the edition by Caplice, *Or.* NS 36 (1967) 9ff., is based on the single source *LKA* 127:9, and its reading and interpretation are uncertain.

lamb," an often quoted phrase whose exact significance still eludes us, and which may have its origin in a mythological tale that has been lost.[273]

The role of Adad, the storm god, as patron of the haruspex is not as clear as that of the sun god, Šamaš, even though both are invoked in the standard first-millennium prayer of the haruspex. There is, however, another tradition according to which it is not these two who stand by the haruspex to ensure correct and reliable omens. Rather, it is to the stars and constellations who alone are present during his lonely vigil before he examines the liver at dawn that the diviner addresses his prayer for a successful extispicy. This is the Prayer to the Gods of the Night we saw.

No other text is as explicit as this prayer about soliciting the influence of the stars to secure a favorable outcome of the divination. Rare in Mesopotamia is also the lyricism of this poetic text, with its setting of the still night. All are asleep, even the great gods; alone are present the diviner preparing himself for the act of sacrifice and divination, and the gods of the night, the stars.

Two slightly divergent versions of this prayer have been preserved from the Old Babylonian period, that is, the eighteenth or seventeenth century B.C.; in one of them ten constellations are invoked by name: "Fire god (possibly Sirius), Erra (the god of plague, possibly referring to Mars), Bow, Yoke, Orion, Dragon, Wagon, Goat, Bison, Hydra";[274] in the other version, omitting the Yoke and Hydra but adding the Pleiades, nine only.[275] Most of them are zodiacal constellations; as in other ancient catarchic magic, few non-zodiacal constellations, such as Ursa Maior and Minor, Sirius, Orion, the Pleiades, and Pegasus, are mentioned.[276]

---

[273] The reference to C. J. Gadd, *Ideas of Divine Rule in the Ancient East* (note 28 above) 57 n. 4, adduced by Nougayrol, *CRAI* 1955 p. 510 n. 5 in this context does not clarify this image.

[274] Girra (wr. ^{d}GIBIL) Erra Qaštum Nīrum Šitaddarum Mušhuššum Eriqqum Enzum Kusarikkum Bašmum. Dossin, *RA* 32 (1935) 180 (= *ZA* 43 [1936] 305).

[275] Ibid. 180 AO 6769. For these two texts see also C. B. F. Walker, "The Myth of Girra and Elamatum," *Anatolian Studies* 33 (1983) 146f.

[276] "Die ausserzodiakalen Gestirne und Einzelsterne kommen als Heilgötter seltener in Frage, ebenso ist in der Astromagie und in der zukunfts-

The prayer, along with its description of the night, reappears about one thousand years later, in the library of Assurbanipal in Nineveh. In the late version the constellations addressed are much the same as those of the Old Babylonian period:

> Enter, gods of the night, great stars,
> Yoke, Orion, Šulpae, [break],
> Wagon, Ferry, Centaurus, Field,
> Enter, gods of the night, goddesses of the night,
> Stars of the south and the north, of the east and the west,
> Enter, Ninsianna, Great Lady, and the innumerable neighboring stars.

Perhaps even as late as the seventh century B.C. the prayer served a practical purpose, and the diviner recited it before he examined the entrails of the lamb.[277] Still, we should not discard the possibility that the text survived not only due to its practical usefulness but in some measure also to its poetic merit, as Oppenheim has suggested. To its lyricism our own sensibility responds, even though in the later and more elaborate prayer the nocturnal setting has become a topos and lost the direct personal, emotional tone, a feature that seems to have been censored by first-millennium taste.

The prayer exists also in a version midway in date between the two, from c. 1200 B.C., found in the capital of the Hittite empire (today Boghazköy). It is embedded in a Hittite ritual, but written in the Akkadian language albeit in an orthography that shows it was written by a Hittite scribe. It has been known

---

deutenden Sternreligion ihre Bedeutung wesentlich geringer als die der Planeten- und Tierkreisbilder. Aber trotzdem kann man auch ihre Bilder und Kräfte sich auf verschiedener Weise nutzbar machen; ihre Energien und ihre Schicksalseinflüsse werden durch mehr oder weniger ausführliche Abhandlungen immer wieder auf den verschiedensten Gebieten dargelegt. Münzen, Gemmen, Ringsteine u. a. m. beweisen, dass auch der Grosse und Kleine Bär, Sirius, Orion, die Pleiaden, Pegasus und andere Gestirngötter in Altertum, Mittelalter und Neuzeit in prophylaktischer oder therapeutischer Absicht benutzt worden sind." W. Gundel, "Religionsgeschichtliche Lesefrüchte aus lateinischen Astrologenhandschriften," *Mélanges Franz Cumont*, Annuaire de l'Institut de Philologie et d'Histoire Orientales et Slaves, vol. 4 (Brussels, 1936), vol. 1 p. 246.

[277] For an edition of the first-millennium text and the literary appreciation of the images see Oppenheim, "A New Prayer to the 'Gods of the Night,'" *Analecta Biblica* 12 (1959) 282ff.

since its publication by A. Jeremias in 1909.[278] It ends with the prayer to the gods of the night, and includes an enumeration of seventeen stars and constellations.[279]

The prayer to the "gods of the night" is addressed to the nocturnal stars and constellations, after the sun, the moon, and the evening star Venus have set: "The gods and goddesses of the country—Šamaš, Sin, Adad and Ištar—have gone home to heaven to sleep, they will not give decisions or verdicts (tonight)."[280]

The setting of another Old Babylonian prayer of the haruspex[281] is also night. It appeals to the planet Venus alone, as the stellar deity Ninsianna, addressing it as a male deity, that is, in the planet's male manifestation;[282] the diviner invokes the celestial power to ask that his examination find favorable signs:

> O my lord Ninsianna,
> accept this offering,
> be present in my offering, and place in it a portent of well-being and life
> for your servant Ur-Utu.[283]

---

[278] A. Jeremias, *Das Alter der babylonischen Astronomie*, KAO 3 (Leipzig, 1909) 33, see Weidner, KAO 4 (Leipzig, 1914) 17f. and *Handbuch* 60, with Addendum p. 144. The ritual in its entirety has been recently reedited by K. van der Toorn, *Sin and Sanction in Israel and Mesopotamia. A Comparative Study* (Assen/Maastricht: Van Gorcum & Comp., 1985), 125ff. For notes and corrections see the review by Wolfram von Soden, *AfO* 34 (1987) 71. Van der Toorn's text is a kind of lamentation (*šigû*), only the last ten lines (rev. 39–48), not translated anew by him, represent the "gods of the night" prayer, for which see the bibliography in Werner Mayer, *Untersuchungen* (note 270 above) 428 no. 2a.

[279] For this star list see *BPO* 2 p. 2.

[280] Oppenheim, *Analecta Biblica* 12 (1959) 296.

[281] Léon de Meyer, "Deux prières *ikribu* du temps d'Ammiṣaduqa," in *ZIKIR ŠUMIM: Assyriological Studies Presented to F. R. Kraus* (Leiden: Brill, 1982) 271–78.

[282] See p. 6 and note 14.

[283] DINGIR be-lí ^{d}Nin-si$_{4}$-an-na
SIZKUR anniam mu-hu-[ur]
ina SIZKUR-ia izizma
UZU te-er-ti šulmi balāṭi
ana Ur-^{d}Utu ÌR-ka šuknamma.

ZIKIR ŠUMIM, p. 274 lines 1–5. I have rendered the word written with the Sumerogram SIZKUR as 'offering' and *têrtu* as 'portent' rather than as

It is also to the "gods of the night" that the haruspex turns if the examination of the entrails discloses missing or otherwise ill-portending parts:[284]

You great gods of the night,
whom Anu and Enlil have created,
you efface the evil signs that have arisen [for me],
you remove from the man's house the ill-portending features that occurred in [*my*] extispicy,
remove from me the evil sign that occurred in [*my*] house,
let that evil bypass me,
and I will sing your praises as long as I live.[285]

The reverse of the tablet records another prayer of the diviner, similar to the just quoted one, but shorter: "I call to you, O great

---

'prayer' and 'oracle' as de Meyer had done. Instead of 'portent' one could use simply 'entrails.'

284 These are described as *šīrū* (UZU.ME) *haṭūti*, rev.(!) 28. Missing parts of the exta are of ill portent and two paragraphs concerning them ("if in month x the gall bladder is missing"; "if in month x the 'finger' is missing") are included in one recension of the series *iqqur īpuš*, see René Labat, *Un Calendrier babylonien des travaux, des saisons, et des mois* (Paris: Champion, 1965) 138f. n. 4, and on the unpublished tablets BM 65137 and 65570. (The tablet fragment K.11142 cited U. Jeyes, JEOL 32 [1991–92] 32 n. 45, preserves only the protasis about the missing "finger" in each of the twelve months; it may belong either to *iqqur īpuš* or to a tablet of liver omens.) A ritual to avert the portended evil has to be performed; see, for an apotropaion against missing parts (*ha-liq-ti* UZU), Caplice, *Or.* NS 42 (1973) 515:8; for the phrase, though with another interpretation ("loss of flesh," following S. Eypper, *Or.* NS 44 [1975] 193), see Parpola, *LAS* 2 p. 156 on *ABL* 361:12 (= *LAS* no. 167 = SAA 10 no. 212); and for amulets against absence of an ominous part in the examination of the exta see *BAM* 367:21, all cited *CAD* Š/3 p. 121 s.v. *šīru* A mng. 4a.

285 attunu ilū rabûtu ša mušī[ti]
ša Anu u Enlil ibnûkunū[ti]
tapassasa ittāti lemnēti ša ittanab[šânimma]
ina bīt amēli tunakkar(a) šīra lemna ša iššaknu ina têr[tiya]
nukkirani ittu lemuttu ša bašû ina bīt [. . .]
lumna šuātu šūtiqanni[ma]
[adi anā]ku balṭāku dalīlīkunu [ludlul]

STT 231 obv.(!) 31–37, see Reiner, *JNES* 26 (1967) 186f.; also Nougayrol, *RA* 61 (1967) 95 sub 1.

The text also prescribes prayers with rituals to Marduk (obverse 7ff.) and Šamaš (reverse 12ff.). I would like to take this opportunity to correct some of the crassest errors in my transliteration: in line 4 read BI.RI = *ṭulīmu* 'spleen'; in line 16, with Benno Landsberger, . . . *tašakkanšu mēsir abāri* (A.BÁR!) (*ina qablišu tarakkassu*).

gods, stand by me in (this) night, undo the evil of the absence of the ominous part that has occurred for me. I am afraid, worried, exceedingly worried. Let that evil not come close to me, not approach me, not attain me!"[286]

The outcome of the inspection of the exta is conveyed in a letter to the person who requested the extispicy, or is recorded in brief, indeed laconic form on small tablets. A number of such reports, which often begin by stating the query posed to the god, have survived from the Old Babylonian period.[287] Around the middle of the second millennium, in Middle Babylonian reports on the inspection of the liver, the star Sirius is also mentioned in the phrase "let him give instructions that ditto (= they pray) to Sirius"; who the parties addressed are, the haruspex or his client, is not stated in the text.[288] While several prayers to Sirius have been preserved, on which more will be said later, none of them specifically asks the star to secure good omens in the extispicy.

It is not only the haruspex who sought the stars' benefic influence as he inspected the entrails of the lamb. At the more popular level of divination, which I have dubbed "fortune-telling,"[289] and which uses means accessible to clients who could not afford a lamb so that it could be called "divination for everybody" (*"la divination pour tous"*) by Jean Bottéro,[290] appeals are made to stars, especially to Ursa Maior, the Wagon of the Babylonian sky. The popularity of the Big Dipper is also attested in the Greek magical papyri which include several prayers to this constellation under its Greek name 'Bear' (Greek ἄρκτος).

---

286 ilū rabûtu alsīkunūši ina mūši izizzanimma lumun [haliq]ti šīri ša iššaknamma pušra [palhā]ku adrāku u šutādurāku lumnu šâšu ay iṭhâ ay iqri[ba ay isniqa?] ay ikšudanni; rev.(!) 8–11.

287 Albrecht Goetze, "Reports on Acts of Extispicy from Old Babylonian and Kassite Times," *JCS* 11 (1957) 89–105; Jean Nougayrol, "Rapports paléo-babyloniens d'haruspices," *JCS* 21 (1967, published 1969) 219–35; Jean-Marie Durand, "Les devins" AEM 1/1 (= ARMT 26) 3–68.

288 lišpurma MUL.KAK.SI.SÁ KI.MIN (= liseppû), *JAOS* 38 77ff.:51, see Reiner, *Studies in Honor of Benno Landsberger on His Seventy-Fifth Birthday, April 21, 1965*, AS 16 (Chicago: University of Chicago Press, 1965) 248 n. 5; the text has been edited anew by F. R. Kraus, *JCS* 37 (1985) 150.

289 In my article "Fortune-Telling in Mesopotamia," *JNES* 19 (1960) 23–35.

290 In *Divination et Rationalité*, J.-P. Vernant, ed., p. 123.

Two prayers to Ursa Maior are prescribed in the instructions for "fortune-telling" to help obtain a reliable portent through a dream. The first runs:

O Wagon star, Wagon of the pure heavens!
Your yoke is Ninurta, your pole is Marduk,
Your side-pieces are the two heavenly daughters of Anu.
You rise in Assur, you turn toward Babylon.
Without you the dying man does not die and the healthy man cannot go on his journey.
If I am to succeed on this journey I am undertaking, let them give me something (in my dream),
If I am not to succeed on this journey I am undertaking, let them accept something from me (in my dream).[291]

And the second:

O Wagon star, heavenly Wagon!
Whose yoke is Ninurta, whose pole is Marduk,
Whose side-pieces are the two heavenly daughters of Anu.
She rises toward Assur, she turns toward Babylon.
Let a dream bring me a sign whether so-and-so, son of so-and-so, will become healthy and well![292]

How the dream would indicate the recovery of the sick person is left unsaid in the second of the prayers to Ursa Maior. The first prayer, however, specifies what the dream content should be to indicate success or failure of the enterprise concerning which the consultation is made. The significance of giving or being given some object is detailed in the Assyrian Dream-book,[293] and the stipulation of the prayer implies the existence of this Dream-book, even though the expected prediction is not affected by the nature of the object given or received, only by the fact that something is either given or received. This simplification of an ominous occurrence is in accordance with

---

[291] *STT* 73:61–64.

[292] *STT* 73:71–75 and dupl., cited *JNES* 19 (1960) 33; the then unpublished duplicate YBC 9884 quoted there is now published as YOS 11 75. Another duplicate is UET 7 118. A list of texts mentioning prayers to Ursa Maior and of their incipits appears in Werner Mayer, *Untersuchungen* (note 270 above) 429f.

[293] See A. Leo Oppenheim, *The Interpretation of Dreams in the Ancient Near East*, Transactions of the American Philosophical Society, New Series, 46/3 (Philadelphia, 1956), with additional material in *Iraq* 31 (1969) 153–65.

many later divinatory consultations, which restrict the answer to 'yes' or 'no.' In the late Assyrian period the haruspex evidently was only interested in learning whether the various features observed were favorable or unfavorable; adding them up he gave a favorable prognosis if the favorable features exceeded the unfavorable ones, and vice versa.[294]

Another method listed in the same text for ascertaining the favorable or unfavorable outcome of some enterprise,[295] which is not specified, consists of pouring water over the head of a recumbent ox and observing its reactions: whether it gets up or not, lifts its tail or not, and the like. This particular technique was not included in the cuneiform divinatory corpus, but a similar procedure is known from Greece: "At Delphi the goats to be sacrificed were tested by sprinkling a few drops of water into their ear or on their coat to see whether the animal will remain unmoved or react to this instigation."[296] Among the Babylonian divinatory texts was included a group, attested in several exemplars, in which the movements and behavior of the lamb led to slaughter before extispicy are observed so as to foretell what the findings of the exta will be.[297]

Answers couched in similar terms, that is, success or failure—literally: *kašād ṣibûti* 'attaining (one's) desire' and *la kašād ṣibûti* 'not attaining (one's) desire'—are elsewhere based on omens derived from the "shape" of shooting stars (the shape possibly denoting the streaks of light or, less likely, the shape of the meteorite found on the ground) in the omen series *šumma ālu* 'if a city,'[298] while in the text concerned with "fortune-telling" and in its partial parallel[299] it is the path of the shooting star—from right to left—that will determine success.[300]

---

[294] See Ivan Starr, *Queries to the Sungod*, SAA 4, pp. xxxiv–xxxv.

[295] *kašād ṣibûti* 'attaining (one's) desire,' i.e., success, and *la kašād ṣibûti* 'not attaining (one's) desire,' i.e., failure, lines 122–38.

[296] "A Delphes, on essayait les chèvres à immoler en leur jetant quelques gouttes d'eau dans l'oreille ou sur le pelage, pour voir si l'animal resterait morne ou réagirait sous cette excitation." Bouché-Leclercq, *Histoire de la Divination* (note 254 above), vol. 1 p. 150.

[297] For these texts see Meissner, *AfO* 9 (1933–34) 118ff. and 329f.

[298] See Caplice, *Or.* NS 39 (1970) 115f.

[299] *LKA* 138, see Reiner, "Fortune-Telling in Mesopotamia," *JNES* 19 (1960) 28f.

[300] For the ominous significance attached to shooting stars see also Chapter V.

Before pouring water on the ox, there is an appeal to the "gods of the night," collectively called *ilū dajānū* 'divine judges':[301]

> I invoke you, divine judges, in the pure heavens;
> I beseech you unceasingly with prayer and prostration.
> Shining torch in the midst of heaven, all the world longs for your light.
> People observe your verdicts, the weak submits to your decrees.
> Divine judges whose pronouncement cannot be changed,
> In this midnight watch I pour pure spring water on the forehead of an ox;
> Let me see your true judgment and your divine verdict so that I may make a pronouncement.
> Let the ox provide a verdict whether so-and-so, son of so-and-so, will have success.

Even though the phrase *ilū mušīti* 'gods of the night' does not appear in the title of the prayer, the ritual instructions that follow it, which prescribe offerings to the "gods of the night," make it clear that the prayer addresses the stars.[302]

It is probably also in order to secure reliable oracular answers that the prayers designated in their subscripts as *ikribu* were composed. Most of them are too fragmentary to ascertain their purpose with assurance. The word *ikribu*, a noun derived from the verb *karābu* 'to pray,' was assumed to designate a special category of prayer accompanying a nocturnal consultation by the diviner, since both the Old Babylonian prayer to the gods of the night and those of the haruspex to the planet Venus under its name Ninsianna cited earlier[303] have, in their subscripts, the title *ikribu*. Other stellar deities are known to have rated *ikribu* prayers, as Nougayrol has reminded us.[304] A text that has

---

[301] *STT* 73:110–117, see Reiner, *JNES* 19 (1960) 35; the epithet 'divine judges' is in lines 110 and 114.

[302] I had surmised, wrongly, in my discussion (*JNES* 19 28) that 'divine judges' designate Šamaš and Adad, the patrons of the diviner; this suggestion was followed by Werner Mayer, *Untersuchungen* (note 270 above) 423.

[303] Léon de Meyer, "Deux prières *ikribu* du temps d'Ammiṣaduqa," in *ZIKIR Šumim: Assyriological Studies Presented to F. R. Kraus* (Leiden: Brill, 1982) 271–78.

[304] Reference to *ikribu* prayers to stellar deities, such as Ištar, Sin, and Sirius, is made by Nougayrol, *Or.* NS 32 (1963) 381 n. 1. For the genre *ikribu* see also Ivan Starr, *The Rituals of the Diviner* (Malibu: Undena, 1983) 44ff.

been known for a long time[305] contains most likely three *ikribu* prayers: one to the Moon god Sin, another to Jupiter, and—the last one—possibly to Venus. The prayer to Jupiter, still incomplete, begins: "Jupiter, holy god, foremost of the gods, more majestic? than the stars in the sky."[306]

While the diviner depends on the stars for eliciting reliable predictions, practitioners of other divination techniques depend on the haruspex to interpret and confirm the ominous signs obtained through other media, primarily from celestial phenomena.[307] Even the prophecies of ecstatics had to be submitted to the test of hepatoscopy, a test for which the hair of the ecstatic's head and the fringe of his cloak were dispatched to represent the person on whose behalf the divination was carried out.

The long known and famous case of the diviner Asqudum in Mari is now better situated with the publication of an entire archive dealing with this haruspex who had to authenticate by performing an extispicy not only the prophecies and dreams of the ecstatics but even the prediction of a lunar eclipse.[308] King Nabonidus' recourse, a thousand years later, to liver omens in order to interpret a lunar eclipse is equally famous and often studied.

Less explicit, and thus in greater need of explanatory comments, are the diviner's interpretations of two ominous celestial phenomena under Assyrian kings: of the lunar eclipse in 714 B.C. during Sargon's eighth campaign, and of the "secret place" reached by Jupiter at Esarhaddon's advent to the throne. Both episodes are recounted in the *res gestae* of the kings, the

---

305 It was published by S. Langdon, "A Fragment of a Series of Ritualistic Prayers to Astral Deities in the Ceremonies of Divination," *RA* 12 (1915) 189ff.; another piece, K.3794, published by E. G. Perry, *Hymnen und Gebete an Sin*, Leipziger Semitistische Studien 2/4 (Leipzig, 1907) as no. 5b, has since been joined to it.

306 dŠul-pa-è DINGIR KÙ SAG.KAL DINGIR.MEŠ MAH UGU M[UL.MEŠ ša] AN-e, *RA* 12 (1915) 190 Ki. 1904-10-9,157 = BM 99127:14.

307 The necessity for such a confirmation is attested among the Romans too according to Pliny the younger: ". . . I will consult a haruspex whose expertise I have often tested." Without delay, he makes a sacrifice, and declares that the exta and the signs from the stars are in agreement. *Epist.* 2.4–5.

308 See now J.-M. Durand, ARMT 26 no. 81, cf. ibid. 495.

so-called "royal inscriptions," styled as first-person accounts. Sargon's account is styled as a letter to the god Assur.[309]

While Sargon was en route to Urartu the moon became eclipsed and the darkness lasted from the first night watch into the second; the haruspex, who as usual accompanied the king on his campaign, was called upon to interpret the meaning of the eclipse, a much-feared ill-portending event.[310] Sargon continued his route only upon being assured that the portent presaged victory—in his case, unlike Croesus,' the prediction fortunately was not equivocal. Sargon's letter contains another allusion to a favorable portent given the king by a certain, not specified, phenomenon of Jupiter, here called "the star of Marduk."[311] The interrelation between celestial portents and liver omens is also attested, as we have seen (p. 12 above), in reference to Sargon of Assyria's third-millennium predecessor, Sargon of Akkad.

King Esarhaddon, Sargon's grandson, reports on how he secured the throne for himself in the midst of the struggle for power among the sons of Sennacherib after the king had been murdered. His rightful succession was foretold in the stars: among other favorable signs the "secret place" reached by the planet Venus is mentioned.[312] When Jupiter shone exceptionally brightly and reached its "secret place"—which seems to correspond to what in Greek astrology was called the planet's "exaltation" (*hypsoma*), the sign of the zodiac in which it has the greatest influence—in the beginning of his reign,[313] this sign was interpreted as a favorable portent for the rebuilding of Babylon.

The two experts in divination, the haruspex and the astrol-

---

309 Thureau-Dangin, *Une relation de la 8e campagne de Sargon . . .* (TCL 3). The cryptic eclipse report appears in line 318.

310 A. L. Oppenheim, "The City of Assur in 714 B.C.," *JNES* 19 (1960) 137f.

311 "The star of Marduk (i.e., Jupiter), who went on to take up his position among stars which made me resort to arms." See A. L. Oppenheim, *Centaurus* 14 (1970) 121 and n. 46.

312 Borger, *Esarh.* 2 i 39–ii 5.

313 Borger, *Esarh.* 17 Bab. Ep. 13; see Schaumberger, in F. X. Kugler, *Sternkunde und Sterndienst in Babel. 3. Ergänzungsheft zum ersten und zweiten Buch* (Münster, 1935) 311f.

oger, are coupled in the accusation cited in the Assyrian letter of the crown prince Šamaš-šumu-ukīn to Esarhaddon.[314] "They gaze at the stars (and) slaughter lambs, (but) do not (or: he does not) tell (anything) about the king, our lord, (and) the crown prince of Babylon. Aplāyu alone is a haruspex, Bēl-ēṭer (and) Šamaš-zēra-iqīša are astrologers; they look day and night at the sky."[315] As Parpola notes, "The elaborate techniques of astrology and extispicy were seriously utilized by the royal palace in order to foresee the future course of events, and all diviners—not only those resident at court—were obliged to inform the king of their findings."[316]

It is, however, the episode concerning the lunar eclipse under Nabonidus, the last of the Babylonian kings (555-539 B.C.), that best exemplifies the continuing predominance of hepatoscopy. As the king recounts it,

> When Nannar requested a high priestess
> the Son of the Prince showed his sign to the inhabited world;
> the Bright-Light manifested his reliable decision.
> To Nabonidus, king of Babylon, provider for Esagil and Ezida,
> the reverent shepherd who shows concern for the sanctuaries of the great gods
> Nannar, the lord of the crown, who bears the signal for all peoples,
> revealed his sign concerning his request for a high priestess.
> On the thirteenth of Ulūlu, the month of the work of goddesses,
> the Fruit became eclipsed and set while eclipsed.
> "Sin requests a high priestess"—such was his sign and decision.
> As for me, Nabonidus, the shepherd who reveres his divine majesty, I reverently heeded his reliable order,
> so that I became concerned about this request for a high priestess.
> I sought out the sanctuaries of Šamaš and Adad, the patrons of extispicy,
> and Šamas and Adad, as usual, answered me a reliable yes,
> wrote a favorable omen in my extispicy,
> the omen pertaining to the request for priestesses, the request of the gods to man.

---

[314] Edited by S. Parpola, "A Letter from Šamaš-šumu-ukīn to Esarhaddon," *Iraq* 34 (1972) 21–34.

[315] MUL.MEŠ emmuru puhādāni inakkisu ina muhhi šarri bēlini mār šarri Bābili la iqabbi mā Aplāyu udēšu bārû Bēl-ēṭer Šamaš-zēra-iqīša ṭupšar UD-mu Anu Enlil šunu mūšu kala ūmu šamê idaggulu, *Iraq* 34 (1972) 22:19–25.

[316] Parpola, *Iraq* 34 (1972) 31. See also Ivan Starr, *Queries to the Sungod*, SAA 4, pp. xxx–xxxv.

Elsewhere[317] I commented on the imagery and poetic language of Nabonidus' inscription. What is of interest here is that the sign given by the Moon god, a total eclipse in the month of Ulūlu in the last watch of the night, a portent that is listed in the compendium of celestial omens *Enūma Anu Enlil* with the apodosis "Sin requests a high priestess," was not sufficient for the king to act on it. The portent derived from a celestial phenomenon had to be checked by the most ancient, most reliable divinatory method, namely extispicy.

The celestial omen observed under Nabonidus was a total eclipse of the moon, an astronomical event not as rare as a solar eclipse, and one that could be predicted with reasonable accuracy shortly before the eclipse was to take place as early as the seventh century B.C. Nabonidus does not specify how the haruspex arrived at his verdict, what the features of the liver were that gave him the answer to Nabonidus' query. The wording of the king's questions indicates that the answer he expected was in terms of yes or no, and indeed he reports that the gods answered his queries with "yes" or "no." Nabonidus, whose efforts to revive and relive the past are well known,[318] no doubt consciously imitated the Sumerian practice of binary consultation in regard to the choosing of a high priestess,[319] even though, as already mentioned, the practice was also prevalent in the late Assyrian period.

While as late as the reign of Nabonidus the two divination techniques went hand-in-hand or complemented one another, there must have begun even then or shortly thereafter the process that culminated in the prevalence of astrology. The establishment of correlations between the features of the liver and stars or constellations, and their assignment to gods and to the twelve months of the year, must have been one of the steps in this development, a step for which we have some evidence from a late Uruk text.

---

[317] E. Reiner, *Your Thwarts in Pieces, Your Mooring Rope Cut. Poetry from Babylonia and Assyria.* Michigan Studies in the Humanities, 5 (Ann Arbor, 1985) Chapter I.

[318] See preceding note.

[319] As suggested by Oppenheim, *Ancient Mesopotamia* (note 179 above) 213.

A rather obscure and poorly preserved small tablet from the Seleucid period found at Warka[320] (ancient Uruk) enumerates the parts of the liver (with which the gall bladder is, as customary, associated) or the marks on it, called "station" and the like, and gives for each a correspondence with a god, a month, and a constellation. To quote some of the better understood lines:

The "station" is Enlil; month I; [Aries].[321]
The "path" is Šamaš; month II; Taurus.
The "sweet mouth" is Nusku; month III; Orion.
The "strength" is Uraš; month IV; Cancer, Plow-star.
The "gate of the palace" is Ninegal; month V; Regulus.
The "bubble" is the storm god Adad; month VI; Raven star.
The gall bladder is Anu; month VII; Libra.
The "finger" (identifiable as the *processus pyramidalis*) is god (broken); month VIII; Goat star.

Similar are the entries for the remainder of the months on the much eroded and hard to read reverse of the tablet.

The last two elements of each entry refer to the month and the zodiacal sign associated with it; these are standard, and some of them recur in the list of MUL.APIN Tablet I.[322] Month I (March–April) is associated with Aries; month II (April–May) with Taurus; month III with Orion in lieu of Gemini; month IV with Cancer; month V with Leo (that is, with Regulus); month VI with the Raven (Corvus), which has its heliacal rising in month VI; month VII (September-October) with Libra; month VIII with the Goat (Lyra) which has its heliacal rising in that month;[323] month X with Bēlet-balāṭi; month XI with Aquarius; and month XII apparently with Venus. (Month IX is omitted altogether.)[324]

---

[320] Egbert von Weiher, *SpTU*, vol. 4 no. 159; the text (W 22666/0) had been very generously made available to me before publication by Professor von Weiher, the epigrapher of the excavation.

[321] Aries can be restored from the commentary that follows, in which the name of Dumuzi is preserved, because the two, Aries and Dumuzi, are paired in the astronomical text MUL.APIN Tablet I column i line 43, in the edition of Hermann Hunger and David Pingree, *MUL.APIN*.

[322] See *MUL.APIN* p. 139f.

[323] MUL.APIN I ii 45 and iii 4; the traces at the end of the entry in line 17 may represent the zodiacal sign Scorpius.

[324] Similar are the correspondences between months and constellations in the "Calendar texts" discussed on pp. 114f.

The novelty of this unique text is its establishing correspondences between the liver examined by the haruspex and the heliacal risings of constellations. As another unique text to be discussed in Chapter V states, correspondences between terrestrial and celestial phenomena can and indeed must be established.

The parts of the liver and the marks on it are enumerated in the sequence they are normally examined in the course of the hepatoscopy. Their associations with the deities listed can be explained in some cases only: in the case of the "bubble" associated with Adad, we can point to the Raven star called the star of Adad;[325] other associations, such as that of the mark called "path" with Šamaš, and of the gall bladder with Anu, have not yet been found in our sources. The sequence of the parts enumerated makes it certain that the starting point of the learned treatise was the manual of the haruspex and that the zodiacal signs were only secondarily associated with them.

The items of the text are accompanied by and thus were obviously deemed worthy of *scholia*; unfortunately, most of the explanations offered are rather opaque.[326]

Unique as this text is in Babylonian scholarly literature, it testifies to an elaboration of the concept of the stellar influence on the configurations that the liver could exhibit, and thereby to the continued vitality of the Mesopotamian divinatory tradition, while its association between stars and planets and parts of the exta, paralleled in the *Apotelesmatika* of Hephaistio from Hellenistic Egypt,[327] points to wide-ranging crosscurrents in the Hellenistic Near East.

---

325 MUL.APIN I ii 9.

326 They give philological equations, for example, to month II, written with the Sumerogram GU_4.SI.SÁ, first the verb SI.SÁ is translated as *ešēri ša alāku* "to be straight, said of going," then GU_4 , but its translation as "bull" is now broken; the connection of the month name with the constellation Taurus coordinated with it may have been further explained in the commentary.

327 David Pingree, ed., *Hephaestionis Thebani Apotelesmaticorum libri tres*, vol. 1 (Leipzig: Teubner, 1973) III 6.14–17.

FIGURE 10. Bronze bell decorated with scenes of exorcisms of demons. Courtesy of Staatliche Museen zu Berlin, no. VAN 48.

CHAPTER V

Apotropaia

Doch Abraxas bring ich selten!
Goethe West-östlicher Divan

īpuš Ea ipšur Ea 'Ea has wrought it, Ea has loosed it,'[328] this phrase from a Babylonian incantation subsumes the essence of Babylonian magic. Ea, the god of both wisdom and cunning and hence the figure of the trickster god, is also the god of magic. The verb from which the form *īpuš* 'wrought' derives, Akkadian *epēšu*, a common verb with the basic meaning 'to do,' is also the technical term for 'bewitching' and many nouns derived from it denote various though for us often undifferentiated machinations, such as *ipšu, upšāšû, upīšū, muppišūtu,* all denoting sorcery, and *muppišu, muppištu, muppišānu,* all denoting practitioners of witchcraft.[329] The second verb form of the saying, *ipšur* 'loosed,' carries the apotropaic message par excellence, both in its Akkadian version (verb: *pašāru*) and its Sumerian counterpart, the Sumerian verb *búr.* It is from this Sumerian verb that the ritual for undoing evil, Sumerian *nam.búr.bi* and its loan into Akkadian, *namburbû,* takes its name. The Sumerian noun is formed with the abstract nominalizing prefix *nam* (in English, the suffix -ing) and the possessive suffix *bi.* The literal translation, 'its loosing,' refers by "it" to a previously

---

328 CT 23 2:13, *Or.* NS 40 (1971) 141:28′ and 143 r. 16, *Or.* NS 42 (1973) 509 r. 26, etc., and the references cited by Parpola, *LAS* 2 p. 41 (but instead of the there cited K.137+2788 read K.157+2788, edited by R. I. Caplice, *Or.* NS 40 [1971] 140).

329 Similar is the usage in Croatian of the verb *činiti* 'to do' and its corresponding noun *čini* (pl.) 'magic,' compare the popular saying *Ne čini čini na mjesečini* 'Don't do magic in the moonlight.' For Middle Latin *factura* 'sortilegium' and the Italian derivatives *fatturare* 'to bewitch,' and the like, and for Greek *praxis* in this meaning see Wilhelm Havers, *Neuere Literatur zum Sprachtabu,* Sitzungsberichte der Akademie der Wissenschaften in Wien, Philosophisch-historische Klasse, 223, Abhandlung 5, p. 161 and n. 1.

described ominous occurrence and the implicit or explicitly stated impending evil that it portends. The suffix character of *bi* is no longer transparent in Akkadian, and hence the loan-word *namburbû* can take Akkadian possessive suffixes, *-šu* 'its' and *-šunu* 'their.' By carrying out the prescribed actions and reciting the appropriate prayers, the evil will be loosed[330] or simply "he/it will be loosed."[331]

This apotropaion was made available to man by the same gods who were willing to forewarn him through some ominous happening; the power of Ea to undo the portended evil expressed in the cited incantation is repeated in a Neo-Assyrian letter reporting on an earthquake and the evil portended by it: 'Ea has wrought it, Ea has loosed it, he who caused the earth-quake has himself carried out the apotropaic ritual.'[332]

One expects that each collection of omens had its parallel apotropaic ritual. But while the omen collections were serialized, that is, arranged in books or chapters with more or less canonical divisions and numbering, this does not seem to have been the case with the *namburbû* texts.[333] Rather, certain apotropaic rituals are inserted immediately after the ill-portending omen, in midst of the omen collection itself; even the catalogues of omen series that cite the title of some chapter may add 'including its apotropaion' (*adi namburbêšu*).[334] There are also individual tablets inscribed with such rituals alone, one or more; their subscripts do not indicate that they are part of a particular series. Still, apparently every evil portent signaled by

---

330 *maškadu ippaššar* 'the *maškadu*-disease will be loosed,' *BAM* 81:7, (the affliction) *ina zumrišu ippaššar* (written with the Sumerogram BÚR) 'will be loosed from his body', BE 31 pl. 51 no. 60 r. ii 8.

331 *pašir*, *BAM* 140:6, *Analecta Biblica* 12 (1959) 286:107, *Dream-book* 343:23, *LKA* 123:14, and passim.

332 ēpuš Ea ipšur Ea ša rību īpušuni šūtma NAM.BÚR.BI ētapaš (in Parpola's translation in SAA 10) 'Ea has done, Ea has undone. He who caused the earthquake has also created the apotropaic ritual against it,' *ABL* 355 r. 9, see *LAS* no. 35 (= SAA 10 no. 56) and *LAS* 2 p. 41.

333 See R. I. Caplice, *The Akkadian* namburbi *Texts: An Introduction*, SANE 1/1 (Los Angeles: Malibu, 1974), and for the edition of the texts idem, *Or.* NS vols. 34–42 (1965–73) passim. A comprehensive treatment of the genre is now available in Stefan M. Maul, *Zukunftsbewältigung*, Baghdader Forschungen, 18 (Mainz on Rhine: Philipp von Zabern, 1994).

334 CT 39 50 K.957:11: EN NAM.BÚR.BI.

an ominous occurrence could be averted by the appropriate ritual, as we gather from those texts that list in a catalogue form[335] the events against whose evil consequences, generally simply termed 'the evil' (Sumerian HUL, Akkadian *lumnu*), such rituals could be invoked. If the origin of the evil was not known, one could perform the rite against 'all evil' (Sumerian HUL.DÙ.A.BI, Akkadian *lumun kalama*).[336]

The ritual itself is called apotropaion (*namburbû*), a name that appears at the beginning or as subscript at the end; occasionally it is introduced by the phrase *annû namburbûšu* 'this is its loosing,'[337] or is followed by a rubric which states its purpose, normally "apotropaion for the evil of such-and-such," for example, "of a snake," or more specifically "of a snake that spattered the man," that is, citing the ominous occurrence that augured ill.[338]

Numerous are the apotropaic rituals that are concerned with ominous everyday occurrences which are listed in the two omen series *šumma ālu* ('if a city')[339] and *šumma izbu* ('if a creature')[340] and which affect the common man in whose household they are observed. They include strange happenings in his house, his field, and his city in the first series, and abnormal, monstruous births in pen and fold, even among humans, in the second. On the other hand, forecasts from celes-

---

335 For such catalogues see Caplice, *Or.* NS 34 (1965) 108ff. and 42 (1973) 514f. (the latter subsequently published in Hermann Hunger, *SpTU*, vol. 1 as no. 6), and Ebeling, *RA* 48 (1954) 10ff.

336 For example, an apotropaion against "any evil" is recommended in the letter *LAS* no. 334 (K.818, = SAA 10 no. 56), see Parpola, *LAS* 2 p. 351.

337 A. Leo Oppenheim, "A Diviner's Manual," *JNES* 33 (1974) 200:56.

338 [NAM.BÚR.BI] ⌈HUL MUŠ⌉ *ana amīli u bītišu la ṭehê* 'apotropaion that the evil of a snake not approach a man and his house,' *Or.* NS 36 (1967) 23 no. 19:10, and ibid. 24 no. 20:7', etc.; [NAM].BÚR.BI HUL MUŠ *ša amīla isluhu*, *Or.* NS 36 21 no. 18:1.

339 So designated by the Akkadian scribes in the subscript to each of the originally more than one hundred chapters, from its incipit *šumma ālu ina mēlê šakin* 'if a city lies on high ground.' The work was edited in part by F. Nötscher, *Die Omen-Serie šumma âlu ina mêlê šakin* (Orientalia vol. 31 [1928], vols. 39–42 [1929], 51–54 [1930]); a new edition is being prepared by Erle Leichty.

340 These are the teratological omens taken from the birth of malformed children or animals, edited by Erle Leichty, *The Babylonian Omen Series* šumma izbu, Texts from Cuneiform Sources, 3 (Glückstadt: Augustin, 1969).

tial phenomena collected in the treatise *Enūma Anu Enlil* or from the inspection of the liver collected in the various chapters of the series *bārûtu* affect primarily the fate of the king and his land, and thus have a national, even universal significance. Only a few rare apotropaic rituals for averting such evils have come down to us,[341] even though the titles that are listed—without their text—in the mentioned catalogues assure us of their existence. It is worthy of note that unknown, at least to me, are apotropaia to avert evil portents derived from observing the shapes taken by oil poured on water, and by observing the configurations of the smoke rising from an incense-burner, that is, lecanomancy and libanomancy, techniques used only in the Old Babylonian period.[342]

Were it not that the absence of a certain type of apotropaic ritual could be due to chance, the existence of apotropaia could serve as a test to distinguish two types of divinatory text. The ability to resort to apotropaic rituals would characterize those omen collections in which the situation or event warns of an impending occurrence, and the absence of apotropaia those which do not foretell the future, but give as it were a diagnosis. To the latter group belong, first of all, the diagnostic treatise "When the exorcist goes to the house of the sick person" (see Chapter III), and those compendia in which the apodosis simply describes the person's character or ḥabits. Among the latter are the texts called "physiognomic omens"[343] and the texts describing physical or behavioral characteristics known as "A Guide to Moral Behavior Styled as Omens,"[344] the omens derived from a persons habits when speaking,[345] and the very similar collection establishing a person's character from his use

---

[341] Note the subscript [*šumma? idāti*] *ittāti aḫâti ana šarri u mātišu bašâ* 'if there exist evil portents for the king and his land,' *4R* 60, edited by E. Ebeling, *RA* 49 (1955) 40:21.

[342] See Chapter IV note 258. For the relation of *namburbû*'s to the omen collections see R. I. Caplice, *The Akkadian* namburbi *Texts: An Introduction*, SANE 1/1 (Los Angeles: Malibu, 1974) 7ff.

[343] F. R. Kraus, *Texte zur babylonischen Physiognomatik*, Archiv für Orientforschung, Beiheft 3 (Berlin, 1939).

[344] F. R. Kraus, "Ein Sittenkanon in Omenform," *ZA* 43 (1936) 77–113.

[345] F. R. Kraus, "Babylonische Omina mit Ausdeutung der Begleiterscheinungen des Sprechens," *AfO* 11 (1936) 219–30.

of a greeting formula.[346] Evidently these attributes, for example, being pusillanimous, or honest, or affectionate (described in the Guide), or scratching one's nose when speaking (mentioned in the second compendium), even if they portended misfortune were not thought to be susceptible of change through a ritual, and neither were the diagnoses[347] of the causes or the outcome of the illness or its determinations about the sex and number of the children a pregnant woman was carrying.

Many a fortuitous happening, seemingly harmless, could carry a warning about a grave impending event, which could be warded off only by appealing to the gods, and what interests us here in particular, astral gods. The evil was no less to be feared if portended by a squeaky pot than by a more momentous occurrence, just as today a black cat crossing one's path is said to bring bad luck.

There is in fact an apotropaion[348] designed to counteract the evil portended by a squeaky pot. The portent is preserved in *šumma ālu* in a sequence of omens dealing with squeaky pots of various contents, among others, "If a pot of water squeaks in a man's house."[349] The site of the ritual, which is the bank of the river or canal, is purified and offerings are made to the gods Ea—god not only of magic but of sweet water as well—and Šamaš. Before the patient recites a prayer to Šamaš, a holy-water vessel, filled with water from the well of the temple of Marduk into which herbs and beads of metal have been scattered, is to be placed "before the [. . .] star and the Wagon."[350] After the prayer to Šamaš there is a break on the tablet, and

---

[346] E. Reiner, "A manner of speaking," in *ZIKIR ŠUMIM: Assyriological Studies Presented to F. R. Kraus on the Occasion of his Seventieth Birthday*, G. van Driel et al., eds. (Leiden: Brill, 1982) 282-89.

[347] The term "diagnosis" in Greek medicine includes the prognosis of the disease, see G. E. R. Lloyd, *The Revolutions of Wisdom*, Sather Classical Lectures, vol. 52 (Berkeley-Los Angeles-London: University of California Press, 1987) 39 n. 123.

[348] *4R* 60 K.2587, edited by Ebeling, *RA* 49 (1955) 36ff.

[349] [šumma i]na bīt amēli karpat mê issi̮, CT 40 4:87, dupl. ibid. 8 K.10407, and passim in this tablet (cited *CAD* Š/2 s.v. *šasû* meaning 1h). The namburbi in *Or.* NS 40 (1971) 134 which enumerates squeaky pots in lines 5-6 along with other Alu omens is not specific.

[350] ina IGI MUL.[x u MUL].MAR.GÍD tašakkan, *4R* 60:24f., see Ebeling, *RA* 49 (1955) 36:24f.

when the text resumes, on the reverse of the tablet, we find addresses to a plurality, as the verb forms indicate; the addressees could be the three gods of exorcism Ea, Šamaš, and Asalluhi, but possibly are the two constellations to which the holy water vessel was exposed, or even all the stars—the gods of the night—as the phrasing of the prayer suggests: "I invoke you from the heaven of Anu, I implore you (etc.)."[351]

The holy water vessel was exposed to the stars in several other apotropaic rituals, one to ward off the evil portended by a snake[352] and two against the evil portended by fire striking a house.[353] No nocturnal prayer to the stars accompanies the exposure; it is the Sun-god, Šamaš, who is addressed when morning dawns.

When a fungus that portends evil appears on the walls of a house a he-goat[354] is sacrificed before the Pleiades, while a prayer to the Seven Gods, that is, the seven stars of the constellation, is recited[355] and a yellow she-goat (ÙZ SIG_7) is sacrificed to Gula, the goddess of healing, whose celestial manifestation, the constellation Lyra, is called the Goat star.[356]

If a man falls on his face and starts bleeding, obviously an ill-portending happening, he will avert the evil consequences by making a food-offering to a certain deity (the name is broken) and to the constellation Sagittarius.[357]

The evil portended by various birds—described in tablets

---

351 alsīkunūši ištu šamê ša Ani ashurkunūši, *4R* 60 rev. 18.

352 HUL MUŠ, *Or.* NS 36 (1967) 24f. no. 20, see note 338.

353 IZI.ŠUB.BA: "you expose the preparation to the stars of the night" (*ana* MUL *mu-ši-tim tuš-bat*) *Or.* NS 36 (1967) 287:9′, 295:25.

354 MÁŠ.GAL *bur-ru-qá*; the qualifying adjective is obscure.

355 Caplice, *Or.* NS 40 (1971) 143 r. 5f.: MÁŠ.GAL bur-ru-qá ina IGI MUL. MUL KUD-is-ma muhra ᵈ7.BI DUG_4.GA-ma . . . Other references to the Pleiades conceived as the Seven gods par excellence are *RA* 18 (1921) 28 and its parallels *KAR* 38 r. 18ff. and K.8863. Offerings are made to the Pleiades in a Hittite text (Bo3298 + KUB 25 32 + . . . ii 1ff. §12), see Gregory MacMahon, *The Hittite State Cult of the Tutelary Deities*, AS 25 (Chicago: Oriental Institute Press, 1991) 62, cf. the "Lamma of the Pleiades" (*ŠA* ᵈ7.7.BI ᵈLAMMA) cited ibid. p. 48.

356 Caplice, *Or.* NS 40 (1971) 143 r. 34: ÙZ SIG_7 ana ᵈGula KUD-is.

357 kurummassu ana [. . .] u PA.BIL.SAG GAR-ma NU TE-šú 'he should present his food-offering to [. . .] and to Sagittarius,' CT 37 46:7 (šumma ālu Tablet 87, to be published by Ann Guinan).

65?-67 of the omen series *šumma ālu,* which deal with the appearance and behavior of birds in a man's house[358]—is averted by an apotropaic ritual with prayers to the stars:

> Incantation: Mighty stars who have resplendent positions in the sky,
> The g[reat?] gods have created you, wise Nu[dimmud (=Ea) has . . .] you.[359]

The names of the gods Enlil, Ea and possibly Šulpae follow; the next fragmentary line—the last line before the break—with its mention of "stars" possibly refers to the stars of the three "paths" of Anu, Enlil, and Ea,[360] that is, all stars rising over the three "paths" on the horizon.[361]

Similar in tenor is the prayer[362] in the parallel text meant to avert the evil portent of a "bird," probably a bat:[363]

> 8. [Incantation: You,] mighty stars, whom Anu and Enlil have [created],
> 9. [Enlil?,] Ea, Jupiter [. . .],
> 10. [You?] mighty stars who [have resplendent] positions in the sky.[364]

In rare occurrences the celestial power is addressed because

---

[358] F. Nötscher, *Die Omen-Serie šumma âlu ina mêlê šakin* (Orientalia 51–54 [1930]) 149ff., and S. Moren, *The Omen Series Šumma Alu* (Ph.D. diss., University of Pennsylvania, 1978), pp. 104ff. and 211ff.

[359] [ÉN MUL.MEŠ gašrūt]i ša ina šamê manzāza šarhu
ilū r[abûtu? ib]nûkunūši eršu Nu[dimmud . . . -kunūši]

in an apotropaic ritual to avert the evil of a dove: Bu. 91-5-9,155 rev. 8–10, edited by R. I. Caplice, *Or.* NS 36 (1967) 282f.

[360] dEnlil dEa d[Šulpae?] lu MUL.MEŠ [. . .]—Bu. 91-5-9,155 rev. 10–11.

[361] See Introduction p. 6 and note 13.

[362] Rm. 510 lines 8–10, edited by R. I. Caplice, *Or.* NS 36 (1967) 284f.

[363] BURU$_5$.HABRUD.DA. The identification with "bat" is suggested by the description BURU$_5$.HABRUD.DA MUŠEN NITA *ina* MI *šá* DU-*ku-ma* (= probably *ittanallaku* and not simply *illaku*) NIM (= *lamṣata*?) *ibarru* '(blood of) a male bat that goes about at night catching flies,' *BAM* 476:10'.

[364] 8. [ÉN attunu MU]L.MEŠ gašrūtu ša Anu u Enlil i[bnûkunūši]
9. [Enlil?] dÉ-a dŠul-pa-è-a [. . .]
10. [. . . MU]L.MEŠ gašrūtu ša ina šamê manzāza [. . .]

Since line 8 of Rm. 510 corresponds to line rev. 8 of Bu. 91-5-9,155, and line 10 to line rev. 7, we conjecture that the mention of Jupiter (Šulpaea) in line 9 was present in the broken part of rev. 9.

of its analog to the earthly event or object. One apotropaic ritual, against the evil portended by a bow,[365] involves the Bow-star. The Bow-star (part of Canis Maior) in this case too represents Ištar, whose celestial manifestation it is, as we know from several sources,[366] since the instructions call for two altars to be set up, one to Ea and one to Ištar, and for a sheep to be sacrificed to Ea and a kid to the Bow-star.[367]

The analogy is less transparent, and possibly more tenuous, in the ritual to be performed by the king to avert the evil portent of "cult city and sanctuary."[368] It directs that a sacrifice be made and a prayer recited to the Kidney-star: "You arrange an altar before the Kidney-star, . . . the king recites with lifted hands before the Kidney-star as follows: Incantation. 'Enki . . .'"[369] The prayer, in Sumerian, addresses the god Ea under his Sumerian name Enki; the relationship of the Kidney-star (which is part of the constellation Puppis) to the god Ea is not known from other sources, but we may surmise it from a learned commentary on the names of the phases of the moon. The commentary[370] lists the names of the various phases of the moon: the moon is called "crescent" from the first to the fifth day, and "resplendent crown" when full. From the sixth to the tenth, the gibbous moon (*amphikyrtos*) is called *kalītu* 'kidney,' and is equated with Ea.[371]

A compilation that is in some way a companion to *šumma ālu* is the series that already in antiquity bore the name *iqqur īpuš*. This series, first edited under the title "An Almanac from ancient Babylonia,"[372] was republished under the equally sug-

---

365 HUL GIŠ.BAN; one exemplar, *LKA* 113, was edited by Ebeling, *RA* 49 (1955) 137f.; another, Sm. 340, by R. I. Caplice, *Or.* NS 39 (1970) 116f.

366 MUL.APIN I ii 7, *BPO* 2 82 *KAV* 218 i 15, ii 16, 19, etc., see C. B. F. Walker, *Anatolian Studies* 33 (1983) 147 n. 14.

367 GI.DU$_8$.MEŠ ana Ea Ištar tukân . . . UDU . . . ana Ea teppaš, unīqu ana MUL.BAN teppaš, *LKA* 113, see note 365.

368 ana HUL māhāzi u eširti ana šarri la ṭehê, *Or.* NS 39 (1970) 132f.

369 GI.DU$_8$ ana IGI MUL.BIR tukân . . . LUGAL ŠU-su ÍL-ma ana IGI MUL.BIR k[īam iqabbi] ÉN ^{d}En-ki . . . lines 12′ff.

370 For references see *CAD* K s.v. *kalītu* meaning 4.

371 See lastly Alasdair Livingstone, *Mystical and Mythological Explanatory Works of Assyrian and Babylonian Scholars* (Oxford: Clarendon Press, 1986) 30f. and 47.

372 E. F. Weidner, "Ein Hauskalender aus dem alten Babylonien," *RSO* 32 (1957) 185–96.

gestive title "A Babylonian Calendar of works, seasons, and months," echoing Hesiod's *Works and Days.*[373] This allusion notwithstanding, there is no work in Babylonian literature that would parallel Hesiod's. As for those texts that indicate the days and the months suitable for carrying out ritual or magic manipulations, they will be our concern later insofar as these moments are affected by astral positions.

The Babylonian almanac or calendar exists in two arrangements, one according to the enterprise envisaged, and the other according to the month. In the first, each activity forms one paragraph, and the prognosis for each month is stated in the style normal for omens. For example, the first paragraph—from which the name of the series was taken—states "If he tears down (*iqqur*) his house in Nisannu (i.e., month I), he . . .; if in Ayaru (month II), . . ." and so on. Hence, each paragraph consists of normally twelve entries, one for each month of the year, and occasionally of thirteen, if it also includes the intercalary month of the Babylonian calendar, that is, the month that was periodically added so that the year, made up of twelve lunar months of twenty-nine or thirty days, could be brought into agreement with the solar year of 365 and a fraction days. The other arrangement[374] excerpts these paragraphs according to months, so that under each month all pertinent activities are listed along with the prognosis for him who would perform them. Not all of these "monthly sets" are extant, though some of the months exist in duplicate copies to show that different traditions singled out different activities worthy of inclusion.

In fact, only the first sixty-odd paragraphs record activities whose outcome may be favorable or not. The last forty paragraphs deal not with intentional undertakings, but with the forces of nature, and the transition between the two sections is formed by paragraph 66′ that deals with fire—presumably lightning—striking a house. From paragraph 67 on the topics are the ones treated in the compendium of celestial omens, the series *Enūma Anu Enlil*, 'When Anu (and) Enlil,'[375] but include

---

[373] René Labat, *Un Calendrier babylonien des travaux, des saisons, et des mois* (Paris: Champion, 1965).

[374] Called "*iqqur īpuš* mensuel" by Labat, and version B by Weidner.

[375] See p. 12, note 36.

only a selection, and the predictions differ according to the month in which a particular phenomenon takes place. The list of ominous celestial events varies with the different sources, ranging from the always present predictions from eclipses of the moon and of the sun, haloes of the moon, first appearance of Venus, and a few meteorological phenomena, among them thunder, rain, and earthquakes, to risings of other planets[376] not attested in every source. In spite of the crude reckoning that can have no claim to astronomical precision—days (in addition to months) are stated only in regard to the visibilities of Venus while the other phenomena are described solely in terms of months, and those schematic thirty-day months—concern with celestial phenomena is manifest in these texts too. The last of the paragraphs concerned with celestial and meteorological events (§104 in Labat's edition) is followed by a paragraph (numbered §105 in Labat's edition) that lists the twelve months and assigns each to a god or goddess. In one exemplar, VAT 9772, which lists only twelve months and omits the thirteenth, the series does not end there but continues with additional material. Unfortunately, the ends of the lines, which are all that survive, show only that further predictions were listed, but not what the phenomena were from which these were derived.

Concatenating several series is not unique to this text. Elsewhere, different lexical texts are combined into a single composition, possibly reflecting the sequence of the scribe's curriculum, e.g., in some recensions to the 24-tablet series *HAR-ra = hubullu* was added, as Tablet 25, the list of professions *lú = ša*;[377] and one copy of a recension of *šumma ālu* omens is followed by omens excerpted from the celestial omen series *Enūma Anu Enlil*[378] while another copy continued with the series *šammu šikinšu*, the incipit of which is quoted as the omen tablet's catch line. The second tablet of the astronomical compendium MUL.APIN has a catch line MUL SAG.ME.GAR

[376] Jupiter and Mercury are attested, see René Labat, *Un Calendrier babylonien des travaux, des saisons, et des mois* (Paris: Champion, 1965) 170f. n. 6, and so is Mars in the list for month IV in BM 26185 communicated to me by Douglas Kennedy.

[377] See Miguel Civil, MSL 12 p. 90.

[378] CT 41 20f. reverse 31–37 contains celestial omens.

^{d}*Šul-pa-è*, an incipit which is attested on several fragments and lists.[379]

Just as there are apotropaic rituals to avert the evil consequences of such everyday occurrences as are enumerated in the series *šumma ālu* and in the series *iqqur īpuš*, others, against the evil portended by celestial happenings, also exist but in a smaller number, the more regrettable as there are Arabic and Indian magical texts with which it would be interesting to compare them. Of a quite different character are the prolonged and public expiatory rites performed when a lunar eclipse occurred.[380]

The existence of rituals to avert quite specific ill-portending celestial phenomena can, however, be inferred from the "universal catalogues"[381] that we may call "HUL-lists" from the words that begin each line: *ina* HUL, Akkadian *ina lumun*, 'from the evil of.' The sequence of celestial phenomena whose evil consequence is to be averted is the same in the HUL-lists as the sequence of topics in the compendium of celestial omens *Enūma Anu Enlil*: Moon, Sun, weather-phenomena (including earthquakes), and stars and planets, also known as the four books Sin, Šamaš, Adad, and Ištar, and the sequence of those paragraphs of the series *iqqur īpuš* that parallel the celestial omen compendium. One catalogue[382] enumerates, possibly with reference to the king, eclipses of, first (in a broken section) the moon, then of the sun and of Venus, as well as flaring up of stars, earthquakes, and various cloud-configurations: "when [. . . an eclipse of either the Moon] or of the Sun or of Venus, or a flaring? [star (or . . .)] or an earthquake [or . . . or a] cloud? or a fireball? or an *ašqulālu*-phenomenon is seen."[383] A list of evil portents taken from stars and planets is preserved in a

379 See Hunger and Pingree, *MUL.APIN* 8f.

380 See Werner Mayer, *Untersuchungen zur Formensprache der babylonischen "Gebetsbeschwörungen,"* Studia Pohl: Series Maior, 5 (Rome: Biblical Institute Press, 1976) 100ff.

381 Termed "general (allgemeine) namburbi-tablets" by Erich Ebeling, *RA* 48 (1954) 3.

382 *LKA* 108, edited by Erich Ebeling, *RA* 50 (1956) 26.

383 enūma LU[GAL . . . AN.TA.LÙ lu ša ^{d}Sin l]u ša Šamaš lu ša Ištar lu mi-ši-i[h? MUL . . .] lu rību [lu . . . lu A]N.GUB (or read AN.DU = andugû?) lu akkullu lu isqulālu IGI, *LKA* 108:13ff., see *RA* 50 (1956) 26.

šumma ālu text[384] and another, taken from meteorological phenomena, in an Assur text.[385] A parallel to these is included in a royal ritual in which the king lists in column ii "either an eclipse of the Moon [or of the Sun$^{?}$] or of Jupiter or an eclipse of . . ., [or . . .] the roar of Adad that came down from the sky, [or . . .] or a flaring$^{?}$ star or a scintillating$^{?}$ star or [. . .] which came close to the stars of the (three) paths"[386] and continues with "any evil that is in my land and my palace."[387] Of the sequel (column iii$^{?}$) only the first few signs of some lines are preserved, and they are, after an introductory "ditto" (KI.MIN) in each line, "the evil of [. . .], the evil of [. . .] signs which [occurred$^{?}$] in the land, the evil of an eclipse [of . . .], the evil of a fireball$^{?}$ [. . .], the evil of [. . .] star,"[388] and two more lines with only HUL preserved.

The ritual for averting the evil portended by an earthquake is also mentioned in the letters of exorcists to the Assyrian king.[389] Other evil portents given by celestial phenomena are

---

384 CT 41 23 i 3–16, edited by Ebeling, *RA* 48 (1954) 10ff., see Parpola, *LAS* 2 p. 73.

385 *LKA* 48a, edited by Ebeling, *RA* 48 (1954) 82 no. 3.

386 $_{10'}$ . . . lu-u AN.MI Sin $_{11'}$ [. . .] lu-u AN.MI ^{d}Šul-pa-è-a $_{12'}$ [. . .] lu-u AN.MI ši-i-qí $_{13'}$ [. . .] KA ^{d}IM ša TA AN-e ur-da $_{14'}$ [. . . lu]-u mi-ših MUL lu-u ṣa-ra-ár MUL $_{15'}$ [. . .] ša ana MUL.MEŠ KASKAL.MEŠ is-sa-ni-qu K.8091 + 10628, known to me from Geers' copies, parallel *BMS* 62, see Ebeling, *RA* 48 (1954) 8. A similar enumeration is found in the text published by W. G. Lambert, "A Part of the Ritual for the Substitute King," *AfO* 18 (1957–58) 109ff., column A lines 11ff.: AN.MI ^{d}Sin AN.MI ^{d}Šamaš AN.MI ^{d}Šul-pa-è-a [. . . AN].MI ^{d}Dil-bat AN.MI ^{d}UDU.BAD.MEŠ 'eclipses of the Moon, the Sun, Jupiter, Venus, (or of) the (other) planets,' see Parpola, *LAS* 2 p. xxii. No eclipse of Jupiter or Mars is mentioned in the celestial omens, but eclipses of Venus are. Apotropaic rituals to avert the evil portended by a lunar eclipse are published by Ebeling, *RA* 48 (1954) 82 as no. 2 and by Caplice, *Or.* NS 40 (1971) 166f. no. 65; the cuneiform text was subsequently published in autograph copy as CT 51 190.

387 See p. 84 and note 341.

388 HUL [. . .], HUL Á.MEŠ [. . .] ša ina KUR [. . .], HUL AN.MI [. . .], HUL an-qu[l-lu . . .], HUL MUL [. . .] K.8091 + 10628 iii$^{?}$ 1'ff.

389 *LAS* no. 16 (*ABL* 34, = SAA 10 no. 10), and nos. 147 and 148 (*ABL* 357 and 1118+, = SAA 10 nos. 202 and 203), see also Parpola, *LAS* 2 pp. 123ff.; the ritual itself was described in the text *KAR* 7 but only the prayer to Šamaš mentioning HUL *ri-i-b*[*i* . . .], 'the evil of the earthquake,' is preserved in it. A ritual performed by the temple singer *kalû* to avert such evil is attested in Thureau-Dangin, *Rituels accadiens* (Paris, Leroux: 1921) 34ff. obverse 16–reverse 1.

known only from references in the royal correspondence from Assyria. One of the letters mentions the evil (portended) by Mars that missed its appointed time and entered Aries.[390] Another speaks of the late rising of Jupiter[391] and a third[392] of its dark aspect at rising. This last example provides an additional proof, if such were still necessary, that the scholars who reported to Esarhaddon were consulting the omen series, since the partly broken omen that the writer cites can be restored from a number of celestial omen tablets, some of which are cited in the commentary to the letter[393] while others[394] are as yet unpublished.

The conjunction of Mars and the Moon was also an occasion for an apotropaic ritual, but only the incipit is extant in the subscript of a namburbi: "if Mars and the Moon go side by side."[395] In yet another apotropaic ritual the "evil" is attributed to Sagittarius (^{d}PA.BIL.SAG).[396] A curious ritual seeking to "remove a star by the door from a house"[397] is written on a tablet that is designated by its subscript as the "123rd tablet" of a composition whose name is broken.[398] The ritual seeks to ward off the evil portent by throwing into the river "[an effigy?

---

[390] HUL Ṣalbatānu ša adanšu ušēti[quni] u ina libbi MUL.LÚ.HUN.GÁ i[nnamiruni], K.818 = *LAS* no. 334 (CT 53 8, = SAA 10 no. 381), and see Parpola, *LAS* 2 pp. 350f.

[391] *ACh* Supp. 2 62 = *LAS* no. 289 = SAA 10 no. 362.

[392] *ABL* 647 = *LAS* no. 67 = SAA 10 no. 67.

[393] The citations adduced by Parpola in his commentary in *LAS* 2 p. 74 include an omen that is also quoted in MUL.APIN II.

[394] K.2184, K.2286, BM 36627.

[395] [¶ ^{d}] ⌈Ṣal-bat⌉-a-nu u ^{d}Sin it-te-e[n-tu-ú . . .] *Or.* NS 40 (1971) 169 r. 12 (preceding lines fragmentary). The restoration comes from BM 99065 (=1904-10-9, 94) in L. W. King, *Catalogue of the Cuneiform Tablets of the British Museum, Supplement*, pl. III no. 130.

[396] R. I. Caplice, *Or.* NS 40 (1971) 177 (pl. XVI) no. 71 82-3-23,37 line 5: ŠU ^{d}PA.BIL.SAG. Note also [ri-h]u-ut ^{d}PA.BIL.SAG ibid. line 7. To avert the evil, offerings are to be made to the god Hendursagga ([. . .] ^{d}Hendur.sag.gá GAR-ma NU TE-šú, line 4).

[397] ka.inim.ma mul é.ta ká.na è.da.ke$_{4}$, *Or.* NS 39 (1970) 113:8.

[398] The restoration *n[am.búr.bi]* in the break has given rise to the conjecture that there existed a composition of at least 123 tablets comprising namburbû rituals, but it seems likely that "the serialization . . . seems to reflect rather a local ordering within the Assurbanipal library than a canonical sequence" (Caplice, *Or.* NS 34 [1965] 107).

of] the star that fell into your house" and reciting a spell in Sumerian[399] and a prayer to Šamaš in Akkadian. How a shooting star could land in a man's house is difficult to imagine, but portents from shooting stars are not only known from standard omen collections[400] but are requested as answers to the petitioner's question in the popular media of divination more akin to "fortune-telling," as I have had the occasion to show.[401]

The compendium *iqqur īpuš* combined the activities and phenomena of everyday life listed in §§1–66 with the portents announced by celestial bodies in §§67ff. The compilers of *iqqur īpuš* simply juxtaposed omens reflecting the two domains of heaven and earth and, correspondingly, public and private forecasts. Rare is a true conflation of the two, of which we saw a late example (p. 78) establishing a relationship between parts of the liver examined by the haruspex and zodiacal and other constellations. An effort to establish a relation between omens portended by various media was begun, however, even earlier. Speculations to this effect are set out in a text already known under Assurbanipal, from whose library its exemplars come. It was edited by Leo Oppenheim under the programmatic title "A Babylonian Diviner's Manual."[402] The text is a rarity not only in regard to its subject matter but especially in its attempt to give a rationale for the correspondences between signs observed in the sky and signs ~~on~~ earth, in contrast to the Mesopotamian approach which, as we have seen, does not normally give reasons or explanations.

The interconnections between celestial and terrestrial omens are stressed several times but they are eventually expressed in the simple terms: the portents on earth and those in the sky correspond. The task of the diviner, as we can infer from the

[399] The Sumerian spell begins with mul É.NUN.ta è.a 'star which has come out of the É.NUN'; É.NUN, Akkadian *agrunnu* (for which see Caplice, "É.NUN in Mesopotamian Literature," *Or.* NS 42 [1973] 299–305) elsewhere is both the underground abyss and the temple that corresponds to it on earth, see ibid. 304f.

[400] See p. 72.

[401] In "Fortune-Telling in Mesopotamia," *JNES* 19 (1960) 28f., and see above p. 72 and note 299.

[402] A. Leo Oppenheim, "A Babylonian Diviner's Manual," *JNES* 33 (1974) 197–220.

statements of the author, is both to interpret the signs as they are observed individually, and to establish a relation between the terrestrial and the celestial omens. It is noteworthy that this "manual," as much as it proclaims the correspondence (in the Baudelairian sense) of terrestrial and celestial omens, is written on tablets some of which are also inscribed with planetary omens. ". . . our difficult text is witness to the renewed vigor the Mesopotamian scholar brought to bear on enlarging and refining previous divination techniques in the outgoing second and incoming first millennium, a vigor which created a plethora of new forms and methods of divination while at the same time it carefully maintained the heritage of the early second millennium achievements."[403]

The text's first explicit statement:[404] "The signs in the sky just as those on earth give us signals,"[405] follows the listing of incipits of "fourteen tablets with signs occurring on earth" and the second, even more insistent, "The signs on earth just as those in the sky give us signals; sky and earth both produce portents, though appearing separately they are not separate because sky and earth are related," is the subscript to a list of incipits of "eleven tablets with signs occurring in the sky."[406] The correspondence between the two domains extends to the consequences of the portents, as the Manual continues with a warning about evil-portending signs: "A sign that portends evil in the sky is evil on earth, one that portends evil on earth is evil in the sky,"[407] and about the necessity of calculating whether it is susceptible of apotropaic rituals or not.[408] The next rubric gives the grand total of the two groups of tablets: "*In summa* twenty-five tablets with signs (occurring) in the sky and on earth whose good and evil portents are in harmony(?). You will find in them every sign that has occurred in the sky (and) has been observed on earth. This is the method to dispel (them): . . ."[409]

---

403 Oppenheim, *JNES* 33 (1974) 210.
404 Translations are those of Oppenheim.
405 199:24.
406 200:38–40.
407 200:41–42.
408 200:43–46.
409 200:53–56.

Even though far from "every sign" can be found in the twenty-five tablets whose incipits follow,[410] we should note the significant statement that there exists "a method to dispel them." This method, for which precisely the term for apotropaion, *namburbû*, is used,[411] is not a simple catalogue of apotropaic rituals similar to the ones quoted on pp. 83f., but rather instructions for establishing, by astronomical calculations, the exact date of the event and for finding in a hemerological table appended to the Manual the month and day when such rituals can be effective.[412]

The already mentioned Uruk text with its correspondences of parts of the liver with times (possibly indicating zodiacal signs) and celestial bodies, the correspondences drawn between the signs of the zodiac and the performance of apotropaic rites (see Chapter VI) and the Diviner's Manual all indicate various tentatives to refine the techniques or, to use Peter Brown's term, "the technology of sorcery in the ancient world,"[413] into more sophisticated methods that culminate in Hellenistic astrology, and thus testify, as I have had occasion to stress earlier, to the continued vitality of the Mesopotamian divinatory tradition.

---

[410] For a discussion of the significance of this statement see Oppenheim, *JNES* 33 (1974) 208.

[411] *annû namburbûšunu* 'this is their "loosing."'

[412] "The namburbû prescribed in our text consists in establishing the exact date of the event observed by means of sound astronomical observations and calculations and by gleaning from the appended hemerological table whether the month or the time of day was propitious or not for the undertaking planned when the omen occurred." Oppenheim, ibid. 209.

[413] Peter Brown, "Sorcery, Demons, and the Rise of Christianity," in *Witchcraft, Confessions & Accusations*, Mary Douglas, ed. (London: Tavistock 1970) 18.

CHAPTER VI

Sorcerers and Sorceresses

Nunc meis uocata sacris, noctium sidus, ueni
Seneca, *Medea* 750

Sorcerer and sorceress[414] could coerce the power inherent in the celestial bodies for evil purposes, as we learn from the very rituals that are designed to counteract the machinations of these magicians. Rituals for curing an ailment or other affliction suspected of having been brought about by such machinations are prescribed when "witchcraft was practised against that man before the such-and-such star."[415] The words 'witchcraft' (*ipšū*) and 'was practiced against him' (*epšušu*) belong, as we saw, to the family of the verb *epēšu*, 'to do,' that is also the technical term for 'bewitching.' Another term for witchcraft or sorcery, *kišpū*, belongs to the family of words that includes the terms for sorcerer (*kaššāpu*) and sorceress (*kaššāptu*), derived from the verb *kašāpu* 'to bewitch.'

In Babylonian sources, the witches carry out their magic "before" a star, and they are not known to bring the stars down from the sky as Medea raved[416] nor do magic texts reveal that

---

[414] For 'sorceress' many descriptive terms, mostly designating these women as coming from foreign parts, are known, see Tzvi Abusch, "The Demonic Image of the Witch in Babylonian Literature," in *Religion, Science, and Magic*, Jacob Neusner et al., eds. (New York/Oxford: Oxford University Press, 1989) 27–58.

[415] ana amīli šuātu ana pan MUL NN ipšū epšušu, *STT* 89:50, etc., see below pp. 103ff.; for references (before Sirius: *BAM* 461 and dupls.; Scorpius: *BAM* 203; Ursa Maior: *AMT* 44,4) see Marie-Louise Thomsen, *Zauberdiagnose und Schwarze Magie in Mesopotamien*, The Carsten Niebuhr Institute of Ancient Near Eastern Studies 2 (1987), 80 nn. 89–91.

[416] Huc ille uasti more torrentis iacens
descendat anguis, cuius immensos duae,
maior minorque sentiunt nodos ferae
(maior Pelasgis apta, Sidoniis minor)

they bring down the moon. To this feat there is only a cryptic allusion in a Neo-Assyrian letter. Nevertheless, it is this allusion that establishes yet another link between the Mesopotamian and Classical cultures, and at the same time makes us aware of the constraints imposed on our understanding by the paucity and the accident of preservation of the data.

The allusion is found in a Neo-Assyrian letter written to King Esarhaddon in the seventh century B.C. which contains the following passage:

> As for the messengers whom the king, my lord, sent to Guzana, who would listen to the disparaging remarks of Taraṣi and his wife? His wife, Zazâ, and Taraṣi himself are not to be spared. . . . Their women would bring the moon down from heaven![417]

We might easily have dismissed the last sentence as a simple hyperbole would it not remind us of the often-celebrated feat of "the Thessalian witches who draw down the moon from heaven"[418] mentioned by Plato, the feat of drawing down the moon that had become in Latin literature the hallmark of sorceresses, expressed by the Latin phrase *detrahere lunam*, or *deducere lunam*.[419]

The power to draw down the moon was attributed especially to the sorceresses of Thessaly, a land of magic compellingly described by Lucan in *The Civil War*:

". . . I want the Snake that lies up there to come down here like a gigantic torrent. I want the two Bears—the big one, useful to Greek ships, and the small one, useful to Phoenician ships—to feel the Snake's enormous coils . . ." Seneca, *Medea* 694ff.

417 *ABL* 633+ :18–23, recopied with new joins CT 53 46 rev. 26f. The cited translation was made in 1930 by Leroy Waterman. Frederick Mario Fales, *AfO* 27 (1980) 144 translates "The women of these people, they would bring down the moon from the sky!"

418 Plato, *Gorgias* 513 A.

419 Sophie Lunais, *Recherches sur la lune. I. Les auteurs latins de la fin des Guerres Puniques à la fin du règne des Antonins.* Etudes Préliminaires aux religions orientales dans l'empire romain, M. J. Vermaseren, ed., vol. 72 (Leiden: Brill 1979), Chapter XI: Le pouvoir des magiciennes sur la lune, pp. 225–33. See also Anne-Marie Tupet, *La magie dans la poésie latine. I Des origines à la fin du règne d'Auguste* (Paris: Les Belles Lettres, 1976), Chapter VII: La descente de la lune, pp. 92–103.

The pregnant fields a horrid crop produce,
Noxious, and fit for witchcraft's deadly use;
With baleful weeds each mountain's brow is hung,
And listening rocks attend the charmer's song.
There potent and mysterious plants arise,
Plants that compel the gods, and awe the skies;
There leaves unfolded to Medea's view,
Such as her native Colchis never knew.[420]

In this land the witches exercise their magic power to draw down the moon:

Magic the starry lamps from heaven can tear,
And shoot them gleaming through the dusky air;
Can blot fair Cynthia's countenance serene,
And poison with foul spells the silver queen.
. . . .
Held by the charming song, she strives in vain,
And labours with the long pursuing pain;
Till down, and downward still, compell'd to come,
On hallow'd herbs she sheds her fatal foam.[421]

A more prosaic translation of the last section, this one by Robert Graves:[422] "Witches have introduced the art of dragging the stars from the sky; and know how to turn the Moon dim and muddy-coloured, as though she were being eclipsed by the Earth's shadow—after which they pull her close to them and torture her until she secretes poisonous foam on the plants growing underneath."

---

[420] The verse translation is that of Nicholas Rowe from the early 18th century.

[421] . . . illic et sidera primum
praecipiti deducta polo Phoebeque serena
non aliter diris verborum obsessa venenis
palluit et nigris terrenisque ignibus arsit,
quam si fraterna prohiberet imagine tellus
insereretque suas flammis caelestibus umbras,
et patitur tantos cantu depressa labores,
donec suppositas propior despumet in herbas.

Pharsalia (also known as *De bello civili*) 6.499–506.

[422] Robert Graves, *Lucan, Pharsalia* (Penguin Books, 1957) 141. A more recent verse translation is that of P. F. Widdows, *Lucan's Civil War* (Bloomington: Indiana University Press, 1988).

The sorceresses' ability to draw down the moon, which is attested even in modern circum-mediterranean popular lore,[423] has been given a rationalist explanation not only in modern times; the means to achieve this feat (with candles, water, and mirrors) had been denounced already in the fourth century by bishop Hippolytus of Rome.[424]

The connection between the Classical topos and the reference contained in the Neo-Assyrian letter has been overlooked for many years.[425] If in Greek and Latin poetry "bringing down the moon from heaven" was already a topos,[426] associated with the sorceresses of Thessaly,[427] or with barbarians, for example by Lucian in his *Lover of Lies* with a Hyperborean, the origin and original referent of this strange image are unknown. We may assume that it was already well known by the seventh century B.C., when it appears in the quoted Neo-Assyrian letter, since, in speaking of the barbarians of Guzana in Syria, the simple allusion to "their women who bring the moon down from heaven" sufficed to brand them as witches. Even further, while Greek and Latin poets often allude to this feat of the sorceresses—the most famous being perhaps the verse "Charms (that is, incantations) are able to draw the Moon

---

[423] See Tupet, op. cit. (note 419) 97ff.

[424] Refutatio omnium haeresium IV 37, L. Duncker and F. G. Schneidewin, eds. (Gottingae: Dieterich, 1859).

[425] In fact, Leroy Waterman in 1930 not only translated the letter as cited, but in his Commentary refers to a certain Sina Schiffer, and if we follow up this reference to the journal *Oriens. The Oriental Review* (January 1926, p. 34, n. 38) Schiffer had founded in Paris to promote collaboration between French and American scholars, but which did not live beyond its first year, we find that he speaks of the Classical origin of "this allegorical locution." Unfortunately, Waterman's Commentary is hardly consulted nowadays, and so his insight into the connection between the letter and the Classical parallels has borne no fruit.

[426] See S. Lunais, op. cit. (note 419).

[427] quae sidera excantata voce Thessala
lunamque caelo deripit
"who, using the Thessalian incantations, tears the stars and the Moon from the sky"

Horace, *Epod.* 5.45–46, cited Lunais p. 227. For the association of Thessaly with magic and sorceresses see also G. W. Bowersock, "Zur Geschichte des römischen Thessaliens," *Rheinisches Museum* 108 (1965) 278f.

from the sky"[428] of Virgil's *Eighth Eclogue*—there is no reference, to my knowledge, to this feat either in the poetry of the Babylonians, or in their astral magic. It is true that the male Moon god of the Sumerians and the Semites has less affinity with the 'wise women' of Mesopotamia than the goddess Selene, Cynthia, or Luna of the Greeks and Romans. Perhaps it is for this reason that it was the power of the stars that Babylonian sorceresses and other magicians were using to carry out their machinations.

The means of affecting the intended victim involve, as in other cultures, the use of figurines made of him[429] or, more directly, imbuing with sorceries, in Akkadian *kišpū*, the food he eats, the water he drinks, and the oil he uses as body ointment. An elaborate ritual extending throughout a whole night, called *Maqlû* 'Burning' is designed to counteract these evil machinations by burning figurines of the person suspected of having wrought sorcery.[430] The ritual begins, appropriately, with a prayer to the "gods of the night": "I invoke you, Gods of the night, with you I invoke the night, the veiled bride, I invoke (the three watches of the night) the evening watch, the midnight watch, the dawn watch."[431] It is from such rituals, and from the proscription of black magic found in the law books (the Code of Hammurapi and the Middle Assyrian Laws) that the machinations of sorcerers and sorceresses can be documented, since instructions for practicing such noxious magic have, for good reason, not come down to us.[432]

The effect of "witchcraft practiced before the such-and-such star" is manifested in a number of afflictions, physical as well

428 carmina vel caelo possunt deducere Lunam, Verg., *Ecl.* 8.69.

429 See Christopher A. Faraone, "Binding and Burying the Forces of Evil: The Defensive use of 'Voodoo Dolls' in Ancient Greece," *Classical Antiquity* 10 (1991) 165–99, also, in a partly different version, in *Talismans and Trojan Horses* (Oxford University Press, 1992) 74–93, Chapter 4.

430 See Tzvi Abusch, "Maqlû," in *RLA* 7 (1989) 346–51.

431 alsīkunūši ilī mušīti, ittikunu alsi mušītu kallatu kuttumtu, alsi barārītu qablītu u namārītu.

432 Note the two unusual and difficult texts containing a self-curse, each addressed to a god, for which see Erich Ebeling, "Ein babylonischer Beispiel schwarzer Magie," *Or.* NS 20 (1951) 167–70 and Wolfram von Soden, *JAOS* 71 (1951) 267f. ad UET 4 171 (the latter text reedited with collations by Michael Streck, *ZA* 83 [1993] 61–65).

as psychological, that are described in the opening words of the treatment. The names of these afflictions are usually written with Sumerograms, that is, a group of cuneiform signs whose literal meaning can usually be derived from their Sumerian constituent elements, but for which the Akkadian equivalent is not always known, and whose exact meaning is by no means securely established.

Nevertheless, the very names of certain diseases or disabilities indicate their astral cause: 'semen of Jupiter,'[433] '"hand" (ŠU) of Sin (i.e., the Moon)' or '"hand" of Šamaš (i.e., the Sun),' and '"seizure" by Lugalirra,'[434] one of the twin gods who, with Meslamtaea, represents the Twin stars, Gemini. The nature of the relationship of the disease to the deity said to have caused it with his "hand" or his "seizure" is usually impossible to determine. As to the "semen" or "sperm" of the stars[435] describing certain illnesses, it may be a name for "dew" (which is elsewhere called "Blood of the stars"),[436] since dew is said to descend from the stars, and dew can be maleficent–"the evil dew of the stars"–as well as soothing.[437]

Most frequently mentioned among the magic afflictions diagnosed as inflicted with the connivance of the stars is the one called 'cutting the breath.'[438] Since according to the rubric of one such ritual "'cutting the breath' has been practiced against

---

433 *rihût Šulpaea.* Names composed with "semen" or "sperm" and the name of a god appear among "secret" names given to herbs in *PGM* XII 401, etc. (see p. 33 above), see Hopfner, *Offenbarungszauber*, vol. 1 §493, and the herbal of Pseudo-Dioscorides mentions the plant 'Sperm of Hermes,' see ibid. §494. Whether the "sperm of the stars" refers to a particular ingredient or is to be understood as "dew" is unclear. Note the designation "Blood of the stars" given to dew by dream-interpreters, among other such fancy names deplored by Artemidorus, *Onirocriticon* 4,22 (note 132 above), cited Hopfner, vol. 1 §496.

434 See the text *STT* 89 cited presently.

435 rihût kakkabim, *AfO* 18 (1957–58) 63 i 12.

436 See the Artemidorus reference cited in a preceding note.

437 See note 249.

438 Another translation is "throat-cutting." The ambiguity stems from the various meanings of the Sumerian element *zi* of the loanword *zikurudû* (from Sumerian *zi.ku(d).ru.da*) and of its Akkadian equivalent *napištu,* that can mean life, breath, and throat as well. For literature and suggested identifications see Köcher, *BAM* IV p. xvi n. 26.

the man in front of Sirius,"[439] the cure is sought from Sirius too. It takes the form of a complex ritual with alternating libations and prayers to (literally: before) Sirius. The rites are performed in a curtained-off enclosure prescribed in other rituals too[440] and the prayer[441] is recited three times with the appropriate "lifting of the hand." The instructions say: "facing Sirius you sweep the roof, you sprinkle pure water, you strew juniper on a censer (aglow) with acacia-embers, you libate fine beer, you prostrate yourself, you draw the curtains, you set out heaps of flour, you purify that man with censer, torch, and holy-water basin, you have him stand inside the curtains on garden herbs?, he lifts his hand, recites this 'recitation' three times, each time he recites it he prostrates himself and tells everything that is on his mind, and then the wrath of (his) god and goddess will be loosed, the sorcery and machinations will be loosed."[442]

Several evil machinations are enumerated in a long text, which is identified as an excerpt from the medical compendium *When you approach the patient,* itself a sub-series of the diagnostic omen series.[443] The patient may suffer from such

439 [KA.I]NIM.MA šumma amēlu ina pan MUL.KAK.SI.SÁ ZI.KU$_5$.RU.DA epussu(DÙ-su), *BAM* 461 iii 4′.

440 For example, "you draw the curtain as a diviner would do," also "(the ceremony performed in) the curtained cubicle on the 13th day," etc., see *CAD* Š/2 s.v. *šiddu* B.

441 In one of the exemplars the prayer is dubbed a "lifting-of-the-hand" prayer (for which see p. 17) and was published, along with the extant part of the pertinent ritual, by Werner Mayer, *Untersuchungen zur Formensprache der babylonischen "Gebetsbeschwörungen,"* Studia Pohl: Series Maior, 5 (Rome: Biblical Institute Press, 1976) 540f. The subscript is preserved in *BAM* 461 and in its fragmentary duplicate *BAM* 462 which gives a more complete version of the ritual but preserves only part of the prayer.

442 ina pan MUL.KAK.SI.SÁ ūra tašabbiṭ mê ellūti tasallah nignak burāši ina pēnti ašāgi tasarraq šikara rēštâ tanaqqi tuškên šiddī tašaddad zidubdubbê tattanaddi amēla šuātu nignakka gizillâ agubbâ tullalma ina birīt šiddi ina muhhi šammi kirî tušzassuma qāssu inašši minûtu annītu 3-šú imannu ēma imtanû uškên u mimma mala libbašu ṣabtu idabbubma kimilti ili u ištari paṭratsu kišpu ipšū ipaṭṭaru, *BAM* 461 iii 5′–13′.

443 According to the subscripts in lines 102 and 215, these are the 23rd? and [24th?] tablets of the composition (DUB 23?.KAM.MA ana GIG ina TE-ka, *STT* 89:102, [DUB.n.KAM.MA ana GIG] ina TE-ka, *STT* 89:215). In the catalogue to the diagnostic omen series published by I. L. Finkel in *A Scientific Humanist. Studies in Memory of Abraham Sachs,* Erle Leichty, M. deJ.

afflictions as the previously mentioned 'cutting the breath,'[444] "seizure" by Lugalirra,[445] 'semen of Jupiter'[446] and "hand" of Sin or "hand" of Šamaš,[447] or 'epilepsy?' [448] and diseases called with such opaque names as 'hatred';[449] other afflictions may have been described in the broken sections. That these were wrought by magic means can be inferred from enumerations of the same afflictions in other sources among effects of witchcraft;[450] in this very text one of them is attributed to the placing of a figurine of the man in a grave with a dead man[451] and another to the fact that wax figurines of him were "laid down"[452]—no doubt also in a grave or some other gruesome place. That some, perhaps all, of the strange-named and sorcery-induced diseases refer to psychological disorders has also been suggested.[453]

One affliction, called by the seemingly transparent name

Ellis, P. Gerardi, eds. (Philadelphia: The University Museum, 1988) 146, this sub-series occupies Tablets III–XIV, and thus the serial number "23" given in the Sultantepe text poses a redactional problem, for which see already O. R. Gurney, *The Sultantepe Tablets*, vol. 1, p. 8. Recently M. Stol has proposed to see in this text an older version of the diagnostic omen series, in *Epilepsy in Babylonia*, Cuneiform Monographs, 2 (Groningen: Styx, 1993) 91ff.

444 *zikurudû* (ZI.KU$_5$.RU.DA) lines 27, 33, 47, etc.

445 ^{d}*Lugalirra iṣbassu* 'the god Lugalirra has seized him,' lines 105, 111, 116, 126, 135.

446 *rihût Šulpaea*, lines 169, 176, 186, 190.

447 line 214.

448 *miqtu* (AN.TA.ŠUB.BA), lines 138, 143, 150, 162.

449 *zīru* (HUL.GIG), lines 82, 89, 93.

450 Compare, for example, the enumeration kišpī ruhû ru[sû upšāšê] la ṭābūti (NU.DÙG.GA.MEŠ) KI.ÁG.GÁ HUL.GIG.GA DI.BA[L.A . . .] KA.DIB.BI.DA KA.GÌR.RA ŠÚR!(text ŠAR).HUN.GÁ [. . .] É.GAL.KU$_4$.RA miqit ṭēmi šan[ê ṭēmi] ŠU.^{d}INNIN.NA ŠU.GIDIM.MA ŠU.NAM.ER[ÍM.MA . . .] ^{d}ALÀD HUL-tim SAG.HUL.HA.ZA m[ukīl rēš lemutti] iškununimma . . ., Egbert von Weiher, *SpTU*, vol. 2 no. 19:24–30, and the similar enumeration in W. G. Lambert, "An Incantation of the Maqlû Type," *AfO* 18 (1957–58) 288–99, on pp. 289f. lines 11–15 and note p. 95 and in CBS 14161:7–8, in E. Leichty, "Guaranteed to Cure," in *A Scientific Humanist. Studies in Memory of Abraham Sachs*, Erle Leichty, M. deJ. Ellis, P. Gerardi, eds. (Philadelphia: The University Museum, 1988) 262.

451 [. . .] *itti mīti šūnul*, line 7.

452 NU.MEŠ-*šú šá* GAB.LÀL š[*u-nu-lu*], line 101.

453 Edith K. Ritter and J. V. Kinnier Wilson, "Prescription for an Anxiety State: a Study of *BAM* 234," *Anatolian Studies* 30 (1980) 23–30.

'seizing of the mouth,'[454] and which therefore has been taken to describe aphasia,[455] that is, an inability to speak, can be shown to have been imputed to evil magic by referring once again to Classical sources. In the *Wasps* of Aristophanes a dog is put on trial, accused of stealing a piece of cheese. When he takes the stand, the dog, famed for his barking, is suddenly and strangely silent. The president of the mock tribunal, concerned lest this silence be interpreted as an admission of guilt, is ready with a precedent for such an incident: he quotes the case of a certain Thucydides, son of Melesias, who suffered the same mishap when *he* was on trial—he suddenly became paralyzed in his jaw.[456] According to the *scholia*, this Thucydides, an excellent orator, after he had heard his accusers make their case in the course of a trial, was not able to plead his own defense, just as if he had a tongue which had been bound from within. In this way he was convicted and afterwards ostracized.

Other stories also recount inexplicable seizures suffered by ". . . even experienced orators while pleading at the bar"; further testimonies[457] come from inscriptions and from the life of Libanius, the famous orator of the fourth century A.D., who was accused of having cast a spell on a rival whose memory failed in the midst of a speech. Libanius himself tells us in his

---

[454] *ṣibit pî* (KA.DIB.BI.DA), line 101.

[455] Also translated 'lockjaw,' see *CAD* Z s.v. *zikurudû*. For a medical prescription for KA.DIB.BI.DA see *17 šammū latkūtu ša* KA.DIB.BI.DA 'seventeen tested herbs for seizing of the mouth,' E. Leichty, "Guaranteed to Cure," in *A Scientific Humanist. Studies in Memory of Abraham Sachs,* Erle Leichty, M. deJ. Ellis, P. Gerardi, eds. (Philadelphia: The University Museum, 1988) 262 CBS 14161:5. Recently, Stefan Maul, in his review of Thomsen's book on Magic, *Welt des Orients* 19 (1988) 165ff., has suggested that the affliction refers to stopping up the mouth of the effigy representing the victim.

[456] "No, it seems to me that it suffered the same misfortune that once befell Thucydides when he was on trial: he suddenly became paralyzed in his jaw."

οὔκ, ἀλλ' ἐκεῖνό μοι δοκεῖ πεπονθέναι,
ὅπερ ποτὲ φεύγων ἔπαθε καὶ Θουκυδίδης
ἀπόπληκτος ἐξαίφνης ἐγένετο τὰς γνάθους.

[457] All adduced by Christopher A. Faraone, "An Accusation of Magic in Classical Athens (Ar. *Wasps* 946–48)," *TAPA* 119 (1989), citing from *scholia* to Ar. *Wasps* 946–48, also Ar. *Acharnians* 703–18, cited p. 151; Libanius, cited p. 153.

autobiography (1.245–49) how at one point late in his life he became gravely ill and was no longer able to read, write, or speak before his students, until there was mysteriously discovered in his lecture hall the body of a chameleon, strangely twisted and mutilated; one of its forefeet was missing, and the other was "closing the mouth for silence." Libanius recognized a case of magic, and what concerns us especially here, he interpreted the placing of the chameleon's forefoot upon its mouth as having effected the silencing of his speech. He regained his health, he says, only after the body of the chameleon was removed from the room.[458]

The "seizing of the mouth" in Babylonian magic texts also was designed, no doubt, to bring about the inability to speak, especially to speak in one's defense before the judges.

The witchcraft responsible for such afflictions was performed, as the medical text expressly states, "before" certain stars: according to one diagnosis, 'a "binding" was "bound" for him before Jupiter on the 21st (or) the 22nd';[459] according to another, 'magic [was practiced] against that man on the 4th? of month XI "before" Centaurus,'[460] or 'magic was practiced against that man on the nth of month XII "before" Scorpius';[461] and, with the name of the star broken: '[magic was practiced] against that man "before" [. . .].'[462] In another diagnosis only the month name is preserved, not the star's: '[magic was practiced] against that man [on the nth?] of month IV ["before" . . .].'[463] This last

---

458 Campbell Bonner, "Witchcraft in the Lecture Room of Libanius," *TAPA* 63 (1932) 34ff. See also Peter Brown, "Sorcery, Demons, and the Rise of Christianity," in *Witchcraft, Confessions & Accusations*, Mary Douglas, ed. (London: Tavistock 1970) 29. Especially relevant are the "judicial curse tablets" that "attempt to bind the opponent's ability to think clearly and speak effectively in court at an upcoming trial. . . . judicial curses are primarily concerned with the cognitive and verbal faculties which are essential to success in the law courts . . ." (Faraone, "An Accusation of Magic," 156f.).

459 ana IGI ^{d}Šul-pa-è ina UD.21.KAM ina UD.22.KAM rik-su ⌈ra-kis⌉-su, *STT* 89 line 31.

460 ana NA BI ITI.ZÍZ UD.4$^{?}$.KAM IGI MUL.EN.TE.NA.BAR.HUM ip-šú [ep-šú-šú], line 50.

461 ana NA BI ina ITI.ŠE ina ⌈UD.x.KAM⌉ [IGI] MUL.GÍR.TAB ip-šú ep-šú-šú, line 54f.

462 ana NA BI ana IGI [MU]L [. . .], line 36.

463 ana NA BI ina ITI.ŠU [. . .], line 74.

paragraph may already refer to 'hatred,' which follows as diagnosis in lines 85, 89, and 93. Even such a usually beneficent power as the Wagon (Ursa Maior) could be used for nefarious purposes, as an unfortunately fragmentary prescription, from which little survives beyond the phrase "[witchcraft was practiced?] against that man before the Wagon,"[464] testifies.

What a star has wrought, a star will undo. To counteract the evil magic, one turns again to the stars: materials to be used in the ritual, just as medications (see pp. 48ff.), are to be exposed to stars, as in the instruction: "you expose it to all? stars";[465] two now broken lines must have held similar instructions.[466]

An effluvium from a celestial body may manifest itself not only as "seizure" or "hand";[467] another image used is "covering" or "clapping down," an image taken from the impact of a net.[468] For example, a diagnosis states: "the name (of the illness) is 'male fly of . . .,' a wind has swept over him, it is 'covering by Sagittarius,' you may make a prognostication,"[469] and another: "its name is 'female fly of . . .,' a wind has swept over him, it is 'covering by the Twins,' you may make a prognostication."[470] The term also occurs in the fragmentary prescriptions "for 'covering by Ištar.'"[471] Unidentified is the disease or symptom called "staff of the Moon."[472]

The stars are appealed to as individual divine beings whose influence is sought in order to avert the sorcerers' machinations, and it is in the same guise that they are invoked to save from other afflictions, or to achieve a desired goal. Their

---

464 ana LÚ BI ana pan MUL.MAR.GÍD.[DA . . .], *AMT* 44,4:2.

465 ana IGI MUL DÙ? tuš-bat, line 17.

466 [. . . tuš]-bat, line 22, ana IGI MUL [. . .], line 60.

467 An illness is called "hand of Venus" in the Neo-Assyrian letter to the king, *ABL* 203 r. 4, see Parpola, *SAAB* 2 (1988) 74 n. 4.

468 *sihiptu*, a noun derived from the verb *sahāpu* 'to cover, overwhelm.'

469 lamṣat hilâti NITÁ MU.NI šāru išbiṭsuma sihi[pti] dPA.BIL.SAG qība (DUG$_4$.GA) GAR-an. The noun *qību* 'command, declaration' is the technical term for prognosis, prognostication.

470 lamṣat hilâti SAL MU.NI šāru iš-[biṭ-su-ma] sihipti dMAŠ.TAB.BA qí-ba GAR-an, *AMT* 44,1 ii 4 and 10 = *BAM* 580 iii 16f. and 22.

471 ana sihipti Ištar [. . .], *BAM* 582 ii 5′ and 7′.

472 GIŠ.PA *šá* dEN.ZU, in *šumma* LÚ GIM GIŠ.PA *šá* dEN.ZU GAR-*šum-ma* 'if (something) like the "staff of Sin" affects the man,' *BAM* 471 ii 21, dupl. *TDP* 192:35.

influence is not yet connected, as it will be in Hellenistic astrology, with their positions, their "houses," and aspects.

Still, there exist a few texts from Babylonia that seem to be precursors of Greek astrology. Two late, largely parallel, lists from Hellenistic Uruk[473] enumerate the "regions" or "areas"[474] of the zodiacal constellations associated with a certain activity which, in order to succeed, has to be carried out in that region. Occasionally an explicit instruction is added: *teppušma išallim* "if you carry it out, it will succeed."

It is again the Greek astrological tradition that provides the clue for interpreting the Babylonian references to the signs of the zodiac. What the texts mean when they refer to these signs is the region of the sky where the Moon stands in that particular moment. The Moon's position is considered auspicious or inauspicious for engaging in a specific activity, and these moments have been collected in so-called *Lunaria* (when written in Latin), preserved from the second century A.D. onward,[475] to which the Babylonian texts represent often very close parallels.

The *lunaria* not only indicate the auspicious moments (with such phrases as *bonum est, utile est*) but also the times to be avoided (with such phrases as *malum est* or *caveat vos*) when engaging in a specific activity. The Babylonian "Lunarium" includes, e.g., "to bring back a fugitive: region of Regulus, or Libra,"[476] comparable to finding a fugitive, indicated for several

[473] BRM 4 19 and 20, edited by A. Ungnad, "Besprechungskunst und Astrologie in Babylonien," *AfO* 14 (1941–44) 251–84. More recently, these texts have been studied by Jean Bottéro, *EPHE, Annuaire* 1974/75 130ff., reprinted in Jean Bottéro, *Mythes et rites de Babylone* (Geneva-Paris: Slatkine-Champion, 1985) 100ff.

[474] The term used is the Sumerogram KI with the reading *qaqqaru* 'ground, area, region,' written syllabically in *LBAT* 1626 rev 6'. It is possible that a better translation would be 'place' (*locus*).

[475] The earliest preserved text is the Περὶ καταρχῶν of Maximus, edited by A. Ludwich, Leipzig, 1877; see Paola Radici Colace, *Le parafrasi bizantine del* ΠΕΡΙ ΚΑΤΑΡΧΩΝ *di Massimo*, Letteratura e Civiltà Bizantina, 4 (Messina: Dr. Antonino Sfameni, 1988). For Greek Selenodromia see the catalogue in Delatte, *CCAG* 10 p. 121; for Latin Lunaria see Emanuel Svenberg, *Lunaria et Zodiologia Latina*, Studia Graeca et Latina Gothoburgensia, 16 (Göteborg: Elanders Boktryckeri, 1963).

[476] BRM 4 20:20, see *AfO* 14 (1941–44) 259 and 265.

days of the *Lunarium of David and Solomon*,[477] and "to enter the palace (scil., to be well received by the ruler): region of Cancer,"[478] comparable to "bonum est ire coram rege uel iudice 'good for going before the king or a judge'" indicated for the position of the Moon in Aries.[479] The hitherto obscure "placing of silver" of the Babylonian texts[480] can be understood in light of the *lunaria*'s "nummos mutuos dare uel accipere 'to give or receive borrowed money'" recommended for the signs Aries, Cancer, Libra, and Capricorn.[481] Success is also sought in love, in business, and in obtaining royal favor, for example "desire:[482] region of [. . .]"; "to obtain gain for the innkeeper:[483] region of Cancer, variant: Aquarius."

Many of the activities listed describe calamities or diseases in order to indicate the proper time for carrying out apotropaia against them, especially when they were caused by maleficent practices. Such entries are, e.g., "Vertigo:[484] region of Gemini"; and "Seizing of the mouth: . . ."[485] (see p. 105); and "reversal of verdict"; "cutting the breath"; "hatred"; and "migraine?,"[486] all well known and often listed among the evil machinations of sorcerers.[487] The acts of black magic by means of which the sorcerer and sorceress sought to achieve their goals include, for example, "to seize a ghost and tie him to a man"[488] and "to

---

477 A. Delatte, *CCAG* 10 pp. 122ff., e.g., ὁ φυγὼν εὑρεθήσεται.

478 BRM 4 20:12, see *AfO* 14 (1941–44) 258 and 263.

479 Cod. Paris. Nouv. Acq. Lat. 299, XIII s., f. 23r–24v, in Svenberg p. 80, 13.

480 *šikin kaspi*, BRM 4 20:19 = BRM 4 19:7. Compare the proscription for month II day 13: *šea kaspa la išakkan* 'he must not "place" barley (or) silver,' *KAR* 178 iv 67.

481 Cod. Vat. Pal. Lat. 834, cited Svenberg (note 475 above) p. 44.

482 ŠÀ.ZI.GA (= *nīš libbi*), BRM 4 20:45.

483 *išdīh sābî šurši*, BRM 4 20:25 = BRM 4 19:14; see above note 267.

484 IGI.NIGIN.NA (= *ṣīdānu*), BRM 4 20:10.

485 KA.DIB.BI.DA (= *ṣibit pî*), BRM 4 20:43 = BRM 4 19:38.

486 DI.BAL.A, BRM 4 20:2, with commentary *nabalkut dīni* ibid. 55; ZI.KU$_5$.RU.DA (= *zikurudû*), BRM 4 20:9; HUL.GIG, BRM 4 20:22 = BRM 4 19:11, with commentary: *ze-'-i-ri* 'hate,' BRM 4 20:66; and SAG.KI.DIB.BA, literally: 'seizing of the forehead,' BRM 4 20:44.

487 See note 450.

488 GIDIM DIB-*bat* KI LÚ *ana* KÉŠ, BRM 4 20:33, explained in the commentary (ibid. 73) as *e-ṭem-mu ṣa-ba-tu it-ti amēli a-na ra-k[a-si]*, see *AfO* 14 (1941–44) 259f.

hand over a figurine of the man to death (or: to a dead man)."[489] These are comparable to the *Lunarium* which specifies the days suitable for making amulets and phylacteria and carrying out magical operations.[490]

Some of the entries must go back to an earlier period, as is shown by the philological commentary appended to one of the two texts to explicate it and to render the Sumerograms in Akkadian; the other text has been provided with an arithmetical scheme, known in Greek astrology under the name *dodekatemoria,* in which two points of the zodiac are related in such a fashion that the *dodekatemorion* of one position is found by adding to a particular degree of the sign (i.e., a number between 1 and 30) its twelve-fold multiple; the resulting number then is expressed by a degree in another sign.[491]

While only two texts are complete, several fragments dealing with "regions" testify that such speculations were fashionable in the late period. Most of the fragments are as yet unpublished; one of them that is published shows the term "region" in one of its rubrics.[492] The names of two zodiacal constellations, Virgo and Capricorn, can be read in this small fragment; it is possible to restore the names of others, along with the activities recommended when the Moon is in their "region," from the two Uruk texts. For example, the Moon in the region of Virgo assures "that he who sees you rejoices at seeing you";[493] the Moon in the region of the ⟨. . .⟩ star[494] is "for being purified through the river (ordeal)";[495] another "so that a 'favorable finger' be pointed behind the man";[496] and for the Moon in the zodiacal signs now broken, it promises "favor? of

[489] *ṣalam amēli ana mūtu paqādu,* ibid. 33 and commentary ibid. 71.

[490] A. Delatte, *CCAG* 10 pp. 71ff.

[491] For the arithmetical scheme of BRM 4 19 see Neugebauer and Sachs, "The 'Dodekatemoria' in Babylonian Astrology," *AfO* 16 (1952–53) 65–66.

[492] [. . .] x.MEŠ *qaq-qa*[*r* . . .], *LBAT* 1626 rev.? 6′.

[493] [*āmirka ana amārika*] *hadê* KI MUL.KI.DIDLI, *LBAT* 1626 rev.? 2′; cf. BRM 4 20:16 = 19:2 Leo.

[494] End of line; no star name seems to be missing after MUL.

[495] ÍD.KÙ.GA KI MUL, *LBAT* 1626 rev.? 3′; cf. BRM 4 20:11 Capricorn.

[496] *ubān damiqti arki amēli* ⌈*tarāṣi*⌉, *LBAT* 1626 rev.? 4′, restored from parallels, tablet preserves ⌈LÁ⌉ [. . .]).

the king"[497] and the unfortunately obscure outcome "the (legal) case of? the (or: his) adversary . . ."[498]

By determining the propitious time for initiating an activity, the genre represents an early example of the process known as catarchic astrology.[499]

The correspondences drawn between the signs of the zodiac and the performance of the apotropaic or prophylactic rites have a forerunner from a much earlier time. The tablet that records them comes from the site of Sultantepe and is dated to 619 B.C.[500] and thus the composition of the text must precede this date. The same catarchic magic that was listed in the late texts is here stated in terms of propitious dates rather than signs of the zodiac.[501]

The most significant difference between the two is the absence in the earlier text of the astronomical data of BRM 4 19.[502] The Sultantepe text goes through the months of the year, singling out the days of the months that are propitious for carrying out the described enterprise.[503] Its recommendations are expressed by the already mentioned formula *teppušma išallim* "if you carry it out, it will succeed" which ends each section. It also includes activities that are now missing or were never included in the late texts, such as, for the first month in its entirety ("from the 1st to the 30th") "desire,"[504] also "for (curing?) migraine and calming desire."[505]

---

497 ⌈*ma*?-*gar*?⌉ (copy: x GAR, with the GAR sign written as the numeral "4") LUGAL KI x, *LBAT* 1626 rev.? 2; cf. BRM 4 20:46, constellation broken.

498 [. . .] MUL SUM? (possibly mistake for MÁŠ 'Capricorn') *dīn*(DI) *bēl dabābi* KI? (or *bēl dabābišu*) x [. . .], *LBAT* 1626 rev.? 5′.

499 See Introduction (p. 13) and above note 475. See also A. Bouché-Leclercq, *L'Astrologie grecque* (Paris, 1899, reprinted Aalen: Scientia, 1979) 458ff.

500 Dated by the name of the eponym Bēl-aha-uṣur in the colophon.

501 *STT* 300, published in 1964 in cuneiform copy by O. R. Gurney, who identified it as a duplicate to BRM 4 19 and noted the differences between them. See also Jean Bottéro, *EPHE, Annuaire* 1974–75, pp. 130ff., reprinted in Jean Bottéro, *Mythes et rites* (note 473 above) 100ff.

502 See above pp. 108ff. and note 491.

503 *STT* 300:7 has a parallel in Egbert von Weiher, *SpTU*, vol. 2 no. 23:1, a ritual concerning the activity *šu.du*$_8$*.a*, which is also listed in BRM 4 20, see Ungnad, *AfO* 14 (1941–44) 272 and von Weiher, op. cit. 124.

504 ŠÀ.ZI.GA, line 1.

505 SAG.KI.DIB TUK-e ù nu-uh-hi ŠÀ.ZI.GA x x, line 2.

Some entries are applicable to more than one month.[506] According to rev. 18, days 27, 28, and 29 of every month are (propitious) for [expelling?] the demon SAG.HUL.HA.ZA, literally: 'who holds the head of evil.'[507]

The medieval *lunaria* that list every day of the month are not much different from the hemerologies that list auspicious and inauspicious days, adding, in the words of Boll and Gundel, only a thin veneer of astrology[508] over the ancient menologies, and the previously adduced *lunaria* or *zodiologia*, which list the twelve zodiacal signs, can similarly be considered offshoots of the ancient menologies.

Such hemerologies and menologies existed in Mesopotamia,[509] both in the redaction in which the days and the months are listed in their calendrical order and marked as either good or bad for initiating certain activities, and in the reverse format, in which the activity is mentioned first, and is followed by the list of the months or days which are recommended for its execution or are to be avoided.[510] The resemblances to the last section (lines 765–828) of Hesiod's *Works and Days*, even though they are few and superficial, have naturally been noted by the editors of these texts.[511]

As for the cultic significance of the days and months of the

---

506 Line 11 to months II and III, line 19 to months IV and V, line 24 to months VI and VII, rev. 15 to months X and XI, and rev. 16 and 17 to months XI and XII. (Months VIII and IX are not so combined.)

507 For this demon see W. Farber, "Saghulhaza *mukīl rēš lemutti*," *ZA* 64 (1974) 87–95.

508 "es ist damit nur ein leichter astrologischer Firniß über die alte Tagewählweisheit gestrichen," Boll-Bezold-Gundel 176.

509 For texts and discussion see S. Langdon, *Babylonian Menologies and the Semitic Calendars*, The Schweich Lectures of the British Academy 1933 (London: Oxford University Press, 1935); René Labat, *Hémérologies et ménologies d'Assur* (Paris: Maisonneuve, 1939), and additional texts published by him in *RA* 38 (1941) 13ff., *MIO* 5 (1957) 299–345, *Sumer* 8 (1952) 17ff.; and by L. Matouš in *Sumer* 17 (1961) 17ff. A new edition of the hemerologies is being prepared by A. Livingstone.

510 Among the *lunaria* too some are arranged according to the activity recommended or to be avoided, see Boll-Bezold-Gundel 176, listing "Krankheits-, Traum-, Aderlaß-, Nativitäts- und Tagewähllunare."

511 The edition of Hesiod by M. L. West (Oxford University Press, 1978), conversely, notes many parallels with the Assyrian and Babylonian hemerologies and Mesopotamian (Sumerian and Akkadian) literary texts.

year from Sumerian times onward, and for the local calendars of the second millennium, it is only recently that efforts have been underway[512] to enlarge and update Benno Landsberger's early work of 1915,[513] since he himself never returned to the subject in a second volume as he had promised.

The cuneiform hemerologies list the days that are favorable—in their entirety or in part—in general or for conducting a particular kind of business or activity, either private, such as building a house, taking a wife, or religious, such as addressing prayers and offerings to a god or goddess. The sequence is calendrical by months and days; some texts are laid out in a grid pattern, indicating "favorable" (ŠE) or "unfavorable" (NU ŠE) in the appropriate column of a table.[514]

Some lists give only a selection of the days of the month. The selection always includes the days that are most dangerous, namely the "evil" days 7, 14, 19, 21, 28. Cultically significant days on which prayers and offerings to gods are prescribed are found especially in hemerologies prepared for use by the king, and perhaps exclusively in those. Astral gods to whom prayers and offerings are to be made are conceived in their astral manifestations: stars, constellations, and planets; offerings to the Moon are prescribed for the 15th day, the day of the full moon in the standardized thirty-day month. A hemerological text from Assur which is the most explicit of all[515] prescribes offerings on the 18th of Nisannu (the first month in the calendar) to the Pleiades (ii 45); on the 19th and on X 10 to Orion (Ṣipazianna, ii 15 and r. ii 48); on III 16 to Marduk, Gula, and Venus (v 44f.); on III 12 and XI 14 to Venus (v 32 and r. ii 53); on IV 18 to the Scorpion (MUL.GÍR.TAB, vi 47); and VI 16 and VII 14 to Jupiter (Šulpae, r. v 50 and r. iv 80).

---

512 Mark E. Cohen, *The Cultic Calendars of the Ancient Near East* (Bethesda, Maryland: CDL Press, 1993); Walther Sallaberger, *Der kultische Kalender der Ur III-Zeit*, Untersuchungen zur Assyriologie und Vorderasiatischen Archäologie, 7 (Berlin: de Gruyter, 1993).

513 Benno Landsberger, *Der kultische Kalender der Babylonier und Assyrer.* Leipziger Semitistische Studien 6/1-2 (Leipzig: Hinrichs, 1915).

514 Compare the layout of the table at the end of the Diviner's Manual cited p. 96.

515 *KAR* 178, edited by René Labat, *Hémérologies et ménologies d'Assur* (Paris: Maisonneuve, 1939).

Conversely, on particular days food and sex proscriptions apply, to avoid acts abhorrent to the astral deity. One of the more common proscriptions, that of eating fish and leeks, is on day 7 of month VII[516] said to be prohibited by "Šulpae, lord of the date grove"; as often, the reference is frustrating because a connection between Šulpae, that is, Jupiter, and date groves is not otherwise attested, nor are we told what these two forbidden foodstuffs have to do with Jupiter, even though offering onions is considered sacrilegious in the Greek magical papyri.[517]

On the 7th of month VII there is a prohibition for having intercourse with one's wife because "she will despoil him of his virility; it is an abhorrence to the Wagon of the sky of Anu."[518] Again, the relationship between sexual abstinence and the Wagon is not explicit, but the connection between the (celestial) Wagon, Ursa Maior, which often represents Venus, and sexual taboo is readily understandable.

The few late texts concerning the relationship of days of the month and the signs of the zodiac[519] presumably reflect Hellenistic speculations. These are the texts for which the term "calendar texts" (German: *Kalendertexte*)[520] was coined. Of two re-

---

[516] Reverse iv 55f.

[517] E.g., *PGM* IV 2584–86, 2650; the fact was noted by Albrecht Dieterich (". . . Zwiebeln haben eine besondere Bedeutung") in *Abraxas*, Festschrift Hermann Usener (Leipzig, 1905, reprinted Aalen: Scientia, 1973) 158.

[518] ina sūn <SAL>-šú la inâl ÚR-šú itabbal ikkib GIŠ.MAR.GÍD.DA šamê Anim, *KAR* 178 r. iv 61f. I have supplied the sign SAL 'woman' in the poorly written and transmitted text; the omission of the word and the consequent translation "he must not lie in his (own) lap," has given rise to several, to my mind wrong, interpretations. The remark "of the sky of Anu" to "Wagon" is presumably added because the text simply says "wagon" (GIŠ.MAR.GÍD.DA), not "Wagon-star" (MUL.MAR.GÍD.DA). For MUL.MAR.GÍD.DA.AN.NA 'Ursa Minor' see the literature cited in W. Horowitz, "The Akkadian Name for Ursa Minor," *ZA* 79 (1989) 242–44.

[519] For the late introduction, c. 500 B.C., of the zodiac of 30 degrees as opposed to references to zodiacal constellations see Neugebauer, *HAMA* 593.

[520] E. F. Weidner, *Gestirn-Darstellungen auf babylonischen Tontafeln*, Österreichische Akademie der Wissenschaften, Philosophisch-historische Klasse, Sitzungsberichte 254, 2. Abhandlung (Wien: Böhlaus Nachf., 1967). Additional fragments are W. Mayer, *Baghdader Mitteilungen*, Beiheft 2 p. 19 nos. 78–79 and W.20030,133, cited H. Hunger, "Noch ein 'Kalendertext,'" *ZA* 64 (1975) 43.

cently published tablets from Uruk that belong to this genre[521] one lists the thirty consecutive days of month IV, the other of month VIII. Each line begins with the name of the month (indicated with the "ditto"-sign from line 2 on) and the number of the day. These two entries are followed by another pair of entries, also designating a month and day, in which the month is expressed, as elsewhere, by the name of the corresponding zodiacal sign, and the day by the number referring to the degree in the sign. From one line to the next the second pair increases by nine signs plus seven degrees ($9 \times 30 + 7$) yielding the number 277. Since no astronomical significance for this number can be found, it has been suggested, among other speculations, that it refers to the number of days in a gestation period. In the first text (no. 104) the sequence begins with I 7 (Aries 7°) for day one, continuing with X 14 (Capricorn 14°) for day two, etc.[522]

Typical of "Calendar texts" is the association of zodiacal signs with a tree, a stone, an herb, and various other items. Sources come from Seleucid Uruk[523] and their relationship with Hellenistic texts is shown by the fact that they assign the same entities to the signs of the zodiac—or rather, of a micro-

---

[521] Egbert von Weiher, *SpTU*, vol. 3 nos. 104 (month IV) and 105 (month VIII).

[522] Not all the designations of the zodiacal signs are the standard ones used in astronomical texts. Both texts (nos. 104 and 105) use the month names BAR (month I) instead of LU or HUN for Aries (I), and ŠU (month IV) instead of ALLA for Cancer (IV). Moreover, the sign GUD 'Taurus' is replaced by MÚL.MÚL 'Pleiades' (II), MAŠ.MAŠ 'Gemini' by SIPA 'Orion' (III), and 1 IKU 'Field' (= Square of Pegasus) (XII?) stands for ZIB (Pisces, XII); both texts also use the abbreviated names GÍR (= GÍR.TAB) for Scorpius, SIPA (= SIPA.ZI.AN.NA) for Orion (standing for Gemini), PA (= PA.BIL.SAG) for Sagittarius, SUHUR (= SUHUR.MÁŠ) for Capricorn. However, according to the catch line of no. 104, the next tablet of the set, dealing with month V, again designates Taurus, as usual, by GUD 'Bull.'

[523] Published in cuneiform copy by F. Thureau-Dangin, TCL 6 12, and edited along with another fragment, now in Berlin, of the same tablet (see figs. 3–5) by E. Weidner in *Gestirn-Darstellungen auf babylonischen Tontafeln* (note 520 above). Included in Weidner's publication is a tablet now in the British Museum, which is catalogued among the Kuyunjik collection, but most likely also comes from late Babylonian Uruk. Landsberger drew attention to it as early as 1915 in *Der kultische Kalender der Babylonier und Assyrer* (note 513 above) 145ff.

zodiac[524] in which each sign is divided into twelve units of 2½ degrees each—as do the Cyranides,[525] as I discuss in Chapter VII. The above-described Uruk texts assign to each of the calendar dates an ointment whose ingredients are related to the zodiacal sign by a pun, either linguistic or purely orthographic, on the name of the sign. Thus, the text prescribes as ointment the following ingredients:

For the first month, corresponding to the zodiacal sign Aries 'Ram,' the ingredients are blood, tallow, and wool from a sheep; for month II, corresponding to the zodiacal sign Taurus 'Bull,' here designated by one of its conspicuous constellations, the Pleiades, they are blood, fat, or hair of a bull; for month III, corresponding to the zodiacal sign Gemini, here, as in the similarly late text cited on p. 80, designated by the name of the constellation Orion, they are to contain the head, blood, and feather of a rooster;[526] for month IV, corresponding to the zodiacal sign Cancer 'Crab,' the blood and fat of a crab; for month V, corresponding to the zodiacal sign Leo 'Lion,' blood, tallow, or hair from a lion; for month VI, corresponding to the zodiacal sign Virgo 'Furrow,'[527] flour made of *šigušu*-barley, the head and feather of a raven; for month VII, corresponding to the zodiacal sign libra 'Scales' . . .;[528] for month VIII, corresponding to the zodiacal sign Scorpius 'Scorpion' . . .; for month IX, corresponding to the zodiacal sign Sagittarius, here designated by the name of the god Pabilsag, the head, feather, and blood of the *anzû*-bird; for month X, corresponding to the zodiacal sign Capricorn, blood, fat, and hair of a goat; for month XI, corresponding to the zodiacal sign Aquarius,[529] the

[524] For the micro-zodiac see A. Sachs, *JCS* 6 (1952) 71.

[525] For recent literature see David Bain, *Dover Fs* 295f.

[526] Written DAR.MUŠEN, which elsewhere corresponds to Akkadian *ittidû* 'francolin' but which here must be an abbreviation for DAR.LUGAL. MUŠEN = *tarlugallu* 'Rooster,' part of the constellation Canis Minor.

[527] The name of the constellation is written, as usual in late texts, with the signs KI.DIDLI that have no known etymology, unless they stand for Akkadian *ašar niṣirti*, literally "secret place," a term designating the sign in which a planet reaches its exaltation (Greek: *hypsoma*). The constellation Raven (Corvus) has its heliacal rising in month VI; compare the text cited p. 78.

[528] The entry is, here and in the next month, the unintelligible KI.KAL-*tim*.

[529] The name of the constellation, written GU, abbreviated from its Sumerogram GU.LA, does not seem to be connected with the word for 'eagle.'

head, feather, and blood of an eagle; for month XII, corresponding to the zodiacal sign Pisces, here designated by 'Field,' the name for the Square of Pegasus, the head and blood (variant: heart) of a dove, the head and blood of a swallow.

The late origin of the text is also evident from the fact that the punning relationship between the prescription and the corresponding sign of the zodiac can be understood only with reference to the classical zodiac. For example, the recipe prescribed for the first month is prepared from a sheep although the expected zodiacal sign, Aries 'ram,' is not mentioned nor is the Akkadian name of the sign, *Agru* 'hired man,' associated with "sheep"; MUL.LU, MÚL.LU, or simply LU with the meaning "Aries" is well attested in Seleucid texts.[530] Note also that the prescription for the second month requires the blood, fat, or hair of a bull, but the month is identified by the constellation MUL.MUL 'Stars,' i.e., the Pleiades, used in late texts instead of the name GUD 'Bull' of the zodiacal sign.

I am not able to solve the problem posed by the unintelligible KI.KAL-*tim* prescribed for months VII and VIII, the signs Libra and Scorpius. However, although less transparent, the connection between the birds that provide materials for the ointments and the month or sign for which these are prescribed, can be astronomically justified;[531] thus month III, Gemini, designated by Orion, is connected with the Rooster, a part of Canis Minor; month VI appropriately with the Raven (Corvus); month XI, Aquarius, with the Eagle (Aquila), and month XII, Pisces, with the Swallow, a name for the western Fish of Pisces. Since the identification of the *anzû*-bird is not certain, its connection with month IX, Sagittarius, cannot be argued.

Heads and feathers of various birds indeed appear as ingredients in various Mesopotamian recipes, both magic and medical, just as they do in medieval magic texts. Among twelve recipes against a disease[532]—its name is broken on the tablet—

[530] See A. Sachs, *JCS* 6 (1952) 71f. ad TCL 6 14:6–20. Among various theories for the origin of the writing LU, the association of LU (a cuneiform sign that may also be read UDU 'sheep') with the zodiacal sign Aries 'ram' was also discussed by Ungnad, *AfO* 14 (1941–44) 256 n. 37.

[531] Following a suggestion of David Pingree.

[532] 12 *bulṭu ša* [. . .], *BAM* 473 i 26; in line 27, an enumeration of medicines for ŠU.GIDIM.MA 'hand-of-the-ghost' begins.

only in the last five are the names of the ingredients preserved, and in the first of these five, the eighth recipe, only the word for "head." The ninth recipe requires the head of a raven,[533] the tenth the head of a goose,[534] the eleventh the head of an *uruballu* bird,[535] and the twelfth the head of an eagle.[536] A salve for headache in another recipe also uses the head of an eagle;[537] a phylactery to assure victory over an adversary must include an eagle's head, eagle feathers, and hair from a lion.[538] The heads of a water-fowl and of a male bat[539] are used in a salve for headache; the head of a bat and feathers and blood from various birds in phylacteries against epilepsy[540] and other afflictions.[541]

These phylacteries are said to have been transmitted from Lú-^{d}Nanna,[542] one of the seven sages who lived under King Šulgi of the Third Dynasty of Ur, who elsewhere too is credited with the confection of powerful drugs and amulets.[543]

533 *qaqqad* (or *rēš*, written SAG) *a-ri-bi*.

534 SAG KUR.GI MUŠEN.

535 *qaqqad* (written SAG.DU) *ú-ru-bal-li* MUŠEN.

536 SAG Á.MUŠEN; the text is *BAM* 473 i 1–25.

537 *qaqqad a-re-e*, *BAM* 481:4.

538 Egbert von Weiher, *SpTU*, vol. 2 no. 22 iv 11–12.

539 *qaqqad* KI.SAG.SAL.MUŠEN *qaqqad* $BURU_5$.HABRUD.DA NITÁ, *BAM* 480 iii 38, cf. *AMT* 76,6:4′–11′ cited *BAM* V p. xxv ad loc.

540 $BURU_5$.HABRUD.DA 'bat' (*BAM* 476:10′), *arabû* (a bird) (line 14′), *arû nahti* 'fledgling eagle' (lines 14′ and 17′), *nahti paspasi* 'duckling' (line 14′), *āribu* 'raven' (line 16). For $BURU_5$.HABRUD.DA 'bat' see above note 363.

541 The head of a falcon (*surdû*) in *BAM* 311:62′ and dupl. *AMT* 46,5:8, of a swallow and a bat BE 8/1 133:6, etc., see, e.g., *CAD* S s.v. *suttinnu*.

542 See Rykle Borger, "Die Beschwörungsserie *bīt mēseri* und die Himmelfahrt Henochs," *JNES* 33 (1974) 183–96, and Claus Wilcke, "Göttliche und menschliche Weisheit im Alten Orient," in *Weisheit*, A. Assmann, ed. (München: Fink, 1991, pp. 259–70) 266.

543 *BAM* 476 r. 11′, also *BAM* 434 iii 78.

CHAPTER VII

The Nature of Stones

Ingens est herbis virtus data, maxima gemmis.*
(μέγα μὲν σθένος ἔπλετο ῥίζης ἀλλὰ λίθου πολὺ μεῖζον
Orphei Lithika 410.)

Zachalias of Babylon, in the volumes which he dedicates to King Mithridates, attributes man's destiny to the influence of precious stones.
Pliny, *NH* 37.169.

Human-headed bulls and other stone colossi guarded, as it is well known, the gates of Assyrian palaces. Their apotropaic function is sometimes inherent in their names already, as that of the guardian figure called *aladlammû* (from the two Sumerian words *alad* and *lamma*, both designating protective spirits); the name of another, *apsasātu*, reflects its shape (from the word for cow, Sumerian *áb*). Both these learned loanwords were coined, along with many others, during the renaissance of learning under the Sargonid kings.

The palace of Alcinous too was guarded, as we know from the *Odyssey*, by apotropaic dogs of gold and silver, fashioned for the Phaeacian king by Hephaestus the Magician.[544] But only the Assyrian king Esarhaddon explains how the guardians fulfilled their function: they were made of the stone ŠE.TIR "repelling the evil one according to their *šiknu*."[545] The available, usual translation of this word *šiknu* as 'form' (in the

* John M. Riddle, *Marbode of Rennes' (1035–1123) De Lapidibus*, Prologus, line 23. (Sudhoffs Archiv, Beiheft 20), Wiesbaden, 1977, p. 34.

544 Christopher A. Faraone, "Hephaestus the Magician and Near Eastern Parallels for Alcinous' Watchdogs," *Greek, Roman, and Byzantine Studies* 28 (1987) 257–80. A revised version is found in Christopher A. Faraone, *Talismans and Trojan Horses* (Oxford University Press, 1992) 18–35, Chapter 2, "Beastly Guardians at the Gate."

545 aladlammê apsasâti ša NA_4.ŠE.TIR ša ki-i šik-ni-šú-nu irti lemni utarru, Borger, *Esarh.* p. 61 §27 Episode 22, A vi 15–16.

alternative translation "which by virtue of their form ward off evil" of the above phrase) seemed to indicate to Faraone, in his comparison of Greek and Near Eastern apotropaic statues, that the Assyrian king attributed the operative force of the statues to their form alone. We have seen, however, that in reference to the handbooks describing herbs or stones a more appropriate translation of the word *šiknu* would be 'nature.' A translation 'nature' also vindicates Faraone's suggestion that "the medium could also be an important factor." His suggestion was based on an inscription of Sennacherib who boasts of having had protective colossal statues[546] fashioned from that same stone ŠE.TIR,[547] which, as the old translation had it, "was normally used only for making neck amulets."[548] Unfortunately, Sennacherib does not say exactly this. Rather, as the more up-to-date translation has it, he identifies "the *pindû* stone which at the time of my forefathers was (considered) too precious to be (worn) around the neck."[549] Still, as Faraone had surmised, it is the material, the substance, the nature of the stone—its *šiknu*—that gives it its power, a power described in the handbook called, after its incipit, *abnu šikinšu* 'the nature of the stone is.' Of the entries of this handbook, which has survived only in fragmentary state,[550] some preserve the description of the stone or mineral, and others also the purpose for which it is suited. For example:

---

[546] For the human-headed lion-colossi (*apsasāti*) made of NA_4.[d]ŠE.TIR see H. D. Galter, L. D. Levine and J. E. Reade, *ARRIM* 4 (1986) 31 sub no. 20.

[547] The Akkadian name is possibly *pindû* or *ezennû*, and not as previously thought *ašnan*.

[548] "*Ashnan*-stone, whose beautiful structure had the appearance of cucumber seeds, and was highly prized for necklaces (*lit.*, stones of the neck), or amulets to bring on rain (*lit.*, stone for commanding favor and bringing on rain) and to keep disease from approaching a man" D. D. Luckenbill, *Ancient Records of Assyria and Babylonia* (Chicago: University of Chicago Press, 1927) vol. 2 no. 430.

[549] *mala aban kišādi šūquru*, OIP 2 127 d 5, in *CAD* K p. 449 *kišādu* meaning 2b.

[550] The surviving fragments are: *STT* 108, *STT* 109, *BAM* 194, *BAM* 378, K.4751 (for these, see B. Landsberger, *JCS* 21 [1967, published 1969] 151 n. 64), and BM 50664; the latter two are edited, with some comments on the series, by Wayne Horowitz, "Two Abnu šikinšu Fragments and Related Matters," *ZA* 82 (1992) 112–21.

the such-and-such stone is for appeasing divine anger;
the such-and-such stone is for entering the palace—namely, to be received with favor by the ruler;[551]
the such-and-such stone is to prevent migraine;
the such-and-such stone which has a greenish tinge is to assure that the god be favorable to the man; and so on.[552]

Descriptions that appear only in the Assyrian kings' narratives probably are citations from this work, as that of the *girimhilibû* stone, which protects one from plague[553] or of the *elallu* stone, which serves to obtain obedience,[554] while that of the ŠE.TIR-stone "which ensures obedience and averts destruction"[555] may be compared with "the stone for averting destruction," attested in a list of amulet stones.[556] The 'nature' of the ŠE.TIR-stone itself does not happen to be preserved in the Stone-book, and many of the Stone-book's descriptions leave the modern reader perplexed and, as so often, with his curiosity unsatisfied. Take the entry: "the stone whose nature is like fish eye is called 'fish-eye'"; no more informative though more picturesque is the description of, for example, the stone *arzallu* as "the stone whose nature is like a stork's wing" or the stone *abašmû* called "stone of sunset";[557] another stone or possibly the same—the name is not preserved—is called "stone

---

551 Two parallel texts sum up a list of 37 stones as 37 NA_4.MEŠ TU É.GAL taš?-ni-ni kar-ṣa la ma-ha-ri '37 stones for entering the palace and not be confronted with calumny,' BM 56148 ii 12, dupl. to *BAM* 367:9, coll. C. B. F. Walker.

552 The text is published as *LKA* 9; the list is on the left side of the tablet, that is, either on the first column of the obverse or the last column of the reverse. The bottom of the tablet is not preserved, so that the purpose of the enumeration is not apparent. Neither are the beginnings of the lines preserved, so that the name of the stone with which the line began is missing; to compound the uncertainty caused by the break at the left margin, it is also often impossible to tell whether a line is a new entry, or whether it continues the preceding line. The text belongs possibly to the *abnu šikinšu* series. Similar are the texts *BAM* 343 and 344, as noted by Köcher, *BAM* IV p. xiii. Compare also Egbert von Weiher, *SpTU*, vol. 4 no. 129.

553 NA_4 girimhilibû . . . NA_4 N[AM.BAD] ana amēli la ṭehê, *Archaeologia* 79 pl. 52 no. 122 N (+ M):5, cited *CAD* E p. 74 s.v. *elallu* A usage b.

554 NA_4 alallu aban qabê u magāri, Borger, *Esarh.* 85:50, cited ibid.

555 aban qabê magāri u rihṣu šūtuqi, Luckenbill, OIP 2 132:73 (Sennacherib).

556 NA_4 rihṣi šūtuqi, *BAM* 343:2.

557 *STT* 108:75 and dupl. *BAM* 378 iv 17′f.

of sunrise."[558] Would that we had the lapidary of Zachalias of Babylon![559]

A place of special interest was allotted to the magnetite, Sumerian KA.GI.NA.DIB.BA, a compound translated into Akkadian as *šadānu* (KA.GI.NA) with an epithet written DIB.BA that may be read *ṣabtu* or *ṣābitu*. Since the reading of the Sumerogram DIB.BA is ambiguous, the epithet either describes the magnetic attraction of the stone: *ṣābitu* 'capturing,' or alludes to the magnetite captured, along with a cohort of rebellious stones, by the god Ninurta in the Sumerian mythological epic tale *Lugale*:[560] *ṣabtu* 'captive.' Akkadian *šadānu* most likely simply refers to the ore's '(coming) from the mountain'[561] but the explanation of the corresponding Sumerogram KA.GI.NA as 'speaking the truth' is probably just popular etymology, based on the possible translation *dabābu* 'to speak' of its component KA, and the translation *kīnu* 'true' or *kittu* 'truth' of its component GI.NA; the stone therefore is given the aitiology "the stone of truthfulness, he who wears it shall speak the truth, only a pious man may wear it."[562] This function of "the stone of truthfulness" evokes of course Pliny's statement that possession of the haematite reveals treacherous designs on the part of the barbarians.[563]

Reference to the "Babylonian Stone-book" is made in a Neo-Babylonian list of stones[564] which culls stone names, both Sumerian and Akkadian, from the standard lexical list *HAR-ra* = *hubullu* without apparent order. It ends with a colophon

---

558 *STT* 108:74.

559 Pliny, *NH* 37.169, quoted in the motto to this chapter, see Robert Halleux and Jacques Schamp, *Les Lapidaires grecs* (Paris: Les Belles Lettres, 1985) xxiv and 320.

560 J. J. van Dijk, *LUGAL UD ME-LÁM-bi NIR-GÁL. Le récit épique et didactique des Travaux de Ninurta, du Déluge et de la Nouvelle Création* (Leiden: Brill, 1983).

561 From Akkadian *šadû* 'mountain.' See A. A. Barb, "Lapis Adamas. Der Blutstein," in Hommages à Marcel Renard, vol. 1, Coll. Latomus 101 (Brussels, 1969) 69 n. 6 for the suggestion that the word recurs in Greek as oreitēs, and that Greek ἔμψυχον ὀρείτης reflects Akkadian *šadānu balṭu*.

562 *BAM* 194 vii 4.

563 Pliny, *NH* 37.60, as cited in R. Campbell Thompson, *DACG* 86.

564 Published in MSL 10 65–68.

comprising a subscript? and a catch line:[565] "(the series) *abnu šikinšu* for learning about stones"[566] followed by the equation NA₄ KALAG = *su-ú, [u]s-su-ru,* the catch line[567] to the stone section of the pharmaceutical series *Uruanna*.[568] The same catch line also appears at the end of Tablet VIII of the synonym list *malku* = *šarru*,[569] showing that the sequel to this synonym list was the stone list, or a particular recension of it.[570]

Besides the handbooks, there exist shorter lists of herbs alone, stones alone, or of a combination of herbs, stones, shells, and various other *materia magico-medica;* these are usually written on narrow tablets,[571] whose shape itself is reminiscent of the lamellae made of lead or other metals.

Certain Akkadian stone names have been adduced to explain Arabic and Greek counterparts.[572] The fame of stones' magical properties and the aitiological explanations pertaining to them have spread beyond Babylonia. The best known of these is the *aitites* or 'eagle-stone.' Its name in Akkadian is *aban erê* (or its phonetic variant *aban arê*), of which the second element, *erû* or *arû*, is both the word for eagle and the infinitive of the verb 'to be pregnant.' It is in the bilingual Sumerian and Akkadian lists that we find the "basic" meaning, or at least the

---

565 vi 17–20.

566 [(x y)] abnu šikinšu [N]A₄ ana lamāda.

567 NA₄.KALAG.GA = NA₄ su-ú, K.4237 i 1, in CT 14 17 (= Uruanna III 143).

568 The stone section—with its entries preceded by the determinative NA₄ 'stone'—follows the herb section, whose entries begin with the determinative Ú 'herb' or GIŠ 'tree'; they are usually separated by a ruling (in Köcher, *Pflanzenkunde* 12 ii 39/40 and Köcher, *Pflanzenkunde* 14 + CT 14 10 iii 18/19). One source, K.4419, in CT 14 43, ends with the plant section, and has a subscript [. . .] NA₄.MEŠ, which Köcher suggests to restore [*arkišu*] NA₄.MEŠ '[there follow] the stones.'

569 Malku VIII 176.

570 For concatenating various series see Chapter V (p. 90).

571 E.g., *BAM* 255, or UET 4 nos. 148–53, mentioned in his review of the volume by A. Leo Oppenheim, *JCS* 4 (1950) 188ff., and especially René Labat, "Ordonnances médicales ou magiques," *RA* 54 (1960) 169–76, with *RA* 55 (1961) 95; such texts are mentioned in Jean Bottéro, *EPHE, Annuaire* 1974/75 p. 110, who is quoted by Köcher, *BAM* V p. xi note 9.

572 See Paul Kraus, *Jābir ibn Hayyān*, vol. 2, Mémoires de l'Institut d'Egypte, 45 (Cairo, 1942) 72ff. (citing Akkadian stone names after R. Campbell Thompson, *DACG*).

meaning that was considered primary: the Sumerian name of the stone is *na₄.peš₄* 'stone for pregnancy.' Nevertheless, in Akkadian context, the name of the stone is often written, in rebus writing, with the Sumerogram NA4.Á.MUŠEN, that is, NA4 = *aban* 'stone (of),' Á.MUŠEN 'eagle-bird' = *erû*. It is of course the homonymity of 'pregnant' and 'eagle,' and the use of the logogram of the latter word for the former, that gave rise to the fable about the stone to be found in the nest of the eagle, brought by the eagle from India or other far-away places,[573] or, according to other sources, found in the head of a fish called 'eagle,'[574] to serve as amulet for pregnant women.[575]

The claim that stones have such beneficial properties was ridiculed by Pliny the Elder when he wrote in his *Natural History* in the first century A.D.: "Zachalias of Babylon, in the volumes which he dedicates to King Mithridates, attributes man's destiny to the influence of precious stones; and as for the 'haematitis' [a stone discussed by Pliny earlier], he is not content to credit it with curing diseases of the eyes and liver, but places it even in the hands of petitioners to the king,[576] allows it to interfere in lawsuits and trials, and proclaims also that to be smeared with an ointment containing it is beneficial in battle."[577]

Beads made of semi-precious stones, shells, and other colored stones (some of which are probably colored glasses[578]) are supposed to protect from evils wrought by demons or witches. Even though in some of the Assyriological literature they are called "amulet stones," this designation may be misleading, as our own associations with the word "amulet" are

---

573 See *RAC* 1 (1950) 94 s.v. "Adlerstein."

574 Kyranides, cited Barb, *JWCI* 13 (1950) 317 n. 8.

575 "In der Literatur wird ein Stein erwähnt, der den Mutterleib mit dem darin befindlichen Embryo durch ein im Inneren befindliches kleineres Steinchen wiedergibt (*AGM* VIII 1/2, P. 11[4]). Natürlich wollte sich die Trägerin dadurch vor Fehlgeburt sichern." E. Ebeling, *RLA* 1 (1928) 121 s.v. "Apotropaeen." See now R. Halleux, *Les lapidaires grecs* (note 559 above) 336f. n. 4 with previous literature. A. A. Barb, "The Eagle-stone," *JWCI* 13 (1950) 316–18 has noted the pun, interpreting the hesitant suggestion of R. Campbell Thompson, *DACG* 105.

576 Compare the stone "for entering the palace" cited earlier.

577 Pliny, *NH* 37.169.

578 A. Leo Oppenheim, *Glass and Glassmaking in Ancient Mesopotamia* (Corning, NY: The Corning Museum of Glass, 1970) 9ff.

different and, moreover, modern authors use the term "amulet" to refer to a variety of things.[579] In fact, the Latin word *amuletum* from which "amulet" is borrowed has no known etymology,[580] and when Greek and Latin texts speak of using such stones and other materials for protection, they simply prescribe "tying them on" as in Latin *(ad)alligare,* Greek *kathaptein* or *periaptein.* It is exactly the same phrase, 'to tie on,' that is used in Akkadian to describe wearing such phylacteries.[581]

Amulets are used mostly not singly, but on a string. Such a string of beads (Akkadian *ṭurru*) is made up of various stones strung on a cord of colored – red, white, black, or multicolored – wool to be worn as charms around the neck, on the right or left wrist, or the right or left ankle. Other charms – amulet stones – may be placed on the chest or the abdomen. A particularly well known example from Hellenistic and medieval magic texts and lapidaries is the charm used to make a woman talk, a phrase that recurs verbatim in a Babylonian magic text.[582] It is only the Hellenistic lapidary that says that by placing the preparation on the sleeping woman's bosom (Greek: *psyche,* a term used for *pudenda*), she will be induced to talk. It is, however, a medieval text that tells us that if you place the stone from the nest of an owl [*la huppe* < *upupa*] on the bosom of the sleeping woman, she will babble out in her sleep if she has a lover.[583]

Prescriptions for various ills include long lists of such beads,

---

[579] E.g., Beatrice L. Goff, "The Rôle of Amulets in Mesopotamian Ritual Texts," *JWCI* 19 (1956) 1–39.

[580] According to A. Ernout and A. Meillet, *Dictionnaire étymologique de la langue latine*[3] (1951) 54 s.v., while others have proposed that it derives from Greek *amylon* 'starch,' reinterpreted by folk-etymology as *amolimentum* 'phylactery' (A. Walde, *Lateinisches etymologisches Wörterbuch* s.v.).

[581] The Hebrew term *qāmiy'a* also means 'Angebundenes,' see Strack-Billerbeck, vol. 4/1 p. 529.

[582] Reiner, "Nocturnal Talk," in *Lingering over Words: Studies in Ancient Near Eastern Literature in Honor of William L. Moran,* Tzvi Abusch et al., eds., Harvard Semitic Studies, 37 (Atlanta: Scholars Press, 1990) 421–24.

[583] Auctarium cavense, 65, p. 645 Pitra (Analecta Sacra II), from Evax lapidary, cited Halleux, Studi medievali 3,15 (1974) 332, and newly edited in Halleux, *Lapidaires* (note 559 above) 288 lxvii and 342. For literature (Pliny, Damigeron, and the similar beliefs in German and French folklore ["Aberglaube"]) see also Max Wellmann, *Marcellus von Side als Arzt und die Koiraniden des Hermes Trismegistos,* Philologus, Supplementband 27/2 (Leipzig: Dieterich, 1934), 7f. and nn. 26–29.

sometimes enumerated in sets for each such string; the lists end by stating the purpose of the string (*ṭurru*), or simply of the group of "stones" (Akkadian *abnu*, usually expressed with the Sumerogram NA_4) and the manner of application. For example, a small tablet enumerates eleven beads, and summarizes them as "eleven stones for blurred vision,[584] to string on red wool, you wrap 'wolf-bane' on seven rolls (*lippī*) of blue wool, while you recite a charm, and tie it on his left hand."[585] To cure a hemorrhaging woman you string on red wool various stones, recite the appropriate magic spell, and tie the string around her waist;[586] another string for the same purpose is to be strung on the tendon of a dead cow or dead sheep, with fourteen—that is, twice seven—knots tied between the beads.[587]

Not all the items are precious or semi-precious stones, or even stones at all. Among the "stones" enumerated there appear beads made of a metal, either of the precious metals silver and gold, or of others, such as copper, iron, or tin, and beads of various minerals such as antimon, and even shells, all of which are normally written by means of their Sumerograms, with initial NA_4 'stone.'

Specifications added to names of stones are rare, except for the qualification "male" or "female" mentioned earlier in connection with the sex of herbs (Chapter II). Male and female varieties of stones are known from Classical texts[588] and from late antiquity; for example, it is said of the topaz that "it is green, . . . hard, compact, transparent. This is the male variety. The female variety is lighter."[589] Male and female stones are named not only in magic texts[590] and in the stone lists,[591] but they are so classified in the "Glass texts," the Assyrian prescriptions for

---

584 Akkadian: *birrat īnī*.

585 *BAM* 351, also 352.

586 *BAM* 237.

587 *BAM* 237 i end.

588 E.g., Pliny, *NH* 36.39, 37.119; see R. Halleux, "Fécondité des mines et sexualité des pierres dans l'antiquité gréco-romaine," *RBPH* 48 (1970) 16–25 and *Lapidaires* (note 559 above) 326.

589 Orphei lithica kerygmata 8.6: Οὗτος (scil.τοπάζιος) ἐστιν ὁ ἄρσην, ὁ δὲ θηλυκὸς ἐλαφρότερος, cited Halleux, *Lapidaires* (note 559 above) 151.

590 E.g., 7 NA_4 šu-u NITA, *BAM* 473 iii 22.

591 NA_4 li-li-i NITÁ and NA_4 li-li-i SAL in the *abnu šikinšu* text K.4751:5–6, see *ZA* 82 (1992) 117f.

producing colored glasses, which speak of male and female frit.[592] Among the rare descriptions of natural markings, one refers to a variety of *ašpû* stone as *ša uskaru kullumu* 'which shows a (moon?) crescent,'[593] and some shells are often specified as having seven spots.[594]

In contradistinction to the amulet of antiquity, which according to one definition is "a stone of inherent supernatural powers that may be engraved and/or consecrated, and that is either used as a seal or worn as a phylactery" and to the talisman, which is "an image either made of metal in the round or engraved on a metal plate, over which image a ceremony of incantations and suffumigations is performed in order to induce a spirit to enter the talisman and to endow it with power,"[595] the Babylonian "stone" bears no engraving or image. The images and engravings on Babylonian cylinder seals have a different origin and aitiology, even though of course some seals may have been worn as amulets,[596] and even though the particular stone that serves as material for a cylinder seal is said to determine the fate of the person who wears such a seal in the omens appended to one exemplar of the *abnu šikinšu* series.[597] Nor does the Babylonian string of stones

---

592 (anzahhu) lu UŠ lu [SAL], A. Leo Oppenheim, *Glass and Glassmaking in Ancient Mesopotamia* (note 578 above) 48 fragm. e §20, see ibid. 49.

593 See E. Reiner, *JNES* 26 (1967) 196 line 7, with note 21; a further attestation is NA_4 *aš-pu-ú šá* UD.SAR PÀD-*ú*, von Weiher, *SpTU* vol. 2 no. 22 iii 32.

594 ayartu ša 7 tikpūša, Egbert von Weiher, *SpTU*, vol. 2 no. 22 iv 19 and other references cited *CAD* T s.v. *tikpu*; for the reading see Landsberger, *JCS* 21 (1967, published 1969) 147.

595 David Pingree, "Astrology," in *Dictionary of the History of Ideas*, vol. 1 (New York: Scribner, 1973) 118–26; see also Et ymagines sapientes apellant telsam, quod interpretatur violator quia quicquid facit ymago per violenciam facit . . . Sunt composite corporibus propriis ad implendum predicta, et hoc in temporibus opportunis; et suffumigacionibus quibus fortificantur attrahuntur spiritus ad ipsas ymagines . . . *Picatrix Latinus* (Pingree) I ii 1.

596 For the question of representations on and the function of seals see the works of Edith Porada, for example, "The Iconography of Death in Mesopotamia in the Early Second Millennium B.C.," in *Death in Mesopotamia*, B. Alster, ed., Mesopotamia, 8 (Copenhagen: Akademisk Forlag, 1980) 259–70. See also the article by B. Goff cited n. 579.

597 *BAM* 194 viii. The text (formerly published as *KAR* 185) has been adduced by B. Goff (note 579 above), but was interpreted as referring to portents from a particular cylinder seal rather than referring to the wearer of such a seal.

normally undergo a ceremony of consecration by which a spirit is induced to enter it and to endow it with power. The power sought to imbue the string or the individual stones is that coming from the stars. For this reason they must be exposed to irradiation by stars.

In a recently published ritual enumerating the proper amulet stones to be used in various predicaments[598] such an exposition to the Goat star is recommended against the evil machinations of an "ill-wisher" or, as the term *bēl lemutti* may also be translated, "adversary." Other strings listed in the same text, but without specifically prescribed nocturnal exposition, protect from such physical ailments as diseases of the eye,[599] but also from harm brought about by enemies, ill-wishers, divine anger,[600] and sorcery.[601] The ritual to protect the client from the disastrous consequences (described in lines 8–16) brought about by an "ill-wisher" begins with column ii line 8.[602] It is divided in two parts; the first section of seven lines (ii 17–23) enumerates seven phylacteries, one in each line, containing two herbs and one stone each, while the next section goes—without a ruling—from the enumeration of stones to the exposition to the Goat star (the star of Gula) and the prayer to Gula, beginning in ii 24 and ending in iii 2, for a total of thirty lines.[603] This last section begins with a list of twelve stones—as a matter of fact, when you count them there are thirteen—and many of them cannot be identified:

> Carnelian, lapis lazuli, yellow obsidian, *mekku, egizangû, pappardilû, papparminû, lamassu*?, antimon, jasper, magnetite, *turminû, abašmu*, twelve(*sic*!) stones (to use) if a man has an "ill-wisher." You string

---

598 Egbert von Weiher, *SpTU*, vol. 2 no. 22. An excerpt tablet that duplicates lines 16–25 is published by M. J. Geller, *AfO* 35 (1988) 21f. Note [x] BE NA4.MEŠ DIŠ HUL.GIG UD.4.KAM šá ITI.NE DÙ-su '[. . .] stones if "hatred" was practiced against him on the fourth of month V', i 30–31 with which may be compared the magic "practiced against the man on the fourth of month XI before the constellation Centaurus," *STT* 89:50, see Chapter VI.

599 *birṣu*, i 3′–15′.

600 i 16′–25′, ii 8′–16′, etc.

601 i 39′–46′.

602 A ruling after line 7′ of column ii introduces a section that runs until column iii line 32, at which point other rituals begin.

603 Thirty and not thirty-one, since line "32" is a *rejet* from line 31.

the stones and phylacteries on a [linen? thread], you set in place a holy-water vessel, you purify the stones and the phylacteries, you place the stones before the Goat star, you set up a censer with aromatics, you libate beer, (you recite) the incantation:

. . .[604]O Bright one, let your angry heart be appeased,
let your innermost relent, O Gula, exalted Lady.
You are the one who created mankind, who bestows lots, food portions, and food offerings,[605]
be present at my lawsuit, let me obtain justice through your verdict,
because of the sorceries, spittle and spatter, evil machinations
of my adversary, let his evil doings turn back against him and affect his head and his body,
and I, your weary servant, will sing your praises.

How stones acquired their renown for protecting from evil and granting success to an enterprise is not known; however, there is a tradition about strings of amulet stones harking back to a famous king of the past. Some are attributed to Hammurapi, Narām-Sin, and Rīm-Sin, just as some "proven salves" bear the name of Hammurapi.[606] A list enumerating fourteen amulet stones, to which several duplicates exist, has as subscript: "14 stones of the necklace of Narām-Sin,"[607] while variants to it attribute the necklace to King Rīm-Sin.

---

604 The first four signs, *ú-šá-an-ni*, are unintelligible to me. They seem to stand for a first or third person past tense of the verb *šunnû* 'to repeat' or 'to change,' or possibly may have to be read *šam-šá-an-ni* or *šam-gar-an-ni*, with the ending *-anni* that could represent a first person dative.

605 Compare the address to the Wagon star in *STT* 73 (see p. 71).

606 For salves attributed to a famous king of the past, see Chapter II p. 41 and n. 170.

607 14 NA4.MEŠ GÚ ᵐNa-ram-ᵈSin, *BAM* 372 ii 5; [1]4 GÚ Na-ram-ᵈSin, *BAM* 357:5′; 14 NA4.MEŠ GÚ ᵐNa-⟨ra⟩-am-ᵈSin, *BAM* 375 II 42; 14 GÚ ᵐNa-⟨ra⟩-am-ᵈSin, *BAM* 376 iv 8; [. . .].MEŠ GÚ [. . .], *BAM* 368 iii 9′; see (also for K.2409+ ii 24′, K.6282+ ii 14) Köcher, *BAM* IV p. xvi ad no. 357, and Köcher, "Ein verkannter neubabylonischer Text aus Sippar," *AfO* 20 (1963) 157ff. Note, however, that not all names written AM-ᵈSin are to be emended to Narām-Sin, since AM as Sumerogram can stand for the Akkadian word *rīmu* 'wild bull,' and hence the spelling can refer to King Rīm-Sin of Larsa, as in, e.g., GÚ AM-ᵈSin in *AMT* 7,1 r. i 6, see Yalvaç, *Studies in Honor of Benno Landsberger on His Seventy-Fifth Birthday, April 21, 1965*, AS 16 (Chicago: University of Chicago Press: 1965) 332, now confirmed by the recently published text CT 51 89, which writes GÚ AM-ᵈSin LUGAL Larsam ([UD].UNUGᵏⁱ) in i 15, as I pointed out in "Magic Figurines, Amulets and Talismans," in *Monsters and Demons in the Ancient and Medieval Worlds.* Papers Presented in Honor

The date of composition of the Stone-book is not known, but it probably is to be placed around the turn, or at the beginning of the first millennium, when much of the speculative literature and *scholia* originated, as opposed to lists of stones and other objects of the material world, which go back to the very origin of cuneiform writing. It is worth noting that of these latter lists only chapters XIV (snakes and other animals), XVI (stones), and XVII (plants) of the lexical series *HAR-ra* = *hubullu* have parallels in the three handbooks characterized by their kenning *šikinšu*. It is therefore significant that the same three kingdoms of nature have a role not only in Hellenistic magic but also, with slight modifications, in Babylonian astral magic.

The relevant part of Hellenistic magic is described in the work called *Cyranides*.[608] Book I "contains twenty-four alphabetically ordered chapters. In each of these are enumerated, both individually and in combination, the magical-medical properties of four entities which share a common letter, these entities being plant, bird, stone, and fish. Each chapter also contains the description of an amulet made of the relevant stone and containing in its design one or more of the other entities."[609] Neither birds nor fish—which, by the way, share one tablet, Tablet XVIII, of *HAR-ra* = *hubullu*—appear in the Babylonian sources; they are replaced by trees, so that in lieu of four entities, Babylonian sources enumerate three only as being pertinent in magic: plants, stones, and trees. The references to this practice are rare and often unclear, but the juxtaposition of these three is diagnostic. For example: "when? you practice? plant, stone, and tree and exorcism, do it along with its commentary?"[610] or "when you want to ascertain the zodiacal sign

---

of Edith Porada, Ann E. Farkas et al., eds. (Mainz on Rhine: Philipp von Zabern, 1988) 33 n. 27. A new duplicate published in Egbert von Weiher, *SpTU*, vol. 4 no. 129 iv 19 writes GÚ AM-^{d}Sin LUGAL ŠEŠ.UNUG^{ki}. The list of amulets *ADD* 1043 (= SAA 7 no. 82) also lists 14 GÚ AM-Sin in reverse line 6.

608 For recent literature see David Bain, "'Treading Birds.' An Unnoticed use of πατέω (Cyranides I.10.27, I.19.9)," in *Dover Fs* 295–304.

609 *Dover Fs* 296.

610 kî Ú NA_4 u GIŠ ù LÚ.MAŠ.MAŠ-ú-tu a-na GIG te$^{!}$-pu-šú it-ti ṣi-ti-šú e-pu-uš, *ZA* 6 (1891) 243:39f., cited A. Livingstone, *Mystical and Mythological Explanatory Works of Assyrian and Babylonian Scholars* (Oxford: Clarendon,

in . . . stone, plant, and tree [. . .]."[611] Trees, plants, and stones were associated with zodiacal signs in late Babylonian texts as they were in Hellenistic Egypt, and to these entities were sometimes added animals, cities, and excerpts or incipits of mantic material, lists of gods and temples, and others.[612] No explicit reference is made, however, to amulets with such pictorial representations.

In a late commentary[613] the mention of plant, stone, and tree is possibly connected with medicine, if my reading[614] "to heal him [. . .] plant, stone, and tree of/which [. . .]" is correct; the next line of the text already makes the association of a zodiacal sign with magic operations[615] for which the main sources are the two Neo-Babylonian texts BRM 4 20 and 19, and the similar texts LBAT 1597 and LBAT 1626, discussed in Chapter VI. The just cited text which associates the three entities plant, stone, and tree with exorcism or magic (Akkadian *mašmāšūtu* or *āšipūtu* 'art of the exorcist') enjoins the practitioner to have recourse to its *ṣītu* or, as the signs can also be read, *ṣētu*. The latter reading, *ṣētu*, designates a commentary arranged like a glossary in two columns, and such a commentary would have given in the second column the synonym or explanation of the word in the first.[616] What the commentary to Ụ NA$_4$ *u* GIŠ may have contained we do not know; possibly it gave equivalences,

1986) 73, and translated by him as "When you perform plant stone and wood and the art of the exorcist for a sick man—one performs (it) with its comment?." For the texts see Ernst Weidner, *Gestirn-Darstellungen auf babylonischen Tontafeln* (note 520 above) 17ff.

611 MÚL.LU.MAŠ ana IGI-ka ina É ŠU^{II} (= pit-qad?) šá NA$_4$ Ú u iṣ-ṣi [. . .], *JCS* 6 (1952) 66:6 (= TCL 6 12), see Sachs, ibid. 71ff.

612 See Reiner, *JAOS* 105 (1985) 592f.

613 *LBAT* 1621.

614 [ana] bulluṭišu ([. . .] TI-šú) Ú NA$_4$ u GIŠ šá Ṭ[U . . .].

615 [K]I.ÁG.GÁ NITA ana SAL MÚL.[KUN.MEŠ] 'love of man for woman: constellation: [Pisces],' *LBAT* 1621:8', restored from BRM 4 20:6, see Ungnad, *AfO* 14 (1941–44) 258.

616 For botanical glossaries cf., e.g., the glossaries in A. Delatte, *Anecdota atheniensia*, Bibliothèque de la Faculté de philosophie et lettres de l'Université de Liège, fasc. 88, vol. 2 pp. 273ff.; the Byzantine Greek Lexikon *kata alfabēton en hô hermēneuontai tina tôn botanôn* (= Delatte, op. cit. 378ff.) was also edited subsequently by M. H. Thomson (note 108 above) as no. 9, "Lexique de synonymes grecs," 133ff.

or common names, to such exotic ingredients as "lion's blood" or "wolf bone" as the magical papyrus *PGM* XII 401ff.[617] cited earlier (p. 32) and so represents one tradition in the explanation of "secret" names.

[617] See Hopfner, *Offenbarungszauber*, vol. 1 p. 124f. §493 and "Mageia" in *RE* 27 (1928) 319.

CHAPTER VIII

Nocturnal Rituals

Stellis atque herbis vis est, sed maxima verbis
Heim, *Incantamenta Magica*, p. 465

Night is a time when spirits roam and danger lurks. ". . . The ominous day was one of the dark, moonless nights of the interlunium at the end of the month between last and first visibility of the moon, nights when it was indeed believed that evil spirits could roam freely."[618] But night is also filled with the emanations of the moon and the stars, and is thereby suited for the performance of rituals and magic manipulations. The moon may have been an ally of sorceresses–it was the full moon that Erichtho, Medea, and other notorious sorceresses "drew down" to make their magic more efficacious, thus making Thessaly, the home of witches, famous from Plato to Lucan[619]–but no Mesopotamian text speaks of the influence of its waxing and waning on the growth of crops or on various human activities. No instructions are extant about procedures known from folklore and that the farmers' handbooks of antiquity–Virgil, Columella, Pliny the Elder–recommend and that are still practiced today under the name "biodynamics":[620] say, planting to be carried out when the Moon is waxing, and pruning when it is waning.[621]

---

618 A. T. Grafton and N. M. Swerdlow, "Calendar Dates and Ominous Days in Ancient Historiography," *JWCI* 51 (1988) 14–42; the quote is on p. 16.

619 For literature see Chapter VI.

620 The New York Times, May 2, 1991, Section B, page 1 (continued on page 7).

621 I know only of one instruction to the farmer based on astronomical data, a letter from the Old Babylonian period that warns not to soak? the sesame seeds in preparation for sowing before the rising of Sirius. The letter, TLB 4 (= Altbabylonische Briefe, 3 [Leiden: Brill, 1968]) no. 65, is quoted by F. R. Kraus, *JAOS* 88 (1968) 116 and again, adding a reference to stars signaling the time to cultivate, by R. Frankena, SLB 4 p. 197. The reference is

Moon and Sun may combine their influences. Accordingly, two dates expressly designated for administering potions and for other ritual acts are the two regularly occurring planetary events, the conjunction and the opposition of the Sun and the Moon. These are of course, in lay terms, the nights of the new moon, a time when a solar eclipse may occur, and of the full moon, that is, the middle of the month, when a lunar eclipse may occur.

Both dates repeatedly appear in medical texts. The night of the new moon is recommended as the time when an herb against witchcraft is to be ingested in beer;[622] another herb is to be used for purifying the man at new moon's day, by putting it into water and exposing it to the stars,[623] and still others by placing it around the patient's neck or giving it to him to eat at new moon's day.[624] A particularly precise instruction directs: "put a potsherd lying in the street [and other materials?] into first-quality beer, drink (it) at new moon's day facing the sun."[625] Moonless nights are, as we saw, particularly appropriate for gathering herbs. Thus, an instruction, unfortunately

naturally to the season, and comparable to the importance of the rising of Sothis (i.e., Sirius) in signaling the flood of the Nile in Egypt, or to the rising of Sirius observed for the timing of agricultural tasks in the *Nabatean Agriculture* as noted by D. Chwolsohn, *Die Ssabier und der Ssabismus* (St. Petersburg, 1856) vol. 2 p. 912. The relevance of the Old Babylonian letter for the identification of the oleiferous plant was most recently adduced by Miguel Civil, *The Farmer's Instructions. A Sumerian Agricultural Manual* (Sabadell [Barcelona], Spain: Editorial AUSA, 1994) with reference to the discussion by Marvin Powell, *Aula Orientalis* 9 (1991) 155–64.

622 ina ūm bubbuli ina šikari šaqû, *KMI* 76 K.4569:1–8 and 14–21, a three-column pharmaceutical text of which the rightmost column, the recommendation for use, is preserved but not the first column, the one that gives the name of the herb, and only part of the second column, the one that specifies the herb's curative power.

623 ina ūm bubbuli amēla(NA) ullulu ana mê nadû ina UL bu-[ut-tu?] ibid. 10.

624 ina UD.NÁ.A ina kišādišu [. . .], *KMI* 76 K.4569:11, amēla šūkulu, ibid. 12–13 and Köcher, *Pflanzenkunde* 1 rev. v 18, 19, 24, 27–29, 30, 32. The two texts are discussed in Pablo Herrero, *La Thérapeutique mésopotamienne*, M. Sigrist, ed. (Paris: Recherche sur les Civilisations, 1984) 19, with a note that we have here "une des rares prescriptions de caractère magique," ibid. n. 33.

625 haṣabtu ša ina sūqi nadât [. . .] ana libbi šikari rēštî tanaddi ina ūm bubbuli ana pan [Šamaš šiti], *BAM* 208:7, restored from *AMT* 85,1 ii 12.

fragmentary, prescribes a procedure "on the day when the moon disappears from the sky"[626] and continues with "you pull up? [. . .] the stars must not see (it?), on the 29th day [. . .] hair from his head" and further directs that an effigy be made (presumably of the evil) and offered to the sun, Šamaš.[627]

An effigy is also used in a ritual to be performed at the first sighting of the new moon, a favorable moment as the subscript tells us: "Incantation to recite in order to turn the evil into good at the first visibility of the moon."[628]

The effigy to be fashioned, at moonrise, is called here not with the usual term 'figurine' or 'statue(tte)'[629] but *passu* 'doll,'[630] specified in two exemplars as a "male doll"[631] and in the third as a "female doll."[632] Whose effigy the "doll" represents is not stated in the preserved portions. The ritual addresses the exorcist with the words "throw the 'doll' behind you into the river, and the evil will be loosed."[633] Whereas one

---

626 *ūm ᵈSin ina šamê ittablu*, *BAM* 580 v 5′ (= *AMT* 44,1 iv 5′); compare a ritual against evil dreams prescribed *enūma Sin ittablu* 'when the Moon has disappeared,' *KAR* 262 rev.(!) 14.

627 *BAM* 580 v 7′–8′.

628 KA.INIM.MA šá IGI.DU$_8$.A ᵈSin HUL SIG$_5$.GA.KAM. This apotropaion has survived in three exemplars. One, which has the ritual on the reverse (*BMS* 24 + 25 + K.14704, new copy in *Šu-ila* no. 59, subscripts in rev. 4′, 15′, edited by Werner Mayer *Untersuchungen zur Formensprache der babylonischen "Gebetsbeschwörungen,"* Studia Pohl: Series Maior, 5 [Rome: Biblical Institute Press, 1976] 529f.) has on the obverse a prayer to the Moon god Sin "with lifting of the hand"; its tenor resembles that of the prayers for calming the angry god (*dingir.šà.dib.ba gur.ru.da*). The second (*BAM* 316) is a large tablet with three columns on each side; it enumerates a number of afflictions, seemingly psychological; the ritual appears toward the end, and is followed by the words "the evil of dreams and (other) evil signs," a phrase that may represent the final rubric. The purpose of the third ritual (*LKA* 25 ii) and the prayer to the Moon preceding it, is, according to its rubric, "to calm the angry god." The prayer to the Moon was edited, along with its several more complete duplicates, by W. G. Lambert, *JNES* 33 (1974) 294ff.

629 NU = *ṣalmu*.

630 See Benno Landsberger, *WZKM* 56 (1960) 117ff.

631 ZA.NA NITA (*BAM* 316 and *LKA* 25).

632 ZA.NA SAL (*Šu-ila* no. 59 obv. 15′, in Werner Mayer, *Untersuchungen* (note 628 above) 530.

633 [ku-tal-l]a-nik-ka ana ÍD ŠUB-ma HUL BÚR, Werner Mayer, *Untersuchungen* (note 628 above) 531 rev. 19′.

text ends here and its parallel[634] is followed by a ritual against evil dreams, in the third text[635] the ritual is followed by a prayer to Orion, fragmentary to be sure, but evidently imploring the constellation to avert illness: "O Orion [. . .], who drives away illness [. . .], you are high in the sky, you rise [. . .], vertigo [. . .], before? you [. . .]."[636]

The full moon also has a role in nocturnal rituals. The day of the opposition of Sun and Moon may vary from the 13th to the 16th, but in the schematic month of 30 days it is set for the 15th. To cure the affliction named ZI.KU5.RU.DA, literally "cutting the breath,"[637] the patient addresses a prayer to the Moon god Sin, presents an offering and recounts his affliction to Sin on the night of the 15th of the month.[638] Offerings to the Moon on the 15th day are also recommended in the hemerologies.[639] A remedy for the ears is to be prepared on the 15th of the sixth month[640] while the next recipes prescribe that the treatment be performed on the 1st of the third month and the 11th of the eighth month respectively.[641]

For some rituals it is essential that both planetary deities, the Sun and the Moon, be equally present. That time is when the full moon sets and the sun rises, at dawn of the day of the opposition of Sun and Moon, in the middle of the month (usually expressed as the 15th day); this is the time for carrying out a ritual against the spirits of the dead that haunt a man.[642] The aim of the ritual is to gain deliverance from afflictions caused

---

634 *BAM* 316 vi 24′–28′.

635 *LKA* 25.

636 ÉN MUL SIPA.ZI.AN.NA [. . .] mukkišu GIG [. . .] E_{11}-la-ta ina šamê nap-[ha-ta . . .], ṣīdānu [. . .] mahraka AN [. . .], *LKA* 25 ii 20–24 (end of obverse?). For other prayers to Orion see p. 56.

637 For literature and suggested identifications see Köcher, *BAM* IV p. xvi n. 26. For rituals against *zikurudû*-magic see Chapter VI.

638 *BAM* 449 ii 2f., also ibid. 11–15.

639 See p. 113.

640 UD.15.KAM šá ITI.KIN, *AMT* 105:10.

641 ina UD.1.KAM ša ITI.SIG4, ibid. 14, and ina UD.11.KAM ša ITI.APIN, ibid. 17. The latter date which does not seem to be astronomically significant may relate, as possibly also the other dates of this text, to some pre-calculated time, such as are known from certain divinatory practices.

642 *BAM* 323:93ff. and parallel 228:28ff.

by a "persecuting ghost";[643] it is performed "on the 15th day, when moon and sun are equally present."[644] The exorcist "clothes the patient in a dirty? garment, draws his blood by slashing his forehead with an obsidian (knife), has him sit down in a reed hut, has him face north, makes an incense offering of juniper and libates cow's milk to Sin toward 'sunset,' and makes an incense offering of 'cypress' and libates fine beer to Šamaš toward 'sunrise.' Then the patient recites as follows: 'To my left is Sin, the crescent of the great heavens,[645] to my right the father of mankind,[646] Šamaš the judge, the two gods, ancestors (lit. fathers) of the great gods, who determine the lots for the far-flung people. An evil wind has blown at me, the persecuting ghost persecutes me, so that I am worried, I am troubled, disturbed (as I face) your verdict. Save me so that I not come to grief.' He recites this seven times, leaves the reed hut, changes his clothes, puts on a pure garment, speaks to Sin as follows: 'Incantation: Sin, light of heaven and earth, take away my sickness!' He speaks this three times and speaks to Šamaš as follows: 'Šamaš, great judge, father of mankind,[647] let the evil wind that has settled on me rise to heaven like smoke, and I will sing your praises'—he speaks this three times and does not [. . .]."[648]

---

643 eṭem ridâti, *BAM* 228:27 and dupl. *BAM* 323:92.

644 ina UD.15.KAM ūm Sin u Šamaš ištēniš izzazzu, *BAM* 228:28 and dupls. 229:21′f., 323:93. The texts have been edited by Jo Ann Scurlock, "Magical Means of Dealing with Ghosts in Ancient Mesopotamia" (Ph.D. diss., University of Chicago, 1988), Prescriptions 56–59; the ritual is edited as no. 59.

645 The word "crescent" is used here as a standard epithet of the moon, since obviously on the 15th the moon is full.

646 The word for 'mankind' is *ṣal-mat qaqqadi* (SAG.DU), literally 'black-headed,' written with the Sumerogram SAG.GI$_6$.GA in line 106.

647 See preceding note.

648 NA BI TÚG.ŠÀ.HA MU$_4$.MU$_4$-aš ina NA$_4$.ZÚ SAG.KI-šú te-eṣ-ṣi-ma ÚŠ-šu ta-tab-bak ina ŠÀ GI.ÙRI.GAL TUŠ-ib-šu IGI-šu ana IM.SI.SÁ GAR-an ana ^{d}Sin ana ^{d}UTU.ŠÚ.A NÍG.NA ŠIM.LI GAR-an GA ÁB BAL-qí ana ^{d}UTU.È NÍG.NA GIŠ.ŠUR.MÌN GAR-an KAŠ.SAG BAL-qí NA BI HAR.GIM DUG$_4$.GA ana GÙB-ia ^{d}Sin UD.SAR AN-e GAL.MEŠ ana ZAG-ia a-bi ṣal-mat SAG.DU ^{d}UTU DI.KUD DINGIR.MEŠ kilallān a-bi DINGIR.MEŠ GAL.MEŠ TAR-su EŠ.BAR ana UN.MEŠ DAGAL.MEŠ IM HUL-tim i-di-pan-ni-ma GIDIM ri-da-a-ti UŠ.MEŠ-an-ni lu <na>-as-sa-ku e-šá-ku u dal-ha-ku ana di-ni-ku-nu šu-zi-ba-ni-ma la ah-ha-bil 7-šú DUG$_4$.GA-ma iš-tu GI.ÙRI.GAL È-ma TÚG.BI ú-na-

The situation is quite clear, even though the ritual does not specify the time when it is to be performed. Since the moon is in the west, that is, setting, and the sun rising in the east, we have here a dawn ceremony.

Appeals to stars and planets as the deities' astral manifestations are known from two late rituals, the New Year's ritual in Babylon and a ritual performed in the temple of Anu in Uruk. Among the deities addressed in the New Year's ritual in Babylon[649] are the goddess Ṣarpanītu (the consort of Marduk, chief god of Babylon) in her astral manifestation,[650] also the Square of Pegasus,[651] Mudrukešda,[652] and the star of Eridu;[653] they are followed by the planets Jupiter,[654] Mercury,[655] Saturn—here called, with an epithet elsewhere reserved for Libra, Star of justice[656]—and Mars,[657] and the stars Sirius,[658] Arcturus,[659] NE.NE.GAR,[660] Numušda,[661] Antares,[662] and finally the Sun and the Moon.[663] The prayer to Babylon's tutelary deity, Bēl (that is,

---

kar TÚG.UD.UD MU$_4$.MU$_4$ ana ^{d}Sin HAR.GIM DUG$_4$ ÉN ^{d}Nanna giš.nu$_x$.gal an.ki.ke$_4$ tu.ra nu.dùg.ga su!.mu.ta ba.z[i] 3-šú DUG$_4$.GA-ma ana ^{d}UTU HAR.GIM DUG$_4$.G[A] ^{d}Utu di.ku$_5$.gal ⌈a⌉.a sag.gi$_6$.ga im.hul gar.ra.ba i.bí.gin$_7$ an.šè hé.è ka.tar.zu ga.an.si.il : 3-šú DUG$_4$.GA-ma NU x [x], *BAM* 323:94–107, partly duplicated by *BAM* 228:24–32, 229:18′–26′. My translation differs in mostly minor details from that of Jo Ann Scurlock (see note 644). The text is also treated by Marten Stol, in *Natural Phenomena*, D. J. W. Meijer, ed. (Amsterdam, 1992) 256.

649 Le rituel des fêtes du nouvel an à Babylone, in François Thureau-Dangin, *Rituels accadiens* (Paris, Leroux: 1921), pp. 127ff.

650 ^{d}Ṣar-pa-ni-tum na-bat kakkabī 'Ṣarpanītu, brightest of the stars,' line 252.

651 *Ikû*, lines 275f.

652 MÚL.MU.BU.KÉŠ.DA, line 302.

653 MÚL.NUN.KI, line 303.

654 MÚL.BABBAR 'White Star,' line 305.

655 MÚL.GUD.UD, line 306.

656 MÚL.GENNA kakkab kittu u mīšar, line 307. Libra and Star of Šamaš designate Saturn in several cuneiform sources, see Hunger in Hunger and Pingree, *MUL.APIN* p. 130 ad i 38f. quoting Parpola, *LAS* 2 pp. 342f.

657 MÚL.AN, line 308.

658 MÚL.KAK.SI.SÁ, line 309.

659 MÚL.ŠU.PA, line 310.

660 Not identified; line 311. The name is possibly to be read *Ne-bí-ru*$_x$, i.e., another name for Jupiter.

661 MÚL Nu-muš-da, line 312.

662 MÚL GABA GÍR.TAB 'Breast of the Scorpion,' line 313.

663 Lines 314 and 315.

Marduk), and his consort Bēltiya in lines 318ff. addresses the goddess (lines 325–32) as the planet Venus or as one of its manifestations as a fixed star: the Bow (MÚL.BAN), the Goat (MÚL.ÙZ), the Star of Abundance (MÚL.HÉ.GÁL.A), the Star of Dignity (MÚL.BAL.TÉŠ.A), the Wagon (MÚL.MAR.GÍD.DA), Coma Berenices? (MÚL.A.EDIN) and Vela? (MÚL.NIN.MAH).

In the temple of Anu at Uruk in a nocturnal ceremony[664] offerings are made on the 16th (of a month that is not identified in the preserved portions of the ritual) to the heavenly manifestations of the temple's main deities: to "Anu of the sky" and "Antu of the sky," as well as to the seven planets,[665] and in the same text daily offerings are made to "Anu and Antu of the sky" and to the seven planets, now named in the sequence Jupiter, Venus, Mercury, Saturn, Mars, the rising of the Sun and the sighting of the Moon.[666]

The heavenly manifestations of Anu and Antu are, for Anu, a star belonging to the constellation Mudrukešda (α Draconis?) and, for Antu, a star in the constellation Ursa Maior.[667] The text itself specifies: "as soon as the star of Great Anu of the sky rises, (and?) Great Antu of the sky rises in the Wagon."[668]

The most elaborate ritual performed at night with appeal to the stars is the "washing of the mouth" (*mīs pî*). It deals with the all-important ceremony of breathing life into the statues of the gods, a process called empsychosis in Greek. In Babylonia,

---

664 Akkadian: bayātu.

665 *Rituels accadiens* (note 649 above) 79, lines 32–34: UD.16.KAM ša arhussu 10 immerē SAG-ú-tú marûtu ebbūti ša qarnu u ṣupru šuklulu ana dAni(DIŠ) u Antu ša šamê ù dUDU.BAD.MEŠ 7-šú-nu ana sa-al-qa i-na te-bi-ib-tum ŠUII ina paramāhi ziqqurrat dAni kīma ša UD.16.KAM ša Ṭebēti inneppuš.

666 ūmišam kal šatti 10 immerē marûti ebbūti ša qarnu u ṣupru šuklulu ana Ani u Antu ša šamê dSAG.ME.GAR dDil-bat dGUD.UD dGENNA dṢal-bat-a-nu KUR-ha Šamaš ù IGI.DU8.A dSin . . . inneppuš, ibid. p. 79 rev. 29–31, and the similar enumeration . . . ina muhhi 7 paššūrmah hurāṣi ana dSAG.ME.GAR dDil-bat dGUD.UD dGENNA ù dṢal-bat-a-nu dSin ù dŠamaš kīma ša innammar mê qātē tanašši-ma (etc.), ibid. p. 119:22–24.

667 *Rituels accadiens* (note 649 above) 85 n. 2. The star list to which he refers is now published in *MUL.APIN*.

668 kīma ša MUL dAnu rabû ša šamê ittapha An-tum rabītu ša šamê ina MUL.MAR.GÍD.DA ittapha "Une cérémonie nocturne dans le temple d'Anu," in *Rituels accadiens* (note 649 above) 119 lines 15–16.

the ceremony is called the "opening of the mouth" (*pīt pî*), which is preceded by the "washing of the mouth" (*mīs pî*) of the divine statue. Divine statues, we know, were made of wood, and overlaid with precious materials, usually gold; incrustations of precious stones adorned them.[669] Their fabrication was, therefore, placed under the tutelage of the patron gods of carpenters, goldsmiths, and jewelers. Only after the inert materials were infused with breath through the mouth-opening ceremony could the statue eat and drink the offerings, and smell the incense.[670]

The vivification of the divine statue comprised several stages. The first stage, the first mouth-washing, was conducted in the workshop; then, the statue was carried in procession to the river bank, where a second mouth-washing took place. The statue was first facing west, then facing east. Offerings were made to the nine great gods, among whom are the major planetary gods, that is, Sun, Moon, and Venus; then to the nine patron gods of the craftsmen; then to other planets and to certain fixed stars and constellations, among them Sirius, Libra, the Wagon, the Goat, and the Scorpion, and finally to the stars rising over the three "paths" along the eastern horizon, that is, *all* the stars.[671] The role of the astral deities in the ritual is not specified; nevertheless, that role is clear from the description of the venue, which is the river bank, and the time: at night, as indicated by the fact that the procession advances by torchlight; the stars and planets were to irradiate the statue crafted of wood and adorned with precious metals and stones and thus infuse these materials with their power. The offerings are

---

[669] Oppenheim, "The Golden Garments of the Gods," *JNES* 8 (1949) 172–93.

[670] ṣalmu annû ina la pīt pî qutrinna ul iṣṣin akala ul ikkal mê ul išatti 'this image without opening of the mouth does not smell incense, does not eat food, does not drink water,' *STT* 200:42f. and dupl. PBS 12/1 6—a near-literal equivalent of Psalm 115's description of idols.

[671] S. Smith, *JRAS* 1925 37ff., also Erich Ebeling, *Tod und Leben nach den Vorstellungen der Babylonier* (Berlin and Leipzig: de Gruyter & Co., 1931) 104–105:25–36; see also W. Mayer, *Or.* NS 47 (1978) 445 W 20030/3:3–5 (copy: *Baghdader Mitteilungen*, Beiheft 2 no. 1). The introductory instructions are partially broken; the text begins: *e-nu-ma šip-ri* DINGIR ⌈BI/GA-*am*⌉ [*x x x ina* IT]I *šal-me* . . . 'when . . . the work on the god, [. . .] in a favorable month . . .,' lines 1f.

described with the words: "you set up a cultic arrangement[672] to the god"; it seems that these "cultic arrangements" or, as we might say, "altars," are the *loci* to which the astral god will descend. It is to be noted that no specific connection is made between the various materials of which the statue is made and the deity that presides over each. Only in Hellenistic times will each planet be associated with a particular metal and stone.[673]

At the head of the offerings to astral deities stands Jupiter:

> You set up two altars for Jupiter and Venus – ditto (= you perform the mouth-washing)
> You set up two altars for the Moon and Saturn – ditto
> You set up three altars for Mercury, Sirius, and Mars – ditto
> You set up six altars for Libra, (called) the Star[674] of Šamaš, the Plow, ŠU.PA,
> the Wagon, the Cluster, the Goat – ditto
> You set up four altars for the Field (the Square of Pegasus), the Swallow, the Star of Anunitu, the Furrow – ditto
> You set up four altars for the Fish, Aquarius, the Star of Eridu, the Scorpion – ditto
> You set up three altars for (the stars) of the Path of Anu, of the Path of Enlil, of the Path of Ea – ditto.[675]

The first seven offerings, in two groups of two and one of three, are meant for the seven planets, even though the place of the sun, Šamaš, is taken by Sirius in the last group, either because he was included in the group of nine gods enumerated

---

[672] riksu.

[673] Bouché-Leclercq, *L'astrologie grecque* (Paris, 1899, reprinted Aalen: Scientia, 1979) 313.

[674] Text: House.

[675] 29. 2 riksē a-na dSAG.ME.GAR u dDil-bat tarakkas KI.MIN

30. 2 riksē a-na dSin u dUDU.BAD.SAG.UŠ tarakkas KI.MIN

31. 3 riksē a-na MUL.GUD.[UD] MUL.KAK.SI.SÁ MUL Ṣal-bat-a-nu tarakkas KI.MIN

32. 6 riksē a-na MUL Zi-ba-ni-tum É dUTU MUL.APIN MUL.ŠU.PA

33. MUL.MAR.GÍD.DA MUL.A.EDIN MUL.ÙZ tarakkas KI.MIN

34. 4 riksē a-na MUL.AŠ.GÁN MUL.SIM.MAH MUL dA-nu-ni-tum MUL.AB.SÍN tarakkas KI.MIN

35. 4 riksē a-na MUL.KU$_6$ MUL.GU.LA MUL.NUN.KI MUL.GÍR.TAB tarakkas KI.MIN

36. 3 riksē a-na šu-ut dA-nim šu-ut-dE[n-líl u šu-ut dÉ-a tarakkas KI.MIN].

earlier in line 25 or simply because it is night. The next three groups include the zodiacal constellations Libra (with its standard epithet, Star of Šamaš) in the first group of six, Virgo in the second group of four, and Pisces, Aquarius, and Scorpius in the third group, also of four. Moreover, the northern constellations Triangulum (the Plow), Boötes (ŠU.PA), Ursa Maior (the Wagon), Coma Berenices? (the Cluster), and Lyra (the Goat) receive offerings in the first group, the Square of Pegasus and the Northern Fish (the Swallow)—paired, as usual, with the Southern Fish (the Ṣtar of Anunitu)—in the second group, and the southern constellation Vela? (the Star of Eridu) in the third. And finally, offerings are made to all the stars, collectively called "those of (the paths of) Anu, Enlil, and [Ea]."

While only the Late Babylonian version of the mouth-washing ritual describes in such detail the appeal to the stellar powers, already the Assyrian kings Esarhaddon and Assurbanipal speak of the initiation of the new cult statues as taking place before not only the gods and the divine patrons of the crafts by means of which these statues were made, but also "before the stars of the sky," as the texts expressly state.[676] In the Assurbanipal-library version of the directions for the mouth-washing ritual only the setting up of an offering table[677] for ^{d}SAG.ME.GAR (Jupiter) and an altar for MUL.ŠU.PA (= Arcturus?) and the incipits of the prayers to be addressed to them are cited: "You Šulpaea"[678] to Jupiter, and "(You,) magnificent one, 'Mountain' of the Igigu-gods"[679] to Arcturus?.[680] It was noted long ago that the Assyrian recension "did not enumerate these [astral] deities, at any rate in quite the same con-

---

676 mahar kakkabī šamāmi, M. Streck, *Assurbanipal*, Vorderasiatische Bibliothek 7/2 (Leipzig: Hinrichs, 1916) 268 iii 20 (= Th. Bauer, *Das Inschriftenwerk Assurbanipals*, vol. 2 [Leipzig, 1933] 84), Borger, *Esarh.* 91 §60 i 13, and parallels §57 r. 21, etc.

677 GI.DU$_8$ = paṭīru, line 14.

678 atta ^{d}Šul-pa-è-a, line 18.

679 š[urbû šadû] Igigi, line 21.

680 Gerhard Meier, "Die Ritualtafel der Serie 'Mundwaschung,'" *AfO* 12 (1937–39) 40–45; the rituals and prayers to the stars appear on K.9729+ obv. 14–21. A new edition of the "mouth-washing" ritual is being prepared by C. B. F. Walker.

nexion,"[681] it is therefore only in the Babylonian, late version that the process takes on the character of what may already be called "astral religion" while the Assyrian recension testifies only to the belief in stellar irradiation, the effect of which has permeated, as we saw, several crucial areas of Babylonian science and religion.

[681] S. Smith, *JRAS* 1925 40.

Index

abnu šikinšu (composition), 122–125
acacia, 38
acrographic, 26, 62
Adad (god), 65, 66, 68, 79, 91
aitites, 123
Akkadian, 26, 28, 44, 45, 48
"all evil," 83
amulet, amulets, 15, 110, 120, 125, 127
amulet stones, 41, 121, 124, 128, 129
Antares, 138
Antu (goddess), 139
Anu (god), 5, 6, 12, 20, 71, 79, 87, 89, 139, 141
aphasia, 105
aphrodisiac, 35
apodosis, 61
apotropaia, 109, 119
apotropaic ritual, 39, 46, 47, 66, 82, 83, 84, 96
apotropaion, 83, 96. *See also* namburbû
Aquarius, 78, 109, 116, 117, 144
Aquila, 117
Arcturus, 138, 144
Aries, 78, 93, 109, 117
Aristophanes, *Wasps*, 105
Arrow star, 3, 17, 19
Asalluhi (god), 86
Assur, 50, 71
Assur (god), 75
Assurbanipal (king of Assyria), 18, 50, 67, 142
astral deities, 9, 141, 113
astral irradiation, 49, 51, 52, 55
astrologer, 76
astrology, 76, 77; catarchic 13, 111; horoscopic 13
astronomer, 65
astronomical observations, 14, 65
astronomy, 14

Babylon, 71, 138
Babylonian calendar, 89; divinatory texts, 72, 84; "Stone-book," 122
"Babylonian Diviner's Manual," 94, 95, 96
bakshish, 38
beads, 126
Bear (constellation), 56, 70
Bēl (god), 139
Bēlet-balāṭi (goddess), 78
Bēltiya (goddess), 139
bestiaries, 25, 29
bewitching, 97
Big Dipper, 3, 56, 58, 70
bilingual (lists), 46
birds, 86–87, 117, 118
Bison (constellation), 66
black magic. *See* magic
Boghazköy, 48, 67
Boötes, 15, 56, 144
Bow star, 66, 88, 139
brontoscopy, 65
Bull, 117. *See also* Taurus

calendar, 8, 22, 89, 113
calendar texts, 114–116
Cancer, 78, 109, 116
Canis Maior, 88
Canis Minor, 117
cannabis, 35
Capricorn, 109, 110, 116
catalogue, 82, 83, 91
catarchic. *See* astrology; magic
Centaurus, 56, 67, 106
centaury, 33
charms, 125
chiromancy, 30
classification, 26
clouds, 91
Columella, 133
Coma Berenices, 139, 144
commentary, 110, 133

concatenation, 90
conjunction, solar-lunar, 134
conjurer, 47
constellations, 3, 79, 94
Corvus, 78, 117
cuneiform, 25
"cutting the breath," 104, 105, 109, 136
Cygnus, 3
Cyranides, 116, 130

dawn, 23
Delebat, 7. *See also* Venus
Delphi, 72
Demon with the Gaping Mouth (constellation), 3
destruction, 121
determinative, 5, 25, 26
dew, 59, 104
diagnosis, 47
diagnostic omina. *See* omens
divination, 2, 11, 14, 72
diviner, 1, 2, 15, 64, 65, 67, 69, 73–74, 94, 95
dodekatemorion, 110
dog, 52
Draco, 139
Dragon (constellation), 66
Dream-book, 71
dreams, 74
"Dreckapotheke," 45

Ea (god), 5, 6, 21, 81, 82, 83, 85, 86, 87, 88, 141
eagle, 124
Eagle (constellation), 117
eagle-stone, 123
earthquake, 90, 91, 92
eclipse (lunar), 8, 11, 12, 22, 74, 75, 76, 77, 90, 91, 134
eclipse (solar), 11, 12, 90, 134
ecstatic, 74
effigy, 135
Ekur (temple), 21
Emar, 41
empsychosis, 140
Enki (god), 88
Enlil (god), 5, 12, 21, 87, 89, 141
Enūma Anu Enlil (composition), 13, 65, 77, 84, 89, 90, 91
Enūma eliš (composition), 22
Ereškigal (goddess), 19
Eridu, 138
Erra (god), 66
Esarhaddon (king of Assyria), 18, 22, 74, 75, 76, 93, 98, 119, 144
Etruscan, 2, 65
Euphrates, 19
Evening star, 3, 6, 23
evil, 20, 22
exorcist, 8, 15, 24, 47, 65, 92, 131
exposition, 109; nocturnal 51–56, 58
exta, 2, 65, 70, 72, 79. *See also* liver
extispicy, 65, 66, 67, 70, 74, 77, 84. *See also* hepatoscopy

female. *See* feminine
feminine: materia medica, 35; stones, 128
Ferry (constellation), 67
Field (constellation), 67
figurines, 24, 105
First-born of Emah (star), 20, 21
fish, 114
Fish (constellation), 117, 144
full moon, 113, 133, 134, 136
Furrow (star), 3

garlic, 27
Gemini, 78, 104, 109, 117. *See also* Twins
genethlialogy, 13
ghost, 137
Glass texts, 127
goat, 86
Goat (star), 3, 52, 55, 56, 58, 66, 78, 86, 128–129, 139, 140, 141, 144
gods of the night, 1, 16, 18, 19, 66, 68, 69, 73, 86
grave, 39, 40
Gula (goddess), 5, 52, 53, 55, 56, 86, 113, 128, 129

haematite, 122
halo (of the moon), 90
Hammurapi (king of Babylon), 41, 129

HAR-gud (composition), 26
HAR-ra = hubullu (composition), 26, 27, 90, 122, 130
haruspex, 2, 63, 64, 65, 66, 68, 69, 70, 72, 74, 75, 77, 79, 94. *See also* diviner
Hattuša, 49
Hecate, 53
hemerologies, 21, 59, 96, 112–114, 136
hepatoscopy, 63, 65, 74, 76, 79. *See also* extispicy
Hephaistio, *Apotelesmatika*, 79
herb, 27, 28, 35, 36, 38, 39, 40, 103, 115, 128
herbalist, 36, 38, 39
herbals, 25, 28–29, 33
Hermetic, 9
Herodotus, 45
Hesiod, 89, 112
Hippolytus, 100
Hittite, 48, 55–56, 67
Hittites, 18
Hydra, 3, 66
hypsoma, 75

iatromathematics, 46
ikribu, 73
illustrations, 30
incantations, 47
intercession (of stars), 17
iqqur īpuš (composition), 88, 91, 94
iron, 38
irradiation, 15, 48, 52, 55, 59, 128, 141
Irragal (god), 20
Išhara (goddess), 35
Isin, 43, 44
Ištar (goddess), 5, 6, 8, 18, 19, 23, 35, 57, 68, 91
Ištar-of-the-Stars (goddess), 23, 24

Jupiter (planet), 4, 7, 17, 18, 19, 20, 59, 60, 61, 74, 75, 87, 93, 104, 105, 106, 114, 138, 139, 141, 144
justice (Star of), 4

Kidney star, 16, 60, 88

lapidaries, 25, 29
lecanomancy, 62, 84
leeks, 114
Leo, 78
Libanius, 105–106
libanomancy, 62, 84
Libra, 4, 78, 108, 109, 117, 138, 140, 141, 144
libraries, 50, 67, 142
lifting-of-the-hand, 17
lightning, 89
lists, 26, 46, 62, 130
litany, 19
liver, 77, 78–79, 94, 96
liver models, 30
loosing, 81
love charms, 24
lú = *ša* (composition), 90
Lucan, 98, 133
Lucian, 100
Lugalirra (god), 104, 105
lunarium, *lunaria*, 108–110, 112
Lyra, 3, 53, 78, 86, 144. *See also* Goat star

magic, 14; black, 3, 14, 101, 109; catarchic, 111
magic circle, 37, 39, 55, 59
magical papyri, 9, 32, 33
magnetite, 122
male. *See* masculine
malku = *šarru* (composition), 123
Maqlû (composition), 101
Marduk (god), 21, 71, 85, 113, 138, 139; Star of, 75
Mars (planet), 4, 7, 8, 18, 22, 60, 61, 66, 93, 138, 139, 141
masculine: materia medica, 35; stones, 126
materia medica, 15, 44, 123
mediator, 15
medicine, 15, 131; Mesopotamian, 44
melothesia, 59
menology, 112
Mercury (planet), 3, 5, 6, 18, 138, 139, 141
Meslamtaea (god), 104
messengers: stars as, 16
meteorological omens, 63

meteorological phenomena, 92
metoposcopy, 30
micro-zodiac, 116
Moon, 4, 8, 9, 12, 18, 88, 91, 93, 98–101, 104, 108–111, 133, 134, 139. *See also* full moon; new moon
Moon god, 18, 74, 77, 101, 107, 113, 136, 140
Morning star, 3, 6, 23
Mudrukešda (constellation), 138, 139
MUL.APIN (composition), 20, 78, 90

Nabatean Agriculture, 42
Nabonidus (king of Babylonia), 76, 77
namburbû, 81, 82, 96
Narām-Sin (king of Akkad), 42, 129
nature, 30, 120
NE.NE.GAR (star), 138
Nergal (god), 7, 18, 22, 60, 61
nether world, 19
new moon, 63f., 134, 135
New Year's ritual, 138
Nineveh, 50, 67
Ninmah (goddess), 22
Ninsianna (goddess), 67, 68, 73
Ninurta (god), 5, 19, 35, 71, 122
Nippur, 21, 43
Nisannu (month), 113
nocturnal exposition, 52, 56, 59
Numušda (god), 1, 40

obedience, 121
omen, 61–63
omen collections, 13, 82–84
omen literature, 13
omens: 11, 82, 90, 94, 95; celestial, 11, 12, 63; diagnostic, 84, 105; liver, 7, 11, 30; meteorological, 63, 72, 92; physiognomic, 30, 84
"opening of the mouth," 140
opposition, 134, 136
Orion, 3, 5, 17, 19, 56, 66, 67, 78, 113, 116, 117, 136. *See also* Sipazianna

patch test, 40
path: of Anu, 5, 87, 144; of Ea, 5, 87, 144; of Enlil, 5, 87, 144; three paths, 5, 87, 140, 144
Pegasus (square of), 66, 138, 141, 144
pharmaceutical, 46; handbook 28
pharmacist, 35
phylactery, 118, 125, 127, 128, 129
physician, 8, 35, 43, 47, 48, 64; Egyptian, 44
physiognomic omens, 30, 84
Pisces, 117, 144
plague, 7–8, 22, 66, 121
planet, planets, 6, 8, 13, 19, 91, 139, 140; rising of, 90
planetary gods, 140
plant, plants, 27, 131; gathering, 36; planting, 133
Plato, 98, 133
Pleiades, 16, 17, 19, 20, 66, 86, 113, 117
Pliny, 35, 39, 122, 124, 133
Plow star, 144
Poem of the Creation (composition), 22
poetry, 15
Pole star, 20
portents, 95
prayer, 73, 74
prayers, 17, 18; 82; *ikribu*, 73–74
pregnancy, 124; testing, 41
prescriptions (medical), 46, 125
prognosis, 40
prognosticate, 47
prophecy, 74
protasis, 61
Puppis, 88

rain, 90
Raven, 78, 79, 117
regions, 108, 110
Regulus, 78, 108
reports (on extispicy), 70
Rīm-Sin (king of Larsa), 41, 129
rituals, 17
Rooster (constellation), 117

sacrifice, 72
Sagittarius, 5, 86, 93, 107, 116, 117
Sargon (king), 12, 74, 75

Saturn (planet), 3, 18, 138, 139, 141
Scales, 4. *See also* Libra
scholia, 27, 60, 79, 105, 130
Scorpion, 17, 56, 114, 139. *See also* Scorpius
Scorpius, 17, 106, 116, 117, 144
(cylinder) seals, 127, 128
secret names, 33, 132
secret place, 75, 116
"seizing of the mouth," 105–106, 109
Selene, 53
semen: of stars, 104, 105
Sennacherib (king of Assyria), 75, 120
Seven Gods, 86
seven sages, 118
shells, 126, 127
shooting stars, 72, 94
signs, 9
Sin, 8, 18, 68, 74, 77, 91, 104, 105, 136, 137. *See also* Moon god
Sipazianna, 56, 113. *See also* Orion
Sirius, 3, 17, 18, 19, 66, 70, 105, 138, 140, 141, 142
Snake (constellation), 3
sorcerer, 2, 8, 14, 97, 109
sorceress, 2, 8, 97, 109, 133
sorceries, 101
Spica, 3
squash, 27
Star of Abundance, 139
Star of Anunītu, 142
Star of Dignity, 139
Star of Eridu, 142
Star of Justice, 138
stars, 12, 13, 17, 18, 19, 57, 86, 87, 91, 93, 97, 133, 140; first, 58; of the night, 24; of the sky, 142
statue (divine), 140
stone, stones, 115, 120, 121, 131; masculine, 131; feminine, 126
Stone-book, 121
storm god, 66
string of beads, 125, 126, 128
substitute king, 9
Sultantepe, 111
Sumerian, 22, 26, 28, 44, 45; lists, 26; writing system, 25
Sumerogram, 104, 110
Sun, 4, 9, 17, 18, 22, 23, 65, 66, 91, 104, 134, 136, 138, 139, 140
Sun god, 86. *See also* Šamaš
sun, 37
sunrise, 22, 23
Swallow (constellation), 117, 142
Syriac, 19
Ṣalbatānu (planet), 7, 8, 18. *See also* Mars
Ṣarpanītu (goddess), 138
Šamaš, 8, 18, 23, 65–66, 68, 79, 85, 86, 91, 94, 104, 105, 135, 137, 141, 142. *See also* Sun
Šamaš-šumu-ukīn (king of Babylonia), 18, 22, 76
šammu šikinšu (composition), 90
Šulgi (king of Ur), 118
Šulpae (planet), 67, 87, 114, 142
šumma ālu (composition), 83, 85, 87, 88, 90, 91, 92
šumma izbu (composition), 83

tablets, 12, 82, 93, 95, 96
Taurus, 78
Theocritus, 24, 42
Theophrastus, 34, 38
Thessaly, 98, 100
Thucydides, 105
thunder, 90
Tiglath-Pileser I (king of Assyria), 50
Tigris, 19
toothache, 21
treaties, 8
treatment (medical), 46
tree, trees, 115, 131
Triangulum, 142
True Shepherd of Anu, 3, 17, 56. *See also* Orion
Twins (constellation), 107. *See also* Gemini

Ulūlu (month), 21, 76–77
Urartu, 75
Ursa Maior, 3, 17, 24, 57, 58, 66, 70, 71, 107, 114, 139, 142. *See also* Wagon
Ursa Minor, 66
Uruanna (composition), 28, 36, 123

Uruk, 78, 108, 115, 116, 138, 139. *See also* Warka
Vega, 53, 56
Vela, 139, 142
Venus (planet), 3, 5, 6, 8, 16, 17, 18, 19, 22, 23, 24, 58, 68, 73, 74, 75, 78, 90, 91, 114, 139, 140
veterinarian, 55
Virgil, 24, 34, 101, 133
Virgo, 4, 19, 110, 116, 142

Wagon (constellation), 3, 17, 20, 56, 57, 66, 67, 70, 71, 85, 107, 114, 139, 140, 142. *See also* Ursa Maior
Warka, 78. *See also* Uruk
warnings, 12, 61, 85
"washing of the mouth," 140
watches of the night, 16, 101
weather, 91
witch, 97, 98, 99, 100
witchcraft, 81, 97, 99, 101, 105
writing of heaven, 9

Yoke star, 15, 16, 57, 66, 67

zodiac, 96, 108, 111, 114, 116, 117
zodiacal constellations, 108
zodiacal signs, 115, 131
zodiologia, 112

www.ingramcontent.com/pod-product-compliance
Ingram Content Group UK Ltd.
Pitfield, Milton Keynes, MK11 3LW, UK
UKHW051853200426
11947UKWH00046B/1800

9 780871 698544